TERRA F

THE EARTH NOT A PLANET.

PROVED FROM

SCRIPTURE, REASON, AND FACT.

BY

DAVID WARDLAW SCOTT,

AUTHOR OF

"*Dora Marcelli;*" "*The Contrast, and other Poems;*" "*Water and the Spirit;*"
"*God Misunderstood;*" "*The Purpose of the Ages;*"
"*Hades and Beyond;*" &c.

———

" For He hath founded it upon the seas, and established it upon the floods."
—*Psalm xxiv.* 2.

———

1901.

British Library Cataloguing-in-Publication Data
A catalogue record for this book is available from the
British Library

A Brief History of Astronomy

Astronomy is the oldest of the natural sciences, dating back to antiquity, with its origins in the religious, mythological and astrological practices of pre-history. Early cultures identified celestial objects with gods and spirits – and related these objects (and their movements) to worldly phenomena. Rains, droughts, seasons and tides were all explained via the heavenly realm. It is generally believed that the first 'professional' astronomers were priests and that their understanding of the skies was seen as 'divine', hence astronomy's ancient connection to what is now called 'astrology'. This area of knowledge, a complex mix of belief and science, has been developed all over the world – from cultures and countries as diverse as China, India, the ancient Egyptians, Mesopotamia, Mesoamerica, the medieval Islamic and the western world. It is, of course, still evolving today.

In the last couple of decades, our understanding of prehistoric European astronomy in particular has radically changed. This occurred with the discoveries of ancient astronomical artefacts such as the world's oldest observatory, the 'Goseck circle.' Located in Germany, the site proves that Bronze Age Central Europeans had a much more sophisticated grasp of mathematics and astronomy than was previously assumed. According to Berlin archaeologist Klaus Goldmann, 'European civilization goes further back than most of us ever believed.' The enclosure is one of hundreds of similar wooden circular Henges built throughout Austria, Germany, and the Czech Republic during a 200-year period around 4,900 BC. While the sites vary in size (the one at Goseck is around 220 feet in diameter) they all have the same features: A narrow ditch surrounding a circular wooden wall, with a few large gates equally spaced around the outer edge. These gaps were used to observe the sun in the course of the calendar year and at the winter solstice, observers at the centre would have seen the sun rise and set through the south east and southwest gates.

The Ancient Greeks further developed astronomy, which they treated as a branch of mathematics, to a highly sophisticated level. The first geometrical, three-dimensional models to explain the apparent motion of the planets were developed in the fourth century BC by Eudoxus of Cnidus and Callippus of Cyzicus. Their models were based on nested homocentric spheres centred upon the Earth. A different approach to celestial phenomena was taken by natural philosophers such as Plato and Aristotle. They were less concerned with developing mathematical predictive models than with developing an explanation of the *reasons* for the motions of the Cosmos. In his *Timaeus* Plato described the universe as a spherical body divided into circles carrying the planets and governed according to harmonic intervals by a world soul. Aristotle, drawing on the mathematical model of Eudoxus, proposed that the universe was made of a complex system of concentric spheres, whose circular motions combined to carry the planets around the earth. This basic cosmological model prevailed, in various forms, until the sixteenth century AD.

Depending on the historian's viewpoint, the acme or corruption of physical Greek astronomy is seen with Ptolemy of Alexandria, who wrote the classic comprehensive presentation of geocentric astronomy, the *Megale Syntaxis* (Great Synthesis). Better known by its Arabic title *Almagest*, it had a lasting effect on astronomy up to the Renaissance. In this work, Ptolemy ventured into the realm of cosmology, developing a physical model of his geometric system, in a universe many times smaller than earlier (more realistic) conceptions It was not until the scholarly endeavours of Nicolaus Copernicus that astronomy developed much beyond this point. Copernicus was the first astronomer to propose a heliocentric system, in which the planets moved around the sun *not* the earth. His *De revolutionibus* provided a full mathematical discussion of his system, using the geometrical techniques that had been traditional in astronomy since before the time of Ptolemy. Copernicus's work was later defended, expanded upon and modified by Galileo Galilei and Johannes Kepler.

Galileo is considered the father of observational astronomy. He was among the first to use a telescope to observe the sky, and after constructing a 20x refractor telescope he discovered the four largest moons of Jupiter in 1610. This was the first observation of satellites orbiting another planet. He also found that our Moon had craters and observed (and correctly explained) sunspots. Galileo argued that these observations supported the Copernican system and were, to some extent, incompatible with the model of the Earth at the centre of the universe. Kepler built on this work, and was one of the first scholars to unite physics and astronomy. Kepler was the first to attempt to derive mathematical predictions of celestial motions from assumed physical causes. Combining his physical insights with the unprecedentedly accurate naked-eye observations made by Tycho Brahe, Kepler discovered the three laws of planetary motion that now carry his name.

Isaac Newton further developed these ties, through his law of 'universal gravitation.' Realising that the same force that attracted objects to the surface of the Earth held the moon in orbit around the Earth, Newton was able to explain – in one theoretical framework – all known gravitational phenomena. In his *Philosophiae Naturalis Principia Mathematica*, he derived Kepler's laws from first principles. Much of modern physics (and indeed modern astronomy, as the two are now very closely linked) builds on these very discoveries. Outside of England however, Newton's theory took a long time to become established; Descartes' theory of vortices held sway in France, and Huygens, Leibnitz and Cassini accepted only parts of Newton's system, preferring their own philosophies. It wasn't until Voltaire published a popular account in 1738 that the tide changed. In America, it was not until the mid-seventeenth century that astronomical thought began to move away from the much respected Aristotelian philosophy.

Today, astronomy is a vast and incredibly complex field of research, studied by scientists all over the globe. Although in previous centuries noted astronomers were exclusively male, at the turn of the twentieth century women began to play a role in the great discoveries. It was during this most recent century that most of our current knowledge was gained. With the help of the use of photography, fainter objects were observed. Our sun was found to be part of a galaxy made up of more than 10^{10} stars (ten billion stars). The existence of other galaxies, one of the matters of *the great debate*, was settled by Edwin Hubble, who identified the Andromeda nebula as a different galaxy, and many others at large distances and receding, moving away from our galaxy. Physical cosmology, a discipline that has a large intersection with astronomy, also made huge advances during the twentieth century; the *hot big bang* model was heavily supported by evidence such as the redshifts of very distant galaxies and radio sources, the cosmic microwave background radiation, Hubble's law and cosmological abundances of elements.

As is evident from this incredibly short introduction to astronomy, it is a branch of knowledge that has changed massively from its early beginnings. Having said this, the study of the stars, skies and heavenly realms has continued to be an enduring source of human fascination. The work of scholars such as Newton, Kepler, Galileo, Ptolemy and Aristotle has had a massive impact on the way we understand the world around us. This collection celebrates the work of these early astronomers. There is still so much to discover, so many assumptions to be questioned - and the scientists of today are heavily indebted to the pioneers of the past, who did just this. We hope the current reader enjoys this book.

PREFACE.

I am now an old man, and, had I consulted my own comfort, would never have penned a line of this book, as for some years I have had cataract in both eyes, so that it was not without difficulty that I could read or write. So great, however, appeared to be the need, and being still anxious to serve my generation, I determined to undertake this work, in order to expose the fallacies of Modern Astronomy, which are so contrary to the Word of God, and so conducive to the promotion of Infidelity. I do not enter the lists arrayed in the panoply of Neo-Science, to fight this great Goliath, but only with a few pebbles of the brook, yet I trust that, with God's blessing, the attempt may not be altogether fruitless.

I am well aware that—" as it was in the days of Noe, so shall it be also in the days of the Son of Man "—*Luke xvii. 26.* But, while we should be ever ready for His Coming, it is not for us "to know the times or the seasons, which the Father hath put in His own power "—*Acts i. 7 ;* and we are exhorted—" in the morning sow thy seed, and in the evening withhold not thine hand, for thou knowest not which shall prosper "—*Ecc. xi. 6.* It may be that these pages may meet the need of some, who have not altogether been misled by unprovable fancies, and who will rejoice to find that the Biblical account of Creation is, after all, the only one which can be depended upon, and that Modern Astronomy, like its kindred theory of Evolution, that dangerous and degraded form of Buddhist metempsychosis, is nothing but " a mockery, a delusion, and a snare." Thus may the eyes of the understanding be cleared of that obstructive cataract, which obscures the sight of many otherwise sound minds, owing to the evil effects produced thereon by " science falsely so called "—*1 Tim. vi. 20.*

Not being a professional Astronomer, I required to read and think much while writing this book, and had to weigh every matter in an even balance, so as to make no statement which is not in strict conformity with Scripture, Reason, or Fact. I am especially indebted to " The Earth (not a Globe) Review," which was the means of first inducing me to begin this work—to Dr. Rowbotham's (Parallax) " Zetetic Astronomy "—to Mr. Carpenter's " One Hundred Proofs that the Earth is not a Globe "— and to Mr. Winship's " Zetetic Cosmogony." I would also express my best thanks to " ZETETES," the late Editor of " The Earth (not a Globe) Review," who, at my request, carefully read my manuscript before its being sent to the Printers, and who, on returning it wrote—" I am pleased to be in perfect accordance with so much that is in your book." I could not expect him to say more, as it rarely happens that men of independent thought can see everything in exactly the same light. The favourable testimony of such an expert in Astronomic subjects as " ZETETES," gives me confidence in placing the result of my labour before the Public, and I sincerely trust that it may not be " in vain in the Lord," but that it will be helpful to those of my Readers who are desirous of searching out the truth of God, as revealed in His works of Creation.

D. WARDLAW SCOTT.

25 Trinity Road,
    Wood Green, London,
        March, 1901.

CONTENTS.

	PAGE
Map of the World as a Plane	*Frontispiece*
Preface - -	iii

CHAPTER I.

INTRODUCTORY REMARKS.

SECTION
1. A few words about Gravitation - - - 1
2. Fundamental difference of opinion among Modern Astronomers - - - 9
3. Testimonies of some able men against the Copernican Theory · · - 17
4. Quotations showing some of the Atheistical Results of Modern Astronomy - - 21

CHAPTER II.

THE ADAMIC CREATION.

1. The Days of Creation not long periods of time, but Six Natural Days of twenty-four hours each - - 31
2. Not two races of Adamites - - - 37
3. Refutation of the Theory of two different authors of Genesis, from the use of the distinguishing words Elohim and JEHOVAH-Elohim - - 43
4. No Discrepancy exists, regarding the Adamic Creation, in the accounts given in Genesis I. and II. 47
5. Primeval Fauna and the Ages - - - 50
6. Chipped Flints - - 55
7. The supposed Glacial Period - - 57

CHAPTER III.

THE NEBULAR HYPOTHESIS: EXAMINATION OF THREE ALLEGED PROOFS OF THE WORLD'S GLOBULARITY.

SECTION   PAGE

1. The Nebular Hypothesis -   63
2. The Circumnavigation of the Earth   67
3. The Appearance and Disappearance of Ships at Sea - 73
4. The Earth's shadow in a Lunar Eclipse -   77

CHAPTER IV.

REMARKS ON SOME OTHER ALLEGED PROOFS OF THE WORLD'S GLOBULARITY.

1. Variability of Pendulum Vibrations   85
2. Supposed Manifestation of the Rotation of the Earth   86
3. Railways and Earth's Centrifugal Force   89
4. Declination of the Pole Star   90
5. Motion of Stars North and South   91
6. The Planet Neptune   93

CHAPTER V.

THE WORLD CIRCULAR, BUT NOT GLOBULAR; HAS IMMOVABLE FOUNDATIONS, THEREFORE NOT A PLANET.

1. Relative Proportion of Land and Water   96
2. The Compass a proof that the Earth is not a Planet   98
3. Dangers of Navigation in Southern Seas, caused by the theory that the World is Globular   102
4. The supposed Revolution of the Earth around the sun proved to be untrue - - - 108
5. The Earth stretched out upon the Waters, which have an Impassable Circumference - 111
6. The Earth proved to have Immovable Foundations - 117

CHAPTER VI.

THE HORIZONTALITY OF LAND AND WATER PROVED.

SECTION   PAGE
1. Railways -   -   122
2. Rivers   -   -   -   -   -   126
3. Canals   -   -   -   127
4. Submarine Cables   .   -   134
5. The Light of Lighthouses seen at a distance   135

CHAPTER VII.

THE SUN, MOON, AND STARS, ACCORDING TO MODERN ASTRONOMY.

1. The Sun -   -   140
2. The Moon -   147
3. The Stars -   -   -   -   152

CHAPTER VIII.

THE SUN, ACCORDING TO THE SCRIPTURES.

1. Light comes out of Darkness   .   -   163
2. Zetetic Measurements respecting the Distance and
        Diameter of the Sun   -   -   167
3. Some Particulars respecting the Sun   -   174
4. Scriptural Proofs of the Rising and Setting of the Sun   180

CHAPTER IX.

THE SUN'S PATH AND WORK IN THE HEAVENS.

1. The cause of Day and Night and the Seasons -   -   184
2. The reason for gain and loss of time at Sea   -   -   186
3. The Seasons of the Year -   -   187
4. The Midnight Sun, and the alternation of Summer and
        Winter in the Northern Centre   -   190
5. The Sun and the Zodiac -   -   -   -   -   195

CHAPTER X.

THE SUN STANDING STILL AND RETURNING BACKWARDS.

SECTION   PAGE

1. The Sun standing still over Gibeon   -   -   - 204

2. The Sun's Shadow turning back ten degrees on the dial
of Ahaz   -   -   -   210

CHAPTER XI.

THE DELUGE—BIBLICAL ACCOUNT.

1. The date, cause, and extent of the Deluge   214

2. God's instructions to Noah respecting the Ark -   217

3. Some objections against the Deluge answered -   219

4. The Earth not a Planet proved by the waters finding
their own level above the highest mountains   221

5. Subsidence of the waters, and safe debarkation of Noah
and all with him from the Ark   - 226

6. The Noachian Covenant   -   229

7. The Last Judgment on the Earth to be by Fire   - 231

CHAPTER XII.

THE DELUGE—TRADITIONAL RECORDS.

1. Marks of the Deluge visible in many lands   -   - 234

2. The Accadian, or old Chaldean, account of the Deluge 237

3. Extracts from old Chaldean Epics, declaring the
revolution of the sun, and the creation of men and
animals   -   -   -   - 247

4. Babylonia identified with the Garden of Eden -   - 251

CONTENTS.

CHAPTER XIII.

THE GREAT DEEP A PROOF THAT THE EARTH IS NOT A PLANET.

SECTION   PAGE

1. The Earth in solution before the Adamic Creation, showing horizontality by its strata - 256

2. The Tides and the Great Deep - - 258

3. The Great Gulf Stream and Currents of the Great Deep 265

4. The Rivers come from and return to the Great Deep - 267

CHAPTER XIV.

FRAGMENTS GATHERED UP.

1. A fixed locality - - 272

2. Up and Down - - - 274

3. Some other reasons why the Earth is not a Planet 278

4. Concluding remarks - - 283

SUPPLEMENTAL INDEX - - - - x

SUPPLEMENTAL INDEX.

PAGE

ABSURDITY of Modern Astronomy shown in its description of
the heavenly orbs - - 142, 144, 145, 154

Accommodation, The argument of, utterly condemned
120, 121, 284, 285

Adams, The two contrasted - - - - - 61

Adventures of Gilmanes, a kind of ancient Hercules - - 238

Ages, referred to in Scripture, before and after this present
world - - - - 53—55

Angels, a different order of beings from men - - 38

Ark, The, shown to be sufficiently large for its requirements 219, 220

„ now acknowledged to have been built on the most
approved principles to combine strength, capacity, and
stability - - 224, 225

„ a type of Christ - - 233

Astronomic Curvature, The law of, unnatural and untrue - 123

„ „ disallowed by the British Government 124

„ method of teaching the young - - 26

Axial Motion not in the Earth, proved by the firing of cannons
and other projectiles - - - - 89, 90, 282

BABYLONIAN SEAL, representing the Temptation in the Garden
of Eden - - - 252

Bacon, Lord, altogether disapproved of the Copernican Theory
18, 19

Balloon, In a, the horizon always appears level with the eye,
thus showing the earth to be horizontal - - - 74, 75

Bera, in Hebrew, primarily means to create that which had no
previous existence - - - 33

Bedford Canal, The, proved by experiments to be level 127—130

„ „ the wager trial respecting it explained 130—133

Boldness required in dealing with error - - - 284, 287

PAGE

CIRCUMNAVIGATION of the world confessed by Keith to be no proof that it is a sphere -   -   -   -   69

Clarke's, Dr. Adam, letter to the Rev. Thomas Roberts respecting the sun standing still over Gibeon -   204

"   his failure to explain that miracle on Copernican lines   -   209

"   as also that of the sun's shadow turning ten degrees backward on the dial of Ahaz   -   -   -   212

Comets not absorbed by the Sun   -   7

Comparison between the old Chaldean and the Biblical account of the Deluge   -   245, 246

"   between the old Chaldean and the modern Evolutionists' idea of Creation   250, 251

Copernicus admitted that his system of the Earth's revolution round the Sun was only a supposition   11, 12

"   Condemned by Pope Urban VIII.   -   14

Critics, The so-called Higher, at variance amongst themselves, and not to be depended upon   -   44—46

"   The late Mr. H. L. Hastings's remarks on same   48, 49

DARKNESS an entity, and not the mere negation of light   164—166

Day, various meanings of the word in Scripture   35—37

Deceit of Modern Astronomers regarding the motion of the Sun   -   -   -   15, 286

Deep, The, thought to be enclosed in a vast rocky basin 98, 119, 120

Diagrams of ships at sea in astronomical books are most misleading   -   -   -   75—77

Dial, The, a daily proof of the Sun's revolution round the World   -   -   -   211

Difference of opinion should be no cause for ill-feeling   -   288

Discrepancies of Astronomers as to the distance of the Sun from the Earth -   12, 13, 141, 142

Distance, The, round the surface of the world at 45 degrees N. Latitude being only half of what it is at 45 degrees S. Latitude, proves that the world is not globular   280, 281

Dove's, Rev. John, vindication of the Scriptures against Modern Astronomy   -   -   -   -   27

PAGE

EARTH, The, proved to be horizontal, immovable, and stretched upon the waters ; therefore it is not a Planet   111—113

,,   distinguished from the Seas by the term Dry Land -   35

Earthquake of Lisbon, its effects on lakes, springs, and rivers at a great distance - -   262—264

Eclipses are calculated from previous observations and tables, irrespective of any particular theory as to the shape of the Earth -   - - -   77, 78, 178

Evolution, a dangerous form of Buddhist metempsychosis, altogether unscriptural, unnatural, and untrue   iii, 51, 112, 250, 251

FINAL dissolution of the Heavens and the Earth 161, 162, 231—233

Foundations of the Earth proved by Scripture - - 117—119

GEOLOGICAL conjectures not to be trusted -   50, 51

Globe, The word not mentioned in the Bible at all - -   113

" Globe, One Hundred Proofs that the Earth is not a," by the late W. Carpenter, quoted -   13, 191, 192, 278—282

Göthe's opposition to the Newtonian hypothesis -   19, 20

Government inconsistent as regards Astronomic teaching   138

HORIZON, The line being *straight* proves the world to be horizontal and not globular - - 74, 75, 91, 281

Hull, The, of a ship leaving port often restored to sight by the telescope, after being lost to the naked eye - - -   75

Humboldt's remarks on the colour of the stars - - 152

,,   ,,   ,,   Deluge - - - - 235, 236

,,   ,,   ,,   Level of the Sea - - -   223

INDIFFERENCE as to the statements of Scripture respecting the stability of the Earth condemned - - 284, 285

Infidelity shown to arise from the false theories of Modern Astronomy - -   - 22—25

JOSEPHUS's testimony as to the fact of the Deluge - -   236

KELVIN's, Lord, " wonderful stone "   - - - - 112

Kepler's famous Laws shown to be erroneous - - - 4, 5

LA PLACE's "grand conception" of the Nebular hypothesis only a myth - -   63, 64

PAGE

Le Verrier's calculations respecting the planet Neptune entirely erroneous - - - - - - - - 94

Lunarians, What the supposed, are supposed to see - 147, 148

MEN are not fastened to a globular earth like needles to a spherical loadstone - - - - 280

Mistake, The sad, into which some Christian writers have fallen in calling this world "a globe" - 274, 275

Mistranslation of Authorized Version (*Genesis i.* 20) respecting the water bringing forth fowl 41, 42

,, of the Hebrew words for "Sun" and "Moon" by Calmet and Parkhurst with respect to the miracle related in *Joshua x.* - 205—207

,, of *Sheol* and *Hades* as "hell" and "the grave" instead of the place of the dead 275, 276

,, of the word *belimeh* as "nothing" instead of "fastenings," in *Job xxvi.* 7 - - 114—116

NEWTON, Sir Isaac, proposed his system only as a supposition 4, 83, 84

,, his career should be a warning to others - 15

OCEAN beds comparatively flat - 97, 98

Original text, The, often the means of solving difficulties - 42

Ovid's reference to a great deluge - - - - - 236

,, remark on men's stupidity - 127

PAIL of water whirled round the head a false illustration of the world revolving round the sun 1—3

Parkhurst failed in his theory of the motion of the Earth by means of conflicting ethers - - 116, 166, 167

Parallels of Latitude increase in width progressively from the Northern centre to the Southern circumference, proving the world not to be globular - 71, 72, 105, 106

Perspective, The true law of, disregarded by Modern Astronomers - - - - - 74, 90, 91

Plurality of Worlds, Sir David Brewster's argument for, from analogy shown to be unsound - - 154

,, Mr. W. Bathgate's argument against this from Scripture - 156, 157

PAGE

Poem, The oldest, in the world - - - 255

Pole, no South whatever - 71, 72, 92

  ,, Star, The, anciently regarded as " Alpha " in Draco, now
as " Alpha " in Ursa Minor 200, 201

  ,, shows the locality of The North - 101, 273

Pre-Adamite Man shown to be an unscriptural myth 37, 38

Precession of the Equinoxes - - - 201, 202

Proctor's, Mr., " Pretty Proof of the Earth's Rotundity,"
shown to be no proof at all - 73, 74

Ptolomy, in 2nd century, A.D., restored the ancient cosmogony
of the Earth being immovable 13, 14

Pyramid, The Great, and the Sphinx 199

Pythagoras, a Heathen philosopher, first broached the idea of
the Earth revolving round the Sun - 13, 143

Queen of Heaven, Astarte or Ashtaroth, the worship of,
identified with that of the Romish Virgin Mary 143

Rainfall, The, and exhalations from the Ocean and other
waters of the Earth, are insufficient to maintain the flow
of rivers, which must be replenished from the waters of
the Great Deep - 270, 271

Refraction, so uncertain in its action, as not usually to be
reckoned in astronomic calculations 137, 212

Rotation of the Earth quizzed by *Punch* - 88

Satan the presumed source of Modern Astronomy 66, 67, 287, 288

Science, Modern, but a development of the old - 285, 286

  ,, more *real* in the Bible than anywhere else -
157, 166, 200, 232, 268, 284

Sphinx, The riddle of the - - 199

Storms, The greatest, do not affect the sea more than about
ninety feet below the surface, beneath which the water is
quite still, thus proving that the sea does not revolve
round the sun - - 267

Stratification of the rocks effected by the dissolution of the
Earth, thus proving its horizontality - 33, 34, 256—258

PAGE

TIT-BITS from Modern Astronomy - 11

,, ,, Professor Huxley on the convexity of water - 73

,, ,, Professor Airy on the Assumptions of Newton 83, 84

,, ,, Sir Norman Lockyer's " to take it as proved " - 84

,, ,, Sir John Herschel's " take for granted " 84

,, ,, the late Mr. Proctor's " we find that the earth is not flat but a globe " 84

,, ,, Herschel's " in the disorder of the senses " 140, 141

Tycho Brahe's testimony against the Copernican system 18, 108, 109

WATER, always finding its own level, proves that the Earth is not a Planet 135, 222—224

Weather much more severe in the Southern than in the Northern Latitudes of the same degree 71

Wesley's, Rev. John, disbelief of Modern Astronomy 19

" Witness, The, of the Stars," by the Rev. Dr. Bullinger, highly recommended, and quoted - 196, 197, 201, 202

Woodhouse's, Dr., testimony respecting Modern Astronomy 20, 21

World, This, of ours, with the exception of that beyond, the only one referred to in the Scriptures 153, 154, 157, 158

XISUTHRUS, the name by which Noah is called in the old Accadian Tablets - - - 238

ZETETES quoted - iv, 76, 77, 172, 173

" Zetetic Astronomy," by the late Dr. Rowbotham (Parallax quoted 71, 80, 103—105, 128—130, 130—133, 155, 168—170

,, Cosmogony," by Mr. Thomas Winship, of Durban, Natal, quoted - 136—138, 171, 172, 174, 188, 189

"The Earth is JEHOVAH's, and the fulness thereof:
The World, and they that dwell therein:
For HE hath founded it upon the seas,
And established it upon the floods."

Psalm xxiv., 1, 2.

TERRA FIRMA:

THE EARTH NOT A PLANET,

PROVED FROM

SCRIPTURE, REASON, AND FACT.

CHAPTER I.

INTRODUCTORY REMARKS.

SECTION		PAGE
1.	A FEW WORDS ABOUT GRAVITATION - - -	1
2.	FUNDAMENTAL DIFFERENCE OF OPINION AMONG MODERN ASTRONOMERS - - -	9
3.	TESTIMONY OF ABLE MEN AGAINST THE COPERNICAN THEORY - - - - -	18
4.	QUOTATIONS SHOWING SOME OF THE ATHEISTICAL RESULTS OF MODERN ASTRONOMY - -	21

SECTION 1.

A FEW WORDS ABOUT GRAVITATION.

I remember being taught when a boy, that the Earth was a great ball, revolving at a very rapid rate around the Sun, and, when I expressed to my teacher my fears that the waters of the oceans would tumble off, I was told that they were prevented from doing so by Newton's great law of Gravitation, which kept everything in its proper place. I presume that my countenance must have shown some signs of incredulity, for my teacher

immediately added—I can show you a direct proof of
this ; a man can whirl around his head a pail filled with
water without its being spilt, and so, in like manner,
can the oceans be carried round the Sun without losing
a drop. As this illustration was evidently intended to
settle the matter, I then said no more upon the subject.

Had such been proposed to me afterwards as a
man, I would have answered somewhat as follows—
Sir, I beg to say that the illustration you have given of
a man whirling a pail of water round his head, and the
oceans revolving round the Sun, does not in any degree
confirm your argument, because the water in the two
cases is placed under entirely different circumstances,
but, to be of any value, the conditions in each case
must be the same, which here they are not. The pail
is a hollow vessel which holds the water *inside* it,
whereas, according to your teaching, the Earth is a ball,
with a continuous curvature *outside*, which, in agreement
with the laws of nature, could not retain any water;
besides, as the Scriptures plainly tell us—*2 Pet. iii. 5*,
the water is not contained in the Earth, but the Earth
in the water. Again, the man who whirls the pail around
his head, takes very good care to hold it *straight* in an
even circuit, for, if he did not, the water would
immediately be spilt. But you teach us that the Earth
goes *upside down* and *downside up*, so that the people
in Australia, being on the other side of the so-called
Globe, have their feet exactly opposite to ours, for
which reason they are named Antipodes. We are not
like flies which, by the peculiar conformation of their
feet, can crawl on a ball, but we are human beings, who
require a plane surface on which to walk; and how

could we be fastened to the Earth whirling, according
to your theory, around the Sun, at the rate of eighteen
miles per second? The famed law of Gravitation will
not avail, though we are told that we have fifteen pounds
of atmosphere pressing on every square inch of our
bodies, but this does not appear to be particularly
logical, for there are many athletes who can leap nearly
their own height, and run a mile race in less than five
minutes, which they could not possibly do were they
thus handicapped. Sir, your assertion respecting the
revolution of the world round the sun, as illustrated
by the pail of water, is utterly worthless, and will never
convince any thinking man; it is, as the late Mr.
Carpenter said of another astronomical theory, " an
outrage upon human understanding and credulity."

Sir Robert Ball, the Astronomer Royal for Ireland,
says, speaking of Gravitation :—

" In the case of the sun, and of the planetary system generally,
the mass of the central body enormously exceeds that of any of
his planets. The sun, for example, is 1047 times as heavy as
Jupiter—the heaviest of the planets ; while, if the luminary were
subdivided into a million equal pieces, the mass of each one of
them would be greater than the mass of the earth. It, therefore,
follows that the centre of gravity of the sun and of the earth
lies close to the sun's centre.

" The universal law asserts that every body attracts every other
body, and therefore there is attraction not alone between planet
and sun, but also between planet and planet. Jupiter is not only
attracted by the sun, and retaliates by attracting the sun, but
Jupiter also attracts the earth, and is in turn attracted by the
earth. In like manner there is a mutual attraction between every
pair of planets, the intensity of which is measured by the product

of the masses of the two planets, divided by the square of the distance apart."*

So with regard to celestial things, and so, we suppose, with regard to terrestrial matters also; by this wonderful law of Gravitation, the man attracts the woman, and the woman attracts the man, the elephant attracts the flea, and the flea attracts the elephant, the cat attracts the mouse, and the mouse attracts the cat, and so on *ad infinitum*. Calculation, by the square of the distance, might, perhaps, to some appear plausible, were there only a few particular objects concerned, but, when there are countless millions of things, both celestial and terrestrial, all struggling at the same time to attract each other, such a law, from the inextricable confusion which it would necessarily create, would not only be an absurdity but an impossibility. Sir Isaac Newton himself does not even attempt to give one proof of the truth of Gravitation; with him it is only *supposition* from beginning to end. Thus he says—

"But the reason of these properties of gravity I could never hitherto deduce from phenomena; and am unwilling to frame hypotheses about them; for whatever is not deduced from phenomena ought to be called an hypothesis, and no sort of hypotheses are allowable in experimental philosophy wherein propositions are deduced from phenomena, and not made general by deduction."

The famous laws of Kepler, once considered to be so helpful in establishing the theory of Gravitation, are now found to have been only *erroneous suppositions*, as Professor W. B. Carpenter writes in the October, 1880,

---

* "The Cause of a Glacial Age," page 62 ; Kegan Paul, Trench, Trübner & Co., Parliament House, Charing Cross Road, London.

No. of the "Modern Review," from which I quote the following extract—

"He 'took as his guide *another assumption no less erroneous, viz.*, that the masses of these planets increased with their distances from the Sun. In order to make this last fit with the facts, he was drawn to *assume* a relation of their respective *densities, which we now know to be utterly untrue ;* for, as he himself says, ' unless we *assume* this proposition of the densities, the law of the periodic time will not answer.' Thus, says his Biographer, ' three out of the four *suppositions* made by Kepler to explain the beautiful law he had detected, are now *undisputably known to be false,* what he considered to be the *proof* of it being only *a mode of false reasoning* by which *any required result* might be deduced from any given principle.' "

Et tu, Brute ! the Newtonian Cæsar may now exclaim, as he falls by the dagger of his old friend Kepler.

Gravitation is a big word, derived from the Latin adjective *gravis,* heavy, and heavy, indeed, has been the trouble which it has caused to Modern Astronomers by its not acting in obedience to the laws made for it by their Delphic Oracle Sir Isaac Newton. It was at first introduced to the public as a mere hypothesis, but, by degrees, became to be considered as a law, though it paid as little attention to the law propounded for it by Newton, as a Red Republican does to that of his country ; for the small Moon refused to circle round the great Sun, nor would even a splint of wood be attracted by an iron mountain. The truth is that Gravitation, Attraction, Cohesion are only scientific names invented to cover men's ignorance of God's works in nature, pretending to explain facts, when, in reality, they explain nothing at all. Far wiser would it have been to have at once confessed that it is only by the Fiat of God that the substances of things are kept together, for it is He alone that upholdeth all things by the word of His power—*Heb. i. 3.* " He hath made the Earth by His power, He hath established the world by His wisdom, and by His understanding hath He stretched out the Heavens "—*Jer. x. 12.* And that Omnipotent God, who binds things together now, will, in His own time, effect their separation, for " the elements shall be dissolved with fervent heat, and the earth and the things that are therein shall be burned up "—*2 Pet. iii. 10.*

Speaking of Newton's law of Gravitation, Sir Richard Phillips said in his " A Million of Facts,"

" It is waste of time to break a butterfly on a wheel, but, as Astronomy and all science is beset with fancies about attraction and repulsion, it is necessary to eradicate them."

Mr. Breach of Southsea remarks—

" Newton's supposed law of Gravitation was lost in the Moon. Newton found that the Moon's perigee ought to require 18 years to perform its revolution in the heavens, while observation showed that the revolution was performed in one-half of this period. He exhausted all his skill and power to overcome the difficulty, but died, leaving the problem unsolved. His successor Clairant also finally abandoned the law of Gravitation as being incapable of explanation."*

In his article " Nature and Law," which appeared in the " Modern Review " of October, 1890, Professor W. B. Carpenter writes as follows—

" We have no proof, and, in the nature of things, can never get one, of the assumption of the attractive force exerted by the

---

* " Twenty reasons against Newtonianism, and Twenty Geographical Proofs that the Earth is an extended Plane "; S. Phillips, 3 Great Southsea Street, Southsea.

Earth, or by any other bodies of the Solar system, upon other bodies at a distance. Newton himself strongly felt that the impossibility of *rationally accounting* for action at a distance through an intervening vacuum, was the weak point of his system. All that we can be said to know is that which we learn from our own experience. Now, in regard to the Sun's attraction for the Earth and Planets, *we have no certain experience at all.* Unless we could be transported to his surface, we have no means of experimentally comparing Solar gravity with Terrestrial gravity, and, if we could ascertain this, we should be no nearer the determination of his attraction for bodies at a distance. THE DOCTRINE OF UNIVERSAL GRAVITATION, THEN, IS A PURE ASSUMPTION."

If Gravitation in the vast body of our Astronomers' Sun were a reality, why does it not attract, or even, as it might be expected to do, absorb such a light body as a Comet, when it comes so near it, instead of letting its long gossamer tail depart unscathed? Miss Giberne, in writing of Comets, remarks—

"They obey the attraction of the Sun, yet he appears to have the singular power of driving the Comet's Tail away from himself. For however rapidly the Comet may be rushing round the Sun, and however long the tail may be, it is almost always found to stream in an opposite direction from the Sun."[*]

Miss Giberne's remarks, if not explanatory, are at least curious, for they suppose the Sun to have the singular power of first *attracting* and then *repelling* the hapless Comet, a peculiar mode of Gravitation not permitted to our poor Earth, which, it is said, could draw down Sir Isaac's apple from the tree, but had no power

---

[*] "Sun, Moon, and Stars," p. 73; Seeley & Co., Limited, 38 Great Russell Street, London.

to send it back to its stalk again. The truth is no Astronomer on Earth, nor anybody else, knows one single fact respecting Gravitation, which is an unknown and an unknowable quantity, and the sooner it is committed to the grave of oblivion, the more scope will be given for the advancement of true science.

Any object which is heavier than the air, and which is unsupported, has a natural tendency to fall *by its own weight*. Newton's famous apple at Woolsthorpe, or any other apple when ripe, loses hold of its stalk, and, *being heavier than the air*, drops as a matter of necessity, to the ground, totally irrespective of any attraction of the Earth. For, if such attraction existed, why does not the Earth attract the rising smoke which is not nearly so heavy as the apple? The answer is simple—because *the smoke is lighter than the air*, and, therefore, does not fall but ascends. Gravitation is only a subterfuge, employed by Newton in his attempt to prove that the Earth revolves round the Sun, and the quicker it is relegated to the tomb of all the Capulets, the better will it be for all classes of society. He draped his idol with the tawdry tinsel of false science, knowing well how to beguile the thoughtless multitude, for, with a little alteration of Byron's famous lines, it is still true that

" Mortals, like moths, are often caught by glare,
　　And *folly* wins success where Seraphs might despair."

Gravitation is a clever illustration of the art of *hocus-pocus*—heads I win, tails you lose; Newton won his fame, and the people lost their senses.

SECTION 2.

FUNDAMENTAL DIFFERENCE OF OPINION AMONG MODERN ASTRONOMERS.

Judging from the manner in which such able champions of Zetetic truth as Rowbotham, Hampden, and Carpenter, who have passed away, have been treated, as also some strong advocates for it who are still alive, I have no great expectation that anything which I may say will have much effect on Astronomers themselves. They may rather be expected to exclaim, in a somewhat similar strain as a certain noble Lord with respect to the " old Nobility "—

> " Let Scripture, Reason, Fact, and Learning die,
> But spare us Newton's grand Astronomy."

Many books have been written on Modern Astronomy, but I am afraid that most of them are planned more as tales of sensational fiction than as handbooks of useful instruction, and require to be read not only with one but with many grains of salt. I have been informed, on good authority, that some of our Astronomers do already know the Plane truth, and surely it behoves such no longer to hide their light under a bushel, but to let it shine before men, so that others may be benefited and that God may be glorified thereby. If, however, they are still determined to conceal their knowledge, they must just be left severely alone. We may hope that some others will come to the front, who will brush away the cobwebs of theory, and build upon the granite of truth. A splendid opportunity is now before such so much-needed men, who might enrich the world with volumes of real value respecting the Heavens, and the Earth, based upon the lines of Scripture, Reason, and Fact.

The system of the Universe, as taught by Modern Astronomers, being founded entirely on theory, for the truth of which they are unable to advance one single *real* proof, they have entrenched themselves in a conspiracy of silence, and decline to answer any objections which may be made to their hypotheses. Such a method of defence appears to me to be neither wise nor effectual, for Truth is great, and must ultimately prevail. It rather resembles the tactics of the ostrich, which, in order to elude his pursuers, hides his head in the sand, thus leaving the greater part of his body exposed to view. Lord Beaconsfield wisely said—"A subject or system that will not bear discussion is doomed." Both Copernicus himself, who revived the theory of the heathen philosopher Pythagoras, and his great exponent Sir Isaac Newton, confessed that their system of a revolving Earth was only a *possibility*, and could not be proved by facts. It is only their followers who have decorated it with the name of an "exact science," yea, according to them, "the most exact of all the sciences." Yet one Astronomer Royal for England once said, speaking of the motion of the whole Solar system— "The matter is left in a most delightful state of uncertainty, and I shall be very glad if any one can help me out of it." What a very sad position for an "exact science" to be in is this! Nothing certain but the uncertain—nothing known but the unknown. Their calculations on celestial things are so preposterous and vague that "no fella" can understand them; just look at the following tit-bits of Modern Astronomic Science—

The Sun's distance from the Earth is reckoned to be about 92,000,000 miles.

The Sun is larger than the Earth 1,240,000 times.

58,000 Suns would be required to equal the cubic contents of the Star Vega.

Struve tells us that light from Stars of the ninth magnitude, travelling with the velocity of 12,000,000 miles per minute, would require to travel space for 586 years before reaching this world of ours!

The late Mr. Proctor said—"I think a moderate estimate of the age of the Earth would be 500,000,000 years.

The weight of the Earth, according to the same authority, is 6,000,000,000,000,000,000,000 tons!

And so on *ad nauseam.*

Now what confidence can any man place in a science which gives promissory notes of such extravagance as these? They are simply bankrupt bills, not worth the paper on which they are written. And yet, strange to say, many foolish people endorse them as if they were good, the reason being that they are too lazy to think for themselves, and, to their own sad cost, accept the bogus notes as if they had been issued by a Rothschild.

"True 'tis a pity—pity 'tis 'tis true."

What a sad illustration is given by the above statements as to the utter worthlessness of Modern Astronomy in the closing days of this boastful Nineteenth Century!

Copernicus wrote—"It is not necessary that hypotheses be true or even probable; it is sufficient that they lead to results of calculation which agree with calculation. . . . Neither let any one, as far as hypotheses are concerned, expect anything *certain* from Astronomy, since that science can afford nothing of the kind, lest in case he should adopt for truth things *feigned* for another purpose, he should leave the science more foolish than when he came. . . . The hypothesis of the terrestrial motion *was nothing but an hypothesis*, valuable only so far as it explained phenomena not considered with reference to absolute truth or falsehood."

If such was the conviction of Copernicus, the reviver of the old Pagan system of Pythagoras, and of Newton, its chief expounder, what right have Modern Astronomers to assert that a theory, which was given only as a *possibility*, is *a fact*, especially when they differ so much among themselves even as regards the very first elements of the problem—the distance of the Sun from the Earth? Copernicus computed it as being only three millions, while Meyer enlarged it to one hundred and four millions of miles, and there are many estimates between these two extremes. In my young days it was reckoned to be ninety-five, but in my old it has been reduced to about ninety-two millions of miles. Such discrepancies remind me of the confusion which attended those who in olden days attempted to build the Tower of Babel, when their language was confounded, and their labour brought to nought. But no wonder is it that their calculations are all wrong, seeing *they proceed from a wrong basis.* They *assumed* the world to be a *Planet*, with a circumference of 25,000 miles, and took their measurements from its supposed centre, and from supposed *spherical* angles of measurement on the surface. Again, how could such measurements possibly be correct while, as we are told, the Earth was whirling around the Sun faster than a cannon ball, at the rate of eighteen miles per second, a force more than sufficient to kill every man, woman, and child on its surface in less than a minute? Then, the Earth is supposed to have various other motions, into the discussion of which I need not enter here, and will only notice that of its supposed rotation round its imaginary axis at the rate, at the Equator, of a thousand miles per hour, with an inclination of 23½ degrees. Let me, however, remind our Astronomers of a pertinent remark made by Captain R. I. Morrison, late Compiler of Zadkiel's Almanac, who, from the position he held, ought to be considered a good authority on such subjects—

" We declare that this motion is all mere ' bosh,' and that the arguments which uphold it are, when examined by an eye that seeks TRUTH, mere nonsense and childish absurdity."*

How contrary are all these fancied motions to the plain teaching of the Scriptures, that the Earth " is founded upon the seas, and established upon the floods " —*Psa. xxiv. 2.* Yea that God's own hand " hath laid the foundations of the Earth "—*Isa. xlviii. 13.*

Pythagoras of Samos, a heathen philosopher, who lived, it is thought, about 500 years B.C., is the first who taught that the Sun is the stationary centre of the Universe, and that the Earth revolved around it as one of its satellites. But his opinion did not make much headway. In the second century A.D., Claudius Ptolemy of Alexandria, a man reported among the Greeks to be of vast learning and wisdom, restored the ancient Cosmogony, that the Earth is in the centre of the

---

* Carpenter's "One Hundred Proofs that the Earth is not a Globe," No. 98 ; John Williams, 54 Bourne-street, Netherfield, Notts.

Universe, is immovable, and that the Sun, Moon, and Stars revolved around it, as instruments to give it light. This system generally prevailed till the time of Nicolaus Copernicus, who was born at Thorn in Prussia, in the year 1472. He studied philosophy and medicine at Cvacova, and afterwards became Professor of Mathematics at Rome. After some years he returned to his native country, and began to investigate the various systems of Astronomy. He preferred that of Pythagoras, and, after more than twenty years' study, he gave his scheme of the Universe to the world. It was then condemned as being so heretical, that he was imprisoned by Pope Urban VIII., and only released when he made a recantation of his opinions. He died in 1543, but his system was followed by Galileo and other able men, and the introduction of the telescope greatly helped on the cause. At last, in 1642, Isaac Newton was born, the son of Mr. John Newton, a gentleman of small independent means, at Colesworth, near Grantham, Lincolnshire. At an early age he showed signs of uncommon genius, and in due time went to Trinity College, Cambridge. In 1669, when only 27 years of age, he was chosen Professor of Mathematics in the University there, and in 1687 he published his "Principia," confirming and improving the system of Copernicus, somewhat after the manner in which the cook in a boarding-school dishes up what the boys call a "resurrection pie," the chief ingredient being the same as it was previously, but with some spice scientifically added to suit the taste of the more fastidious palate of the day. This work brought him into great repute as an astronomer, and afterwards led to his being made Master of the Mint and Knighted.

As years rolled on so did Sir Isaac's fame, and, as
Harry Hotspur bewitched the world with his horseman-
ship, so has this much-lauded philosopher beguiled the
multitude with his Astronomy.   But error is error still,
and cannot last for ever, and many, who since his day
have honestly examined his system, have been compelled
to reject it, as being utterly unworthy of belief, and I
trust that many more may do so, when they begin to
think for themselves.   A sadder instance of the perver-
sion of splendid talents I do not know than the case of
Sir Isaac Newton.   He spent a long life in teaching a false
system of Astronomy, unsupported by any fact in nature,
and in direct contradiction to the plain statements of the
Bible, that priceless mine not only of all true religion,
but of all sound philosophy.   May his sad example serve
as a warning to others.

Pythagoras, Copernicus, and Sir Isaac Newton considered the Sun to be *stationary*, and, in that idea, for
many years other Astronomers followed suit, but

" A change came o'er the spirit of the dream,"

and they now say that IT DOES MOVE, not, indeed, round
the world, but towards a point in the constellation
" Hercules," though some imagine it to be journeying
towards Alcyone in the Pleiades.   In proof of this most
serious change of opinion, which wholly alters the base
of their system, and which, had they been honest,
should, on the discovery, have been at once publicly
acknowledged, I beg to give the following extract from
pp. 280, 281 of " Sun, Moon, and Stars "* by Miss Agnes
Giberne, a very enthusiastic writer on Astronomical

---

* Seeley & Co., Limited, 38 Great Russell Street, London.

subjects, with a laudatory Preface by the Rev. C.
Pritchard, M.A., F.R.S., &c., Savilian Professor of
Astronomy, in the University of Oxford.

"The rate of its (the Sun's) speed is not very certain, but it
is generally believed to be one hundred and fifty millions of
miles each year. Possibly he moves in reality much faster.

"When I speak of the Sun's movements, it must of course
be understood that the earth and planets all move with him,
much as a great steamer in the sea might drag in her wake a
number of little boats. From one of the little boats you could
judge of the steamer's motion quite as well as if you were on
the steamer itself. Astronomers can only judge of the Sun's
motion by watching the seeming drift of stars to the right or left
of him; and the watching can be as well accomplished from
earth as from the Sun himself.

. "After all, this mode of judging is and must be very uncertain.
Among the millions of stars visible we only know the real distance of ten or twelve, and every star has its own real motion
which has to be separated from the apparent change of position
caused by the Sun's advance.

"It seems now pretty clear that the Sun's course is directed
towards a certain point in the Constellation Hercules. If the
Sun's path were straight he might be expected by and by, after
long ages, to enter that constellation. But, if orbits of suns, like
orbits of planets, are ellipses, he will curve away sideways long
before he reaches Hercules."

Miss Giberne also remarks that a German Astronomer
believes that the Sun and the stars in The Milky Way
are travelling to Alcyone, the chief star in the Pleiades,
but wisely adds—"Much stronger proof will be required
before the idea can be accepted."

Now let me seriously ask—How can any thoughtful

man give the slightest credence to a system which holds
such absurd and contradictory hypotheses as Modern
Astronomers tell us to believe?   What confidence can we
place in those who deliberately reject, not only the direct
evidence of their senses, as shown by their talk about
" apparent motions," the reality of which they refuse to
admit, but also the plain testimony of the Scriptures,
and " have turned aside unto vain jangling, desiring
to be teachers of the law, understanding neither what
they say, nor whereof they affirm "—*1 Tim. i. 6, 7.*   One
might almost as soon credit the godless aberrations of
the Evolutionist, who derives man from a monad, afterwards passing through various gradations, not one of
which has ever yet been discovered, and which are said
to occupy millions of years, till he obtains the hairy
form of a chimpanzee, and then, after still further
developments, comes to the state of a real man, fitted,
as the survival of the fittest, to become the honoured
President of the Royal Society.   Oh how true is the
divine Word—" The world by wisdom knows not God "
—*1 Cor. i. 21.*   " He taketh the wise in their own
craftiness "—and again—" He knoweth the thoughts of
the wise that they are vain "—*1 Cor. iii. 19, 20.*

SECTION 3.

TESTIMONY OF SOME ABLE MEN AGAINST THE
COPERNICAN THEORY.

It is not surprising that able men, who have studied
he subject of Modern Astronomy, have rejected with
:ontempt the theory of the Earth being a revolving

2

Planet. Let me cite a few instances from *well-known* names. Tycho Brahe, the distinguished Danish Astronomer, who flourished soon after Copernicus, writes as follows—

"The heavy mass of earth, so little fit for motion in every respect, could not be displaced in the manner they propose, and moved in three different ways like the Celestial bodies, without .a shock to the known principle of physics, even if they could set aside the express testimony of Scripture."

The great Lord Bacon, the profoundest thinker of his age, was completely opposed to the Copernican system of Astronomy, as may be seen in several passages of his "Novum Organum," from one of which I quote the following—

"In like manner, let the motion inquired into be that other Motion of Rotation, so celebrated among Astronomers, resisting and opposed to the diurnal motion, viz., from west to east, which the old Astronomers attributed to the planets, and also to the starry heavens, but Copernicus and his followers to the Earth; and let it be asked whether any such motion be found in Nature, or whether it be not rather a theory fabricated and assumed for the convenience and abbreviation of calculation, and to favour that beautiful project of explaining the heavenly bodies by perfect circles. . . . And most certain it is, if we may reason like plain men, for a while (dismissing the fictions of Astronomers and the schools, whose fashion it is unreasonably to do violence to the senses, and to prefer what is most obscure), that this motion does appear to the senses as we have described it; and we once caused it to be represented by a sort of machine composed of iron wire."*

---

* "Essays, Civil and Moral, Advancement of Learning, Novum Organum," &c., p. 351, edition 1892, Ward, Lock, Bowden & Co., London.

In his " Confession of Faith," Lord Bacon also says—

" I believe that God created the heavens and the earth, and gave unto them constant and perpetual laws, which we call ' Laws of Nature,' but which mean nothing but God's laws of Creation."

The Rev. John Wesley, in various parts of his Journal, expresses his disbelief in the Copernican or Newtonian theory of the Universe. For brevity I quote only one passage—

" The more I consider them the more I doubt all systems of Astronomy; I doubt whether we can with certainty know either the distances or the magnitude of any star in the firmament, else why do Astronomers *so immensely differ* with regard to the distance of the Sun from the Earth? some affirming it to be only three and others ninety millions of miles."*

I shall just add the vigorous testimony of Göthe—

" It may be boldly asked where can the man be found, possessing the extraordinary gifts of Newton, who could suffer himself to be deluded by such a *hocus-pocus*, if he had not in the first instance wilfully deceived himself? Only those who know the strength of self-deception, and the extent to which it some-times trenches on dishonesty, are in a condition to explain the conduct of Newton and of Newton's school. To support his unnatural theory Newton heaps fiction upon fiction, seeking to dazzle where he cannot convince." †

In a Scientific Lecture, delivered in 1878, at Berlin by Dr. Schœpper, proving that the Earth neither rotates nor revolves, he quoted the following still stronger pro-test of Göthe against the delusions of Modern Astronomy.

---

* Works of Rev. John Wesley, vol ii., p. 392; Mason, London.
† "Proceedings of the Royal Institution," vol. ix., part iii., p. 353.

" In whatever way or manner may have occurred this business,
I must still say that I curse this modern theory of Cosmogony,
and hope that perchance there may appear, in due time, some
young scientist of genius, who will pick up courage enough to
upset this universally disseminated delirium of lunatics."

I could easily cite other good authorities to similar
effect, but I think enough have been already given, to
show that the absurdities of Modern Astronomy have not
been palmed upon the world without a strong protest
from thoughtful minds, and I sincerely trust that the
following pages may prove useful to some honest thinkers,
not only in exposing the fallacies of this chimerical
science, but in showing the true position of the world,
as proved by facts in nature, and as unfolded in the
Word of God. That Word is the only true exponent
which we possess for opening up to us the Wisdom and
the Power of God, as displayed in the works of nature,
as well as in the still higher revelation of His divine
purposes of grace, in bringing at last the whole creation
into complete harmony with Himself. ·

It gives me real pleasure to subjoin, from January,
1893, No. of " The Earth (not a Globe) Review," the
following extract, written by the late Dr. Woodhouse,
formerly Professor of Astronomy at Cambridge—

" When we consider what the advocates of the Earth's
stationary and central position can account for, and explain the
celestial phenomena as accurately to their own thinking as we
can ours, in addition to which they have the evidence of THEIR
SENSES and SCRIPTURE and FACTS in their favour, which we have
not; it is not without a show of reason that they maintain the
superiority of their system. . . However perfect our *theory* may
appear in our own estimation, and however simply and satis-

factorily the Newtonian *hypotheses* may seem to us to account for all the celestial phenomena, yet we are here compelled to admit the astounding truth, if our premises be disputed and our facts challenged, the whole range of Astronomy does not contain one proof of its own accuracy."

SECTION 4.

QUOTATIONS SHOWING SOME OF THE ATHEISTICAL RESULTS OF MODERN ASTRONOMY.

How sinful and foolish is it for any one to reject the unerring Word of God for the unproved and unprovable hypotheses of men! I do not think I should close this chapter without a few words of serious but loving warning to professing Christians, in the hope that they at least may be kept from the snares of Modern Astronomy, Evolutionism, Spiritualism, Ritualism, Demagogism, and other evils of the day, arising chiefly from the cancerous infidelity which is eating out the very heart of true religion, preparatory to the revelation of " the Man of Sin, the Son of Perdition, who opposeth and exalteth himself above all this called God, or that is worshipped, so that he, as God, sitting in the temple of God, showing himself that he is God "—*2 Thess. ii. 3, 4.*

There are many ministers of the Gospel, some of whom I personally know, who teach things contrary to Bible truth, but I refrain from giving names, trusting that they may yet repent. Indeed the mass of society is being leavened with the virus of dishonesty and

infidelity, not only in this country, but throughout the
world. The old landmarks are being rapidly removed;
the very Deluge is repudiated by many. Our civilization
is only a veneer. I have been informed that there are
conventicles for the express worship of Satan both in
London and Paris. Demonology and Witchcraft, of
course *under other names*, are rampant. Men think themselves very clever, but are duped on every hand. What
Isaiah said of Israel may be applied to this corrupt and
vainglorious age—" The whole head is sick and the
whole heart is faint. From the sole of the foot even
unto the head, there is no soundness in it, but wounds
and bruises and putrifying sores "—*Isa. i. 5, 6.* To
show that I am using no exaggerated language, I beg to
quote a few specimens out of the many which might be
given.

" The common notion had been that the Earth was flat, and
heaven a little way above the clouds, and the place of the dead
—the wicked dead, if not all the dead—somewhere underneath.
These were ancient ideas, and the fact that we find them in the
Bible is one proof that the Bible is an ancient book."

A " Reverend " of Cardiff.

" If Moses can be shown to be caught redhanded, in ignorance
and error; what shall we think of the Christ who quoted and
referred to him as an authority?"

Present Day Atheist.

" If it shall turn out that Joshua was superior to La Place,
that Moses knew more about geology than Humboldt, that Job
as a scientist was superior to Kepler, that Isaiah knew more than
Copernicus, then I will admit that infidelity must become speech-
less for ever."

Ingersoll's Tilt with Talmage.

"We date from the First of January, 1601. This era is called the Era of Man (E. M.) to distinguish it from the theological epoch that preceded it. In that epoch the Earth was supposed to be flat, the Sun was its attendant light, revolving about it. Above was Heaven, where God ruled supreme over all potentates and powers; below was the kingdom of the dead, hell. So taught the Bible. Then came the *new* Astronomy. It demonstrated that the Earth is a globe revolving about the Sun, that there is no 'up and down' in space. Vanished the old Heaven, vanished the old Hell; the Earth became the home of man. And when the modern Cosmogony came, the Bible and the Church, as infallible oracles, had to go, for they had taught that regarding the universe which was shown to be untrue in every particular."

Lucifer, Dec. 23rd, E. M. 287 (1887).

"We are trembling on the eve of a discovery, which may revolutionize the whole thought of the world. The almost universal opinion of scientific men is that the Planet Mars is inhabited by beings like or superior to ourselves. Already they have discovered canals cut in its face in geometrical form, which can only be the work of reasoning creatures. They have some snowfields, and it only requires a telescope, *a little stronger* than those already in existence, to reveal the mystery as to whether sentient beings exist in that planet. If it be found that this is the case, the whole Christian religion will crumble to pieces. The story of the Creation has already become an old wife's tale. Hell is never mentioned in any well-informed society of clergymen, the Devil has become a myth. If Mars is inhabited the irresistible deduction will be that all the other planets are inhabited. This will put an end to the fable prompted by the vanity of humanity, that the Son of God came on earth and suffered for creatures who are the lineal descendants of monkeys. It is not to be supposed that the Hebrew carpenter went about as a kind of theosophical missionary to all the planets of the Solar system re-incarnate, and suffered for sins of various pigmies or giants as the case may be who may dwell there. The Astronomers would do well to *make haste* to reveal to us the magnificent *secret* which the world impatiently awaits."

Reynolds' Newspaper, 14th August, 1892.

" There are always enough faddists in this world to afford an unfailing source of amusement. Have we not the Theosophists, and the Zetetic Society? The latter body claim to have discovered that the earth is a motionless and circular plane, over which the sun and moon and stars revolve at moderate distances above it. It would be unnecessary to take notice of this preposterous theory except to lament that any person of intelligence should waste his time upon so gross an absurdity. The capability of the members of this Society for scientific demonstration may be guessed, when I say that they take their science from the Bible. Now the Old Testament is full of the most elementary scientific inaccuracies. Modern science has proved over and over again that the writers of the Old Testament knew nothing about the physical condition of the earth, and certainly nothing of heaven, which indeed is not mentioned."

Reynolds' Newspaper, 17th May, 1896.

" To speak in plain terms, *as far as Science is concerned,* THE IDEA OF A PRESENT GOD IS INCONCEIVABLE, as are also all the attributes which religion recognizes in such a being."

The late Mr. R. A. Proctor, in " Our Place in the Infinities," p. 3.

" While, however, the idea of Government by a God is not excluded by general consent from the dominion of science, the notion of Government by Law has taken its place, not only in popular thought, but in the minds of many who claim the right to lead it, and it is the validity of this which I have now to call in question. . . . PHILOSOPHY FINDING NO GOD IN NATURE, NOR SEEING THE NEED OF ANY.

"The advanced Philosophy of the present times goes still farther, asserting that THERE IS NO ROOM FOR GOD IN NATURE."

Professor W. B. Carpenter, in " Modern Review" for October, 1880.

Even in Churches once reputed for their orthodoxy, false science has had a most withering effect. Thus the last Moderator of The Free Church of Scotland lately said—

"The fact remains that a restless, uneasy, uncertain feeling in regard to religious truth is abroad. . . The whole trouble has arisen from the mistaken assumption that the opening chapter of Genesis was meant to be an authoritative account of the method and order of creative work; it is not prose, but poetry, the great Creation Hymn."

A Professor in the same Church remarks in his " Studies of Theology "—

"Even the myth in which the beginnings of human life are represented. . . The plain truth—and we have no reason to hide it—is, we do not know the beginnings of man's life, of his history, of his sin; we do not know them historically on historical evidence, and we should be content to let them remain in the dark, till science throws what light it can upon them."

Quotations such as the above require no comment, as they speak for themselves, and show to what a debased state of infidelity many persons have been already brought, attributable in a great measure to the false teaching of Modern Astronomy. They have forsaken God, " the fountain of living waters, and have hewn out cisterns, broken cisterns, that can hold no water "— *Jer. ii. 12. Gutta cavat lapidem non vi sed sæpe cadendo.*

How true is this saying which I learned sixty-seven years ago at the Edinburgh Academy—a drop hollows a stone not by force but by often falling. So is it with regard to Modern Astronomy. Children are taught in their geography books, when too young to apprehend aright the meaning of such things, that the world is a great globe revolving around the Sun, and the story is repeated continuously, year by year, till they reach maturity, at which time they generally become so absorbed in other matters as to be indifferent as to whether the teaching be true or not, and, as they hear of nobody contradicting it, they presume that it must be the correct thing, if not to believe at least to receive it as a fact. They thus tacitly give their assent to a theory which, if it had first been presented to them at what are called " years of discretion," they would at once have rejected. This astronomic method of instilling error into young minds, recalls to my remembrance Pope's apt lines respecting vice—

> "Vice is a monster of such hideous mien,
>   As to be hated needs but to be seen;
>   But, grown at length familiar with its face,
>   We first abhor—then pity—then embrace."

The consequences of evil-teaching, whether in religion or in science, are far more disastrous than is generally supposed, especially in a luxurious *laisser faire* age like our own. The intellect becomes weakened and the conscience seared, as has, alas! only too sadly been shown in the results developed by Modern Astronomy and Sacerdotal Ritualism. These delusions are paving the way for the full-blown infidelity of the last days, when the great nations of the Earth will be gathered against

JEHOVAH and His Anointed—*Psa. ii. 2*—and will be swept away, " like chaff of the summer threshing-floor " —*Dan. ii. 35.* Clearly the Rev. John Dove, a learned and esteemed minister at Glasgow, saw this, when, indignant at the falsities of Copernican Astronomy, he wrote his " Vindication of the Divine Cosmogony," about 150 years ago. He faithfully remarked as follows—

" Are there any abettors of this heathen philosophy (the Copernican) still among us? Yes, ten thousand ; not only among the unlearned, but among our Church dignitaries, our classical scholars and teachers ! All on account of their ignorance and unbelief.

" What will be the end of these things ! I am no conjurer, but it is easy to determine what will be from what has already taken place. It has been the fate of all kingdoms, nations, and people from the beginning of time, upon their rejecting or perverting the revelation of God, to fall into anarchy, confusion, and infidelity. The Bible is, as it deserves to be, the great charter of our liberty. The loss of the Scriptures, or severing from or perverting the doctrines or history contained in them, has invariably been attended with discomfiture and ruin, and always will ! And if their successors continue their resistance, as they have done hitherto, it cannot fail to deluge the kingdom with Atheism, destroying all social virtue, and turning it into a field of blood."

It is my object in writing this book to warn people in these dangerous times, and to expose the absurdities of Modern Astronomy, for, if these are made apparent, " surely in vain the net is spread in the sight of any bird " —*Pro. i. 17.* I am afraid it is more than probable that many of my Readers may have already been more or less entangled in its meshes, but I earnestly hope that now, by thinking for themselves, they may make a resolute effort to be free, so that they may be enabled to say— "Our soul is escaped as a bird out of the snare of the fowler; the snare is broken and we are escaped"— *Psa. cxxiv. 7.*

CHAPTER II.

THE ADAMIC CREATION.

SECTION   PAGE

1. THE DAYS OF CREATION NOT LONG PERIODS OF TIME, BUT SIX NATURAL DAYS OF 24 HOURS EACH - - - - - - - - 31

2. NOT TWO RACES OF ADAMITES - - - 37

3. REFUTATION OF THE THEORY OF TWO DIFFERENT AUTHORS OF GENESIS, FROM THE DISTINGUISHING WORDS ELOHIM AND JEHOVAH-ELOHIM - - - - - - - - 43

4. NO DISCREPANCY EXISTS REGARDING THE ADAMIC CREATION IN THE ACCOUNTS GIVEN IN GENESIS I. AND II. - - - - - - 47

5. PRIMEVAL FAUNA AND THE AGES - - - - 50

6. CHIPPED FLINTS - - - - - - - 55

7. THE SUPPOSED GLACIAL PERIOD - - - - 57

A STRONG effort has been made by some Astronomers, Geologists, and others to transform the six natural days of the Adamic Creation into six long and indefinite periods of time. The late Mrs. Duncan, in her " Pre-Adamite Man,"* has, perhaps, been the most successful in propounding this theory, and although she has apparently written in a reverent manner, she has, to my mind, permitted imagination to usurp the place of truth. Being an Astronomer of the Modern School, she believed

* James Nisbet & Co., Ltd., 21 Berners Street, London.

in a Planetary Earth, and has thereby got into inextricable confusion, by supposing the Earth to have turned on an axis from the beginning, and to have revolved around the Sun before, according to God's Word, there was any Sun to revolve around, as that luminary was not formed until the *Fourth* day of creation.

The word " Adam " is usually said to be derived from the Hebrew word *dam*, red, because Adam was made from the dust of the ground, but Mrs. Duncan with, in my opinion, much more propriety, takes it from the root *dem*, likeness, because God said—" Let us make man in our image, *ke-demut-nu*, after our likeness "—*Gen. i. 26*. A similar expression respecting man having been formed in this glorious likeness is found in at least five other passages of Scripture,* as if on purpose to confute those errant Evolutionists who trace man's pedigree through the monkey, and who are guilty of very great sin in thus daring to travesty the infallible Word of God.

Mrs. Duncan imagined her Pre-Adamites, of the sixth day or period, to be a genus of Men-Angels (superior in every respect to us Adamites), who lived in great peace and felicity on the Earth until nearly the close of the seventh or Sabbatic age, when, in consequence of some terrific rebellion, they were brought to irretrievable ruin. Then followed the catastrophe of the supposed Glacial Period, which made the Earth a completely desolated wilderness of ice, after which, in the eighth day or period, our own inferior race of Adamites was created. As such ideas are most misleading, I think it well to offer a few observations on the points named in the heading of this Chapter.

---

* Gen. v. 1; ix. 6; 1 Cor. xi. 7; Col. iii. 10; Jam. iii.

In order to make the meaning of certain words clearer to the general reader, it will be necessary to explain them from the original. I make no pretensions to scholarship, but I know quite enough both of Hebrew and of Greek, to enable me to consult the best Lexicons, of which I have a good supply, so that my Readers may be assured that I shall give the true sense of the words referred to in these languages. I prefer reading Hebrew without points, as these form no part of the original of that concise but most expressive tongue. In the original, Hebrew letters are read from right to left, but for the English reader they are printed here from left to right, so as to be in keeping with the mode of reading English.

— —

SECTION 1.

THE DAYS OF CREATION NOT LONG PERIODS OF TIME, BUT SIX NATURAL DAYS OF 24 HOURS EACH.

The last clause of the Hebrew text—*Gen. i. 5,* cannot be better translated than it is in our Revised Version—

ve-yehe   oreb   ve-yehe   beqer   yum   ehhed

"and there was evening and there was morning day one"; the day being thus bounded by an evening and a morning, including, of course, the intervening hours between these times, proves that it could only have been a natural day of twenty-four hours duration; and this limit is repeated in every one of the six days of the Adamic Creation. Besides, we know that the Seventh or

Sabbath Day, in which God rested from His works,
consisted of twenty-four hours only, as shown by the
following passage, proclaimed on the giving of the Law
at Sinai—

" Remember the Sabbath Day to keep it holy. Six days
shalt thou labour and do all thy work, but the Seventh Day
is a Sabbath unto JEHOVAH thy God. In it thou shalt not do
any work, thou nor thy son nor thy daughter, nor thy man-
servant nor thy maid-servant, nor thy cattle, nor thy stranger
that is within thy gates, for in six days JEHOVAH made the
heavens and the earth, the sea and all that within them is,
and rested the Seventh Day; wherefore JEHOVAH blessed the
Seventh Day and hallowed it "—Exod. xx. 8—11.

Now we know that the Sabbath of the Jews, or
rather of Israel, as the Jews form only a portion of
Israel, commenced at sunset of Friday and ended at
sunset of Saturday, a period of twenty-four hours, and
as that Sabbath, as has been shown, is, as regards
duration, identified with that of the Adamic Creation,
it follows, things that are equal to the same thing being
equal to one another, that the Sabbath of the Adamic
Creation consisted of twenty-four hours also, and, as
each of the six days of Creation is evidently of the same
length as that of the Sabbath, each being bounded by
an evening and a morning, we are Scripturally, as well
as logically led to the conclusion, that each of the six
days of the Adamic Creation consisted of twenty-four
hours only.

Another important fact it is useful to notice also,
that God created the substance of the Heavens and the
substance of the Earth BEFORE the commencement of

the Adamic Creation. The word *bera*, to create, refers to a creation which had *no previous existence, asah* being generally used to express a *re*-formation, and proves the utter falsity of the Evolution myth. *Bera* shows that neither matter nor created life are, in the *strict* sense of the word, *eternal*. Of God only it can be said—*ho Patēr echei zōēn en heauto*—" The Father hath life in Himself "—*John v. 26*, i.e., SELF-EXISTENCE, INHERENT IMMORTALITY. Our immortality is only *derived;* it is a *gift,* bestowed upon believers through our Lord Jesus Christ, who says—" Because I live ye shall live also "—*John xiv. 19. Bera* is only used thrice in Genesis i.

Verse 1, To declare the creation of the Heavens and the Earth.

Verse 21, To express the introduction of life.

Verse 27, To denote the creation of the first man, Adam ; thus proving that there was no Pre-Adamite man.

In Genesis i. 1 we read,

Be-rashit	*bera*	*Alëhim*	*at*	*he-shemim*
" In the beginning	created	God	the substance of	the heavens

	ve-at	*he-arets*	
	and the substance of	the earth."	

When the beginning of Creation actually commenced no human being knows, nor has any means of knowing, because it has not been revealed.

This first verse of Genesis stands by itself alone, and refers to a creation long anterior to that which followed. The word *bera* implies creation in the completeness of order, so we may justly conclude that, in consequence of some great catastrophe, of the cause of which we are not informed, but which might possibly be the introduc-

3

tion of sin through Lucifer, this first creation was broken up, for, in the second verse, we read—

ve-he-arets	hiteh	tehu	ve-behu
and the earth	BECAME	without form	and void.

By giving the true force to the word *hiteh*, *became* instead of *was*, as rendered by our Translators, we see that the world was not *originally* created *tehu ve-behu*, without form and void, but that, according to the Word of God, it had BECOME so, and this is corroborated by another passage in the Divine Record, where it is written—

"For thus saith JEHOVAH that created the heavens. He is God, that formed the earth and made it; He established it, He created it not without form" (*tehu*)—*Isa. xlv. 18.*

This is the very word that is used for that expression in *Gen. i. 2.* The state of the wrecked world, as it doubtless appeared at the time of the Adamic Creation, is referred to by the Apostle Peter as follows—

hote	ouronoi	ēsan	ekpalai	kai	gē	ex
"That	the heavens	were	of old	and	the earth	out

hudatos	kai	di' hudatos		sunestōsa
of water,	and	by means of water		compacted together

tō	tou	Theon	logō.
by	the	Word	of God."—*2 Pet. iii.* 5.

This condition of things will, I think, account for the formation of the strata which have so long puzzled Geologists and others, and it goes to prove that the Earth is not a Planet but a " Terra Firma," " founded upon the seas and established upon the floods "— *Psa. xxiv. 2.*

The Psalmist, speaking of God in His creative works, beautifully sings—

"Who laid the foundations of the earth,
That it should not be moved for ever,
Thou coveredst it with the deep as with a vesture;
The waters stood above the mountains,
At Thy rebuke they fled,
At the voice of Thy thunder they parted away:
They went up by the mountains,
They went down by the valleys,
Unto the place which Thou hast founded for them."

Psa. civ. 5—8.

I would mention here a custom, which our Modern Astronomers have, of calling the dry land and the waters of the seas collectively under the one term *Earth*, when they refer to their supposed revolution round the Sun. It looks very like, as if they attempted by this artifice, to hide the monstrosity of the idea that the waters which, at the very least, occupy thrice the extent of the land, are carried millions of miles round the Sun, without being emptied into the air, notwithstanding their pretended law of Gravitation. The Scriptures most distinctly mark the difference between these two divisions of Creation, thus—" God said Let the waters under the heavens be gathered together into one place, and let the dry land appear; and it was so. And God called the dry land Earth, and the gathering together of the waters called He Seas "—*Gen. i. 9, 10.*

The word "day" in Scripture has a variety of meanings, and its particular interpretation, in each passage where it occurs, must be gathered from the context. Thus, to give a few illustrations—" For, in the day that thou eatest thereof thou shalt surely die "—*Gen. ii. 17,* which threat received its fulfilment on the very day in which Adam sinned, for he then *began to die,* this expression being in exact accordance with the Hebrew, *moot tamut,* " dying thou shalt die."

" One day is with the Lord as a thousand years, and a thousand years as one day "—*2 Pet. iii. 8.*

This, I think, foreshadows the continuance of this world in its present state for six thousand years from its creation, after which will be ushered in the thousand years of the Millennial Sabbath referred to in *Rev. xx. 2—5.*

Sometimes the number of a " day " represents the number of a " year," thus—

" After the number of the days in which ye searched the land, even forty days, each day for a year, shall ye bear your iniquities, even forty years, and ye shall know my breach of promise "—*Num. xiv. 34.*

" As Jonas was three days and three nights in the belly of the great sea-monster, so shall the Son of Man be three days and three nights in the heart of the earth "—*Matt. xii. 40.*

This passage refers, of course, to literal days, being expressive of the actual time that Christ continued in Sheol after His crucifixion. The idea, that our Lord was crucified on the *Friday,* and thus only remained a *part* of three days and three nights in Sheol, is, in my opinion, opposed both to Scripture and sound criticism. See the undermentioned pamphlets on that subject.*

---

* " Good Thursday, not Good Friday," by Rev. James Gall; Gall & Inglis, 20 Bernard Terrace, Edinburgh, and 25 Paternoster Square, London.
" The Good Friday Problem," by D. Nield, 7 Angus Avenue, Wellington, New Zealand; Brown & Co., Woodend, East Finchley, London.

The Reader if he pleases can find scores of illustrations relative to the specific meaning of the term " day " by reference to Cruden's Concordance under that word.

As a good illustration as to the work of the six days of Creation, I beg to refer my Readers to " Questions and Answers in the Bible and Nature," by my friend Lady Blount. They will be found in an Appendix to another work by her Ladyship, called " Adrian Galileo," in which, pp. 50—52, and 59—68, there are also some excellent observations on the Earth being a Plane and not a Planet. *

There need, therefore, be no doubt respecting the exact length of the Six Days of the Adamic Creation, for no less than six times in the First Chapter of Genesis God has called them—" Evening—morning," which limits each to the Natural Day of twenty-four hours; and, further, He corroborates the fact, by reference to the Seventh Day, " the Sabbath of JEHOVAH thy God "— *Exod. xx. 10*, which we know consisted, and still consists of twenty-four hours only.

————

SECTION 2.

NOT TWO RACES OF ADAMITES.

The Bible never hints at *two* races of Adamites, but speaks only of one, that from which we are descended, through our progenitor Adam. There has never yet

---

* Since the above was written Lady Blount has become Editress of a small but good Monthly Magazine called " The Earth," to which I beg to refer any reader who may be interested in the form of " the world we live in." Lady Blount's address is 68 Merton Road, Wimbledon.

been found the smallest vestige of a Pre-Adamite man, or of anything which he might be supposed to have left behind, in any fossil, rock, cave, or excavation in any part of the whole world. Like the Evolutionists' still undiscovered "missing link" to connect our own race of men with the monad, tadpole, or monkey, the remains of Pre-Adamite man have never yet been found, and the solution of the myth may be safely left to the time of the Greek Calends.

Angels are an entirely different order of beings from men, and, in the Old Testament, are called *Beni Elohim,* "Sons of God," who, we are told, when the foundations of the Earth were laid, "shouted for joy"—*Job xxxviii. 7.* The Poet may imagine that

"Angels are men in lighter garments clad,"

and, under certain particular circumstances, they have been mistaken for men, but, in Scripture, the distinction between them and ourselves has always been essential, and must so continue. It is only when redeemed men are raised from the dead, or changed at the Coming of our Lord, that they are said to be made *isangeloi,* equal to the angels in the respect that "they shall die no more"— *Luke xx. 36.* But I believe that, as our Lord Jesus Christ took our nature, and was in all points tempted as we are, yet without sin, we, through our special union with Him, shall form a distinct order for ever. God's government is Regal, not Republican—each in his own rank, not one dead level. "There is one glory of the sun, and another glory of the moon, and another glory of the stars, for one star differeth from another star in glory—so also is the resurrection of the dead"— *1 Cor. xv. 41, 42.*

Angels take an intense interest in man's redemption, as we find by their many appearances, related both in the Old and in the New Testaments, especially in connection with our Lord. They desire to look into the things pertaining to the Gospel salvation—*1 Pet. i. 12*, doubtless believing that, as our blessed Lord "gave Himself a ransom (*huper pantōn*) for ALL, the testimony to be borne in fitting times "—*1 Tim. ii. 6*, the period will at last arrive, when their own formerly lapsed companions, when repentant, will be restored, and, in holy adoration, with all other created beings bow, not at, but IN (*en*) the Name of Jesus, God being All in All—*Phil. ii. 9, 10; 1 Cor. xv. 20—28; Rev. v. 13.*

But, putting altogether aside the idea of Pre-Adamite MAN, it is not impossible that, before the commencement of the Adamic Creation, he who is called "the Anointed Cherub that covereth "—*Ezek. xxviii. 14*, may have held the sovereignty of the pristine world with millions of angels under him; but he rebelled against God through pride, and induced a vast multitude to follow his evil example. He was cast out of his principality, and his adhering legions with him, while those who kept their fealty to God were doubtless removed to some other habitation. The world might then have been destroyed by the complete dissolution of its component parts, which would eventually form the strata in the Great Deep. I do not speak at all positively on these matters, because we have no direct revelation on the subject, but there are certain hints, given here and there in the Scriptures, from which, perhaps, we might be led to infer that Satan may have been Lord Paramount of this world in its original creation. This might account for the ceaseless enmity which he has shown against the inhabitants of this new world from the days of Adam until now, and more especially against the Lord Jesus Christ, who, in the intensity of His matchless love, gave Himself as a Sacrifice for our redemption—even " for the life of the world "—*John vi. 51.* Thrice our Lord speaks of Satan as " The Prince of this world "—*John xii. 31; xiv. 30; xvi. 11,* and the Apostle Paul termed him—" The God of this world "—*2 Cor. iv. 4,* and " The Prince of the power of the air, the spirit that now worketh in the children of disobedience "—*Eph. ii. 2.* Doubtless he would have a special antipathy to man as his successor in the Lordship of this world, and, by his glozing lies, only alas! too successfully

> " Brought death into this world and all our woe,"

so that, in this sense, he had the power of death. But that death is only temporal, for our gracious Lord, through His own voluntary death upon the cross, came " to bring to nought him that had the power of death that is, the Devil, and might deliver all them, who through fear of death were all their lifetime subject to bondage "—*Heb. ii. 14, 15.* Blessed, indeed, are they who believe that Jesus is the Christ, the Son of God, and that believing they " may have life through His Name "—*John xx. 31.*

Mrs. Duncan's supposition that there were *two* Adamic creations will stand the test neither of Scripture nor of honest criticism. She says—

" In (Genesis, A.V.), Chapter I., verses 20, 21, we read that on the fifth day ' God said, *Let the waters bring forth* abundantly the moving creature that hath life, and *fowl that may fly* above the earth in the open firmament of heaven. And God created great whales and every living creature that moveth which the waters brought forth abundantly after their kind, and *winged fowl after his kind*, and the evening and the morning were the fifth day.' But, in Chapter II., verses 18, 19, we have the following account, '*And out of the ground* the Lord God formed every beast of the field, and *every fowl of the air*, and brought them unto Adam to see what he would call them, and what Adam called every living creature that was the name thereof."*

The translators of our Authorised Version of the Bible gave a *Mis*-rendering of the Hebrew of *Gen. i. 20*, when they said that the *waters brought forth* the fowl, and Mrs. Duncan herself confesses that other translators have rendered the Hebrew of that verse so as not necessarily to imply more than that the fowl were created on the same day as the fishes,† but she should have been more careful, and not have sought to build a matter of such vast importance as *two* Adamic Creations on the *mere conjecture* that the fowl were brought forth out of the water instead of the ground. And she was the more worthy of blame for this, as, being the wife of a Professor of Hebrew in Edinburgh, she was, as it is said in Scotland, "at the lug o' the law," that is, in a position where she could obtain the best information on the subject. It so happens that the *Hebrew* text is quite clear on the matter, and makes no discrepancy between *Gen. i. 20* and *Gen. ii. 19*. Thus, *Gen. i. 20* should be translated as follows—

| *yeshretsu* | *he-mim* | *sherets* | *nepesh* | *hheyeh* |
| Let bring forth | the waters | the moving creature | the soul | living; |

* " Pre-Adamite Man," pp. 1, 2 (4th Edition).
† Ditto, p. 2.

ve-oup   *youpep*   *ol*   *he-arets*   *ol-peni*
and fowl   let fly   above   the earth   on the face of

reqio   *he-shemim*
the firmament of   the heavens.

The late Dr. Robert Young, *in loco*, gives a similar rendering, and so does the Revised Version of the Bible —" Let the waters bring forth abundantly the moving creature that hath life, and let fowl fly above the earth in the firmament of heaven."

It is astonishing what light may be thrown on obscure, and even apparently discrepant passages of Scripture, by consulting the original. That truly would be the Higher Criticism, and well worthy of respect, which, instead of distorting the Bible with imaginary difficulties, would honestly seek to explain it, by elucidating the text and context from the original. The Word of God, like all His works of Creation, can bear the strictest scrutiny, and, the more closely it is examined, the more will the accuracy of its diction, and the depth of its meaning be observed.* The translators of the Revised Version have made some good emendations, but, in their desire not to offend the so-called Orthodoxy of the day, they have not always gone to the root of the matter, especially in their rendering of certain words relative to the future. My friend, Mr. Joseph Bryant Rotherham, Author of " The Emphasised New Testament," is now engaged in making a new translation of the Old Testament, which I sincerely trust may, when published, be found to be more literal and correct than any hitherto undertaken.

---

* I know of no book where this fact is so clearly and so fully illustrated, as in the Rev. Dr. Bullinger's magnificent work, "Figures of Speech, used in the Bible"; it is a veritable mine of Scriptural research and learning. It may be obtained from Dr. Bullinger, 25 Connaught Street, London.

SECTION 8.

REFUTATION OF THE THEORY OF TWO DIFFERENT AUTHORS OF GENESIS, FROM THE USE OF THE DISTINGUISHING WORDS ELOHIM AND JEHOVAH-ELOHIM.

Some critics bring forward an argument for a dual authorship of Genesis, from the term Elohim being used for God in the first Chapter, and the words Jehovah-Elohim subsequently. They call the one the Elohistic and the other the Jehovistic account of Creation, and this they do in hopes of setting aside the authority of Moses, by thus trying to show that not he, but *two other unknown* historians were the writers of Genesis.

The Bible, in the original is most precise in its use of proper terms. *Pasa graphē Theopneustos*, " all Scripture is God-inspired " or " God-breathed "—*2 Tim. iii. 16.* " Thy word is true from the beginning "—*Psa. cxix. 160,* and, instead of the above named words exhibiting any signs of TWO different historians, Moses, by the inspiration of God, is found to be the *sole Author* of Genesis. In the first Chapter God reveals Himself by the plural noun Elohim, expressive of His being the Almighty God of Creation and Judgment, and, in the following as Jehovah-Elohim, the self-existing God, in covenant with His creature Adam. For a full exposition of this interesting subject, I beg to refer my Readers to the able work mentioned below, by my late friend, the Rev. J. M. Denniston, M.A.* He says, p. 3—

"For appreciating the two names we must remember that Elohim is an ordinary, wide-spread word for *Deity;* while *Jehovah* is a *special* divinely-given word with a meaning which, after a time, was fully opened up, and a distinct history con-nected with the Covenant as first made with Shem. Hence we may infer that from the very first the name had a certain significance and value of its own."

YAVEH, or JEHOVAH—I am that I am—the periphrase of which is the great name "Alpha and Omega"—the First and the Last, means that God is in Covenant with His people, as will be seen from the following passage, when Israel was on the point of being delivered from the bondage of Egypt—

"And God spake unto Moses and said unto him—I am JEHOVAH: and I appeared unto Abraham, unto Isaac, and unto Jacob as God Almighty, but by My name JEHOVAH I was not known to them. And I have also established My Covenant with them to give them the land of Canaan, the land of their sojourning, wherein they sojourned. And moreover I have heard the groaning of the children of Israel whom the Egyptians keep in bondage, and I have remembered My Covenant. Wherefore say unto the children of Israel—I am JEHOVAH"— *Exod. vi. 2—6.*

The critics do not agree among themselves, so that their testimony is not reliable, and only genders strife and confusion. They are not even consistent in their folly;

---

* "Elohim and Jehovah, or the Employment of the divine names from Genesis i. to Exodus vi."; Morgan & Scott, 12 Paternoster Buildings, London.

for example, while they make Elohim and Jehovah-Elohim
the ground for two different authorships in Genesis, they
pass over in silence *other parts* of Scripture, especially
in Job, where the distinction, in the use of these two
words, is still more marked. Thus, in the first two
chapters of that wonderful book JEHOVAH only is used,
and in the last five it is again the prominent word for
God, while in the thirty-five intermediate chapters, with
one exception, the word Elohim is used. To the discerning Christian the reason for thus using these two
names is plain ; in the first two and the last five chapters,
Job's trust in JEHOVAH's Covenant faithfulness was
unshaken, while, in the thirty-five intervening chapters,
he was troubled with his grievous trial, and thought only
of God as the Elohim, Almighty in power. Further,
these learned critics, while they make use of these words
Elohim, and JEHOVAH-Elohim as the ground for assigning
two different authors to Genesis, stultify themselves by
saying that no book in the Bible is more clearly the
work of *one* author than Job, where these words are far
more forcibly distinguished than in Genesis.

The reason why these so-called Higher-Critics make
such a fierce attack on Genesis appears to be because,
as that is the *beginning* of the Scriptures, they think
that, if they can raise doubts as to *its* authority, they
can thus throw discredit on all the rest. But their
attempt is useless ; in vain do they dash their frothy
wavelets against the impregnable Rock of Truth. In
vain do they try to erase the name of Moses from the
authorship of that First Book of the Pentateuch, for the
facts which he unfolded undeniably remain, and his
authority has been endorsed by our Lord Himself over

and over again—*Matt. xix. 3—9; Mar. x. 2—9; Luke xvi. 29—31; John v. 45—47.* Let these Critics first agree among themselves before they venture to shoot another arrow—

"But no clearer proof could be given of the truth of our contention as to the disagreement among the Critics with regard to the various theories and opinions than the fact that, during the space of forty-seven years up to 1891, the 'Critics' had propounded no less than *seven hundred and forty-seven* different theories! How many more theories may have been propounded by the 'Critics' since 1891 we know not, but the above given number (747) were found and tabulated and published by the late T. M. Marshall, D.D., LL.D., in the year 1891."*

A more suitable name for these Higher Critics would, I think, be *Hyper-Critics*, for their criticism is evidently very far from being *high*, but it goes "over" or "beyond" proper criticism, just as the Hyper-Calvinist, in his dogmatic assertions, out-Herods Calvin himself. Their criticism, like the literal meaning of the Greek word *hamartia*, sin, is "a missing of the mark." They remind me, in the assistance which they so freely offer to sceptics, of the foolish young lady who, in her frantic desire to help her lover in climbing the steep,

"Flung to him down her long black hair,
Exclaiming wildly—'There, love, there'"—

and we need not be surprised, therefore, if both sceptics and critics ignominiously fall below.

---

* "The Higher Critics and their mistakes," by P. & R. H.; Marshall Brothers, Keswick House, Paternoster Row, London.

SECTION 4.

NO DISCREPANCY EXISTS REGARDING THE ADAMIC CREATION IN THE ACCOUNTS GIVEN IN GENESIS I. AND II.

There is no real discrepancy, as Mrs. Duncan supposes,* in the account of the creation of man as recorded in *Genesis i. 26—31* and *Genesis ii. 7—25;* the first briefly states that he was created in the image and likeness of God, and the second gives the details of his formation, just as a historian might mention the result of an important event in one chapter of his book, and narrate the particulars respecting it in another. It was doubtless considered unnecessary to repeat in the Second Chapter what had already been mentioned a few verses before in the First, of man having been created in the image and likeness of God, but to give a circumstantial account of the formation of Adam and his wife Eve. But, that the man of the Second Chapter is identical with that of the first, is proved a little further on where it is written—" This is the book of the generations of Adam. In the day that God created man; in the likeness of God made He him, male and female created He them, and blessed them, and called their name Adam in the day when they were created "— *Gen. v. 1, 2;* after which follows the generations of Adam's descendants from Seth to Japheth. It is thus

---

* " Pre-Adamite Man," Chapter I.

CERTAIN that there were not TWO separate creations of Adamites.

Mrs. Duncan was a clever, and I believe a good woman also, but she was misled by the wild chimeras of Geologists, and wrote some things which had better never have been written, as they only distract without enlightening the mind. All criticism, especially that on Biblical statements, to be of any real value, should be accurate and just, but, of late years, it has too frequently become so incorrect and diffuse, as to go beyond all bounds of reason, and is, therefore, worthless. It is, as Shakespeare speaks of glory—

> "Like a circle in the water,
> Which never ceaseth to enlarge itself,
> Till by broad spreading it doth come to nought."

A good illustration of such kind of criticism is given in the following quotation from the pen of that excellent Christian writer, the late Mr. H. L. Hastings of Boston, U.S.A.

"We have had already specimens of their work, and a more amazing tangle of inconsistency and contradiction can hardly be found in ancient or modern literature. The old dispute concerning the authorship of the Iliad and the Odyssey, which some one summed up as being demonstrated, that the poems 'were *not* written by Homer, but by another man of the same name and living at the same time and place,' was lucidity itself when compared with the revelations of the Higher Critics concerning the original authorship of the forty-six books of the Old and New Testaments. There are plenty of people who may be unable to judge of the correctness of the position occupied by any one of these learned men, but there can be no possible difficulty about deciding that, when each one of a dozen contra-dicts all the others, they cannot all be infallible, and here is the opportunity of the common reader to exercise a little common sense."*

It would be well if these learned Critics studied the Bible a little more closely than they appear to have done, as, in many instances, their knowledge of that Book, in comparison with their shameless effrontery in warping it, seems to be as scanty as Falstaff's ha'p'worth of bread to the unconscionable quantity of sack. In rejecting Moses they reject the upholder of Moses—the Lord Jesus Christ, and to them may be applied the withering reproof administered by our Lord Himself to the Jews—" Had ye believed Moses ye would have believed in Me, for he wrote of Me, but, if ye believe not his writings, how shall ye believe My words? "—*John v. 46, 47.*

There is, however, one good thing which these Critics, though unwittingly, have done; they have led some learned and earnest Christians to pay a closer examination to certain disputed facts mentioned in the Bible, with the positive result that that blessed Book, now rests on a stronger basis than ever. Many state-ments, which these Critics most unwarrantably declared to be false, have been now proved, by the discovery of ancient monuments, tablets, and other sources of infor-mation, to be absolutely true. Gladly, had space permitted, would I give some telling instances of these wonderful confirmations of God's Word, but must

---

* " The Higher Criticism," by the late H. L. Hastings, Boston, U.S.A.; Agents, Marshall Brothers, Paternoster Row, London.

content myself by referring my Readers to the works
mentioned below* which are well worthy of their attentive perusal.

SECTION 5.

PRIMEVAL FAUNA AND THE AGES.

The statements of Geologists, whether Dr. Pye Smith
or Sir Roderick Murchison, Dr. Dick or Sir Charles
Lyell, Drs. Buckland or Mantell, Hugh Miller, and others,
are all unsatisfactory, because they are only *suppositive*,
having no solid basis on which to build their assertions.
Skertchley himself, in his " Geology," p. 101, remarks—

---

* "Inspiration and Accuracy of the Holy Scriptures," 8vo, 7/6; and " Modern
Discoveries and the Bible," 8vo, net 6/-; both books by the Rev. John Urquhart.
    " The Higher Critics and their Mistakes," by P. and R. H.; Special Edition
for gratuitous distribution.
    " The Higher Criticism the greatest Apostasy of the Age," 1/6 net, by D. K.
Paton.
    " Daniel in the Critic's Den," by Dr. Anderson, 3/6.
    Leech's " Is my Bible true ? " 2/6.
    " The New Apologetics, or the Down-grade in Criticism," by Dr. Watts, 6/-
    " How God inspired the Bible," by Dr. J. Paterson Smyth, 2/6.
    " The Grand Old Book," by Rev. A. McCaig, 3/6.
    " Many Infallible Proofs," by Dr. A. J. Pearson, 2/-
    " Remarks on 'The Mistakes of Moses,'" 4/-; and " The Higher Criticism,"
3d.; both by the late H. L. Hastings, of Boston, U.S.
All obtainable from
Marshall Brothers, Keswick House, Paternoster Row, London.
    " History of Babylonia," by the late George Smith, Esq., of the British
Museum ; Edited by the Rev. A. H. Sayce, M.A.; 2/-.
    " Assyria, from the Earliest Times to the Fall of Nineveh," by the late George
Smith, Esq., of the British Museum; 2/-.
    " Sinai, from the Fourth Egyptian Dynasty to the Present Day," by the late
Henry S. Palmer; revised by the Rev. A. H. Sayce, M.A.; with map, 2/-.
    " Persia, from the Earliest Period to the Arab Conquest," by the late
W. J. W. Faux, M.A.; a new and revised edition, by the Rev. A. H. Sayce,
M.A.; 2/-.
    " The Higher Criticism, and the Verdict of the Monuments," by the Rev.
A. H. Sayce, M.A.; 7/6.   *Published by*
The Society for Promoting Christian Knowledge,
Northumberland Avenue, London.

"So imperfect is the record of the earth's history, as told in the rocks, that we can never hope to fill up completely all the gaps in the chain of life. The testimony of the rocks has been well compared to a history, of which only a few imperfect volumes remain to us, the missing portion of which we can only fill up by conjecture. What botanist would but despair of restoring the vegetation of wood and field from the dry leaves that autumn scatters? Yet from less than this the geologist has to form all his ideas of past flora. Can we wonder then at the imperfection of the geological world?"

Yet, notwithstanding this admitted imperfection, some geologists have drawn conclusions, which from want of proper data, are, of course, incapable of proof, with as much assurance as if they themselves had witnessed the formation of the primeval rocks. Sir Archibald Geikie lately said that, in his opinion,

"100,000,000 years would suffice for that portion of the Earth's history which was registered in the stratified rocks of the crust. But if the Palæontologists found such a period too narrow for their requirements, he could see no reason on the geological side, why they should not be at liberty to enlarge it, as far as they might find to be needful for the evolution of organized existence on the globe."[*]

From fossil marks, some of which are scarcely discernible, from a jaw-bone, a tibia or a claw, they have constructed animals of such grotesque appearance as, to use an expression common in my young days, "would be enough to frighten the French." Models of some of these relics of a by-gone age were made some years ago under the direction of Mr.

---

[*] "Report of the British Association" at Dover, from *The Daily Graphic* of September 18th, 1899.

Hawkins, and have been placed in the grounds of the Crystal Palace, Sydenham, and which, as the showman would say, " are as large as life and twice as natural."

With the late Dr. Chalmers and some others, I believe that the first verse in the Bible—" In the beginning God created the Heavens and the Earth "— by no means precludes the idea of a creation *prior* to the Adamic, though *when* such creation was it is quite impossible to tell; but, from the testimony of infallible Scripture, and from the records of the past, I myself have not the shadow of a doubt that the creation, or if preferred the *re*-creation of the world in which we live, commenced at the very time assigned to it in the Mosaic history, less than six thousand years ago. I can afford, therefore, with perfect equanimity, to let the Geologists discover as many as they can of the Fauna of an Earlier Earth, megatheria, plesiosauri, iguanodons, ' pterodac- tiles, &c., &c., of land, or water, or air, but here the line must be drawn, for there never yet has been found, and I am certain that there never will be found, the smallest trace of a supposed Pre-Adamite man, or a single bone of any of Adam's race or of any relics pertaining thereto, in any geological strata of the Earth, thus showing that there never was any Pre-Adamite Man, and that the present world of the Adamic Creation is not one hour older than it is represented to be in the Scriptures of Truth.

Such animals, as those above referred to, would no doubt have had their use in the preparation of the world for man's future habitation, as God makes nothing in vain, for, that the world was systematically made ready for the occupation of man, is evident from the particular stratification of the rocks, the chalk, the limestone, the slate, the building stone, the coalfields, &c., as well as from the position of the metals, iron, lead, tin, &c., as also from its gold, silver, and copper, and from its diamonds, rubies, sapphires, and other precious stones. It is truly a marvellous world within and without, above and below, specially adapted by God's own wisdom, love, and care for the habitation and use of man. Well may we exclaim with the Psalmist— " Oh! that men would praise JEHOVAH for His goodness, and for His wonderful works unto the children of men! " —*Psa. cvii. 8.*

From a careful consideration of the *aiōnes* or ages, which are so often referred to in the Greek of the New Testament, but which unfortunately are so obscurely rendered in our Authorised Version, it appears certain that there were ages *before* the Adamic Creation, as there will be ages *after* this present dispensation has passed away. Let us look briefly at the two following remarkable expressions respecting them.

1. *Sunteleia tou aiōnos*, the end or completion of the age.

2. *Chronois aiōniois*, in age-past times.

1. *Sunteleia tou aiōnos.*

Matt. xiii. 39, " The harvest is *the completion of the Age.*"

Matt. xiii. 40, " So shall it be at *the end of the Age.*"

Matt. xxiv. 3, " Tell us when shall these things be? and what shall be the sign of Thy coming, and of *the completion of the Age.*"

Matt. xxviii. 20, " And lo! I am with you all the days even unto *the completion of the Age.*"

Heb. ix. 26, " But now once, at *the completion of the Ages,*

He hath been manifested to put away sin by the sacrifice of Himself."

From the foregoing passages we gather that Christ will be spiritually with His people till the harvest, or completion of this present age or dispensation, when He will again personally appear to take them to be with Himself for ever. In the last quoted passage the word for " ages " is in the *plural*, from which it would seem that it there refers to *tous aiōnas epoiēsen*, the ages which He had made *previous* to this world, according to *Heb. i. 2* —" through whom also He hath made the Ages."

2. *Chronois aiōniois.*

Rom. xvi. 25, "Now to Him who is able to stablish you according to my gospel, and the preaching of Jesus Christ, according to the revelation of the mystery, kept in silence through *Age-past times,* but now is manifested."

2 Tim. i. 9, "Who saved us, and called us with a holy calling, not according to our works, but according to His own purpose and grace, which was given in Christ Jesus *before Age-past times.*"

Tit. i. 2, "In hope of eternal life which God, who cannot lie, promised *before Age-past times.*"

It is evident, from the above passages, that God chose His saints of the present age or dispensation, according to the eternal purpose of His will *long before* they had any· actual existence except in His own mind. They were redeemed, not with corruptible things as silver and gold, " but with precious blood, as of a lamb without blemish and without spot, *even the blood* of Christ, who was foreordained *pro katabolē kosmou,* before the foundation of the world, but was indeed manifested *ep eschatōn tōn chronōn* at the last stage of the times for your sake "—*1 Pet. i. 19, 20.*

We thus see that there were *ages*, and we may, therefore, presume *creations, before* that of our Adamic world. All that I contend for is, and on this point I am immovable, that *our present world* was not brought out of the Great Deep of waters, and that there was no creation of man, nor of any of the now existing species of land animals, BEFORE the time indicated by Moses in Genesis, which period has not yet reached six thousand years.

The study of the ages is one of the deepest importance towards understanding the eternal purposes of God with respect to His Creatures, and, with deference, I beg to refer any of my Readers, who might desire their farther consideration, to a volume written by myself, mentioned below,* as I know of no other work in which the subject has been so fully treated.

SECTION 6.

CHIPPED FLINTS.

More than half a century ago there was quite a furor among Geologists respecting Chipped Flints, which had recently been discovered, and which were too hastily described as being arrow heads, spear heads, and axe heads, according to their size, made by Ante-Diluvians

---

* " Hades and Beyond, with some Sidelights by the way," chapters iv., v., ix., x., xi., xiv., xv., and xviii. A copy of this work will be forwarded, post free, to any given address, by sending a postal order for 3/6 to D. Wardlaw Scott, 25 Trinity Road, Wood Green, London.

who lived in what they called the " Flint-Age." Sober-
minded people, however, had very grave doubts about
the matter, as these flints were found in so many
different places, and besides in localities so unlikely ever
to have been the abode of men, and also in such vast
quantities that the supposition of their ever having been
made by human hands was too preposterous to be
seriously entertained.   Mrs. Duncan thought at one time
that they might be relics of her Pre-Adamites, and in
the first Edition of her book, wrote accordingly.   However when she afterwards went to examine some of these
flints for herself, she had to acknowledge that she had
made a mistake, and abandoned the idea, as Mr. Jonathan
Oldbuck had to give up his Roman Camp, after the
revelations of Eddie Ochiltree.   She writes, as follows,
in the Preface to the third Edition of her " Pre-Adamite
Man "—

"It seems desirable also to state that the argument (for
Pre-Adamite Man), is in no respect founded on alleged discoveries of implements in the drift of the Pre-Adamite Age,
which came to the Author's knowledge after the work had
passed through the printer's hand, and was added by her to the
proof-sheets only as a possible corroboration of her theory;
and she begs now to add that, having since visited St. Achiel,
near Amiens, and having obtained some of the alleged Ante-
Diluvian implements on the spot, together with a portion of
the sand in which they were embedded; she has been led to
doubt very much whether these objects after all owe their
peculiar appearance to the hand of man.   It is remarkable that
the particles of sand, put under a powerful microscope, present
very much the same appearance as those larger chipped flints,
suggesting the idea that the same process of attrition which

shaped the one may have produced the marks of chipping on the other. At all events she is not confirmed by this visit, but rather the reverse, in the belief that she is entitled to appeal to this source as confirmatory of her views, but she does not believe that her argument will be much affected by the circum-stance, the substantial foundation on which it rests being based, as the title bears, on conclusions derived from Scripture and Science."

Such is the sad collapse of one of the "side-issues" of that "most exact science" of Modern Astronomy now under our consideration.

———

SECTION 7.

THE SUPPOSED GLACIAL PERIOD.

The supposed Glacial Period, of which Mrs. Duncan and certain geologists make so much, is one of the most improbable myths that was ever concocted in the human mind. Mrs. Duncan introduced it without even the slightest pretence of proof towards the close of her Sabbatic Age, the *whole* of which, according to the received meaning of the term Sabbatic, should have been a period of unbroken rest and peace, when, on account of the rebellion of her Pre-Adamites, this catastrophe was suddenly launched upon the world. The Geologists thought it might be a good pretext by which they might get rid of the Universal Deluge, but the attempt has been in vain, for ice could not have produced the effects left by the Noachian Flood. Sir Robert Ball, in his book, " The Cause of an Ice Age," previously mentioned, has done his best to bewilder people's minds upon this subject, but he does not appear to have made much headway even among Scientists, and no wonder, as his work is one of the most unconvincing ever written. For example, he says, p. 32, " I have found it necessary to *assume* the existence of several Ice Ages." It is all *assumption*, no real proof being given for even one Ice Age, and the book is utterly opposed to Scripture, Reason, and Fact. Indeed this poor waif of a theory is very ill, and it will not be long before it is sent to a dishonoured grave. My remarks may seem severe, but they are needed.

With Sir Robert Ball the Earth is, of course, only a Planetary Ball, rolling round the Sun, land and water being mysteriously held together, at the Astronomic rate of 65,000 miles per hour. Mrs. Duncan was content with one Glacial Period for the destruction of the world of her Pre-Adamites, but Sir Robert thinks there have been *several*, with more yet to follow ; considering them to be caused by perturbations in the orbit of the Earth, through the influence of certain planets. Thus he says, p. 172—

"It has been my object to show the reasons for thinking that the planets, especially Jupiter and Venus, have been the primary agents in the formation of Ice Ages; we have substantial grounds for attributing to the agency of the Planets the familiar indication of glaciation."

With Sir Robert Ball's theory, the Bible unfortunately appears to be " an unknown quantity," as it is never alluded to at all. Had he consulted it, he might have saved himself the trouble of writing his book, for God

declares in His covenant with Noah after the Deluge—
" While the earth remaineth seedtime and harvest, and
cold and heat, and summer and winter, and day and night
shall not cease "—*Gen. viii. 22.*

Sir H. H. Howorth, in his work " The Glacial Nightmare and the Deluge," would, indeed appear to have
already given this theory the *coup de' grâce ;* he writes as
follows—

" One of the chief objects of this work is to show that the
Glacial theory, as usually taught, is not sound; but that it
ignores, and is at issue with, laws which govern the movement
of ice, while the geological phenomena to be explained refuse
to be equal with it. This is partially acknowledged by the
principal apostles of the Ice theory. They admit that ice,
as all know it in the laboratory, or ice as we know it in the
glaciers, acts quite differently to the ice they postulate, and
produces different effects; that we are bidden to put aside our
puny experiments, which can be tested, and turn from the
glaciers, which can be explained and examined, to the vast
potentiality in shape of portentous ice-sheets beyond the reach
of empirical tests, and which, we are told, act quite differently
to ordinary ice. That is to say, they appeal from sublunary
experiments, to *a priori* arguments drawn from a transcendental
world. Assuredly this is a curious position for the champions
of uniformity to occupy. . . .

" I hold that the Glacial theory, as ordinarily taught, is
based not upon induction but upon hypotheses, some of which
are incapable of verification, while others can be shown to be
false, and it has all the infirmity of the Science of the Middle
Ages. This is why I have called it a Glacial Nightmare holding
it to be false. I hold further that no theory of modern times
has had a more disastrously mischievous effect on the progress
of Natural Science. . . .

"I not only disbelieve in but I utterly deny the possibility of ice being moved over hundreds of miles of level countries, such as we see in Poland and Russia, and the prairies of North and South America, and distributed drift as we find it there. I further deny its capacity to mount long slopes or to traverse uneven ground. I similarly deny to it the excavation of lakes and valleys, and I altogether question the legitimacy of arguments based upon a supposed physical capacity which cannot be tested by experiment, and which is entirely based upon hypothesis. This means that I utterly question the prime postulate of the Glacial Theory itself."[*]

From the preceding arguments in this Chapter, I think we may now safely draw the following conclusions—

1. That the days of the Adamic Creation were Natural days of twenty-four hours each.

2. That there were not *two* different creations of Adamites, but only *one*, that of our progenitor Adam.

3. That Moses was the *sole* Author of Genesis, notwithstanding all the carpings of the Hyper-Critics.

4. That there is no discrepancy regarding the Adamic Creation in the accounts given of it in Genesis I. and II.

5. That although there might possibly have been creations before the Adamic, there was no Man created *prior* to Adam, at the time assigned by Moses.

6. That the Chipped Flints were not made by human hands.

7. That the supposed Glacial Period is a myth, unworthy of true Science.

---

[*] "The Glacial Nightmare and the Deluge: a Second Appeal to Common Sense from the extravagance of some recent Geology," by Sir H. H. Howorth, K.C.I.E., F.R.S.

From the above deductions we may be assured, in accordance with the Infallible Word of God, that the Earth was emerged from the waters of the Great Deep, in which it has ever since continued stationary, not quite six thousand years ago. And further that the Sun was not in existence when at first the Earth was so emerged, as it was not formed until the *Fourth* day after that occurrence—consequently that the Earth cannot by any possibility be a *Planet* revolving round the Sun; but, on the contrary, that the Sun is only a satellite of the Earth, journeying daily around it to give it light and heat, and regulate its times and seasons.

There are, indeed, *two* Adams, but very different are they from those described by Mrs. Duncan in her Pre-Adamite Man—

"The first man Adam (our progenitor) became a living soul; the last Adam (our Lord Jesus Christ) a life-giving Spirit. Howbeit, that is not first which is spiritual, but that which is natural (soulical); afterwards that which is spiritual (pneumatical). The first Adam is of the earth earthy; the Second Man is out of Heaven "—*1 Cor. xv. 45—47.*

Blessed are the children of the first Adam who put their trust in the atoning sacrifice of the Second, even the Christ who,

"having once for all been offered for the bearing of the sins of many, shall appear a second time, apart from sin, unto those who are ardently waiting for Him unto salvation "—*Heb. ix. 28.*

CHAPTER III.

THE NEBULAR HYPOTHESIS. EXAMINATION OF THREE ALLEGED PROOFS THAT THE WORLD IS GLOBULAR.

SECTION   PAGE

1. THE NEBULAR HYPOTHESIS - - 63

2. THE CIRCUMNAVIGATION OF THE EARTH - 67

3. THE APPEARANCE AND DISAPPEARANCE OF SHIPS AT SEA - 73

4. THE EARTH'S SHADOW IN A LUNAR ECLIPSE - - 77

IT was only to be expected that our Modern Astronomers, in the absence of any *real* evidence, would invent some *imaginary* proofs, to show that the world is a Planet. They have accordingly given several, which are usually introduced

"With words of learnèd length and thundering sound."

Before examining the three referred to at the heading of this Chapter, which, being thought to be their best, are generally brought forward on all suitable occasions, I shall give a specimen of what some of these gentlemen consider to be a proof.

Mr. Schiedler, in his "Book of Nature," says,

"By actual observation we know that other heavenly bodies are spherical, hence we unhesitatingly assert that the earth is so also."

It is true that things which are equal to the same thing are equal to one another, but Mr. Schiedler, in his attempted proof, coolly takes for granted the very first premise of the proposition, namely, that the heavenly bodies and the Earth *are the same kind of things*, which even a child knows not to be so, and which the Scriptures emphatically deny—*1 Cor. xv. 40*. He might as well have said—"An elephant has ears, I have ears, therefore I am an elephant," a fact which would certainly not be proved by this halting syllogism, although, perhaps, from his absurd conclusion that the Earth is spherical, because the heavenly bodies are, some persons might be led to infer that he does not possess the reasoning faculty of that sagacious quadruped.

SECTION 1.

THE NEBULAR HYPOTHESIS.

Many, if not most, Modern Astronomers hold what is called La Place's "Grand Conception," namely, The Nebular Hypothesis, which, as stated by the well-known writer Figuier, is as follows—

"The Nebular *theory* ASSUMES that the Sun was originally a mass of incandescent matter. . . . . In consequence of its immense expansion and attenuation, the exterior rim of vapour expanding beyond the sphere of attraction is *supposed* to have been thrown off by centrifugal force. This doctrine is applied to all the planets, and ASSUMES each to have been in a state of incandescent vapour with a central incandescent nucleus. As the cooling went on, each of these bodies MAY BE SUPPOSED to have thrown off similar masses of vapour, which, by the operation of the same laws, would assume the rotary state, and as satellites revolve round the parent planet."

This theory, as will be seen by the words I have underlined, is one of *mere assumption*, without one single proof being given as to its truth. He who credits it must have the gullibility of the gudgeon, and he who can digest it would require the stomach of an ostrich. It makes God's primary creation of the Universe to be only *nebular*, and all subsequent creation to be *self-formative*, whether land or water, man or animals, coals or gold, grasses or trees. It is downright Atheism; as the Psalmist observes—" All his thoughts are—there is no God "—*Psa. x. 4.* " Science as such," as Mr. H. D. Brown truly remarks in his excellent pamphlet on " Creation," " knows not God."*

If those holding this hypothesis had only read aright the very first verse in the Bible—" In the beginning God created the heavens and the earth "—they would have seen that the derivation of the Earth as a Planet from a nebulous incandescent mass, is utterly untrue and contrary to all reason, because, according to the above emphatic declaration, the Heavens and the Earth were *distinctly created by God Himself*. They thus bring themselves into the fearful position of denying The Word of God.

Carrying out the general idea of nebulosity, some Astronomers imagine the Moon to have been at one time a portion of the Earth, while in a state of incandescence. Mr. Laing, however, who poses chiefly as a

---

* Alfred Holness, 14 Paternoster Row, London.

Geologist, casts doubts upon that subject. Thus he says, p. 43 of his "Modern Science and Modern Thought "—

"In this state of things the Moon is supposed to have been thrown off from the earth. . . . Now these conclusions may be true or not as regards phases of the earth's life prior to the Silurian period, from which downwards Geology shows unmistakably that nothing of the sort, or in the least approaching it, has occurred."

It is sad to see the absurdities and contradictions into which false science leads its votaries. It is like a bad locomotive, over which the driver has lost all control, which rushes with the train down an incline, till at last it leaves the rails altogether, smashing not only itself, but drawing carriages with it and thereby causing serious disaster to many of the unfortunate passengers.

The Nebular Hypothesis, we are told, requires many millions of years for the development of the Universe. Lord Kelvin at one time estimated 400,000,000 of years for the world to be brought to its present state of maturity, and, when some demurred to that enormous period, he obligingly struck off 380,000,000, so that he then gave the requisite time as 20,000,000 of years! Apart from revelation we can form no calculation whatever as to the time occupied in creation by God, that being utterly different from the manufacturing process of men. With us both wine and bread take a considerable time to be made, but, by Christ, the wine at the marriage feast of Cana, and the bread with which He fed the multitudes in the wilderness, were made in a moment. The Psalmist in describing the Earth as

5

being God's handiwork, says—"He spake, and it was done. He commanded, and it stood fast "—*Psa. xxxiii. 9*, referring doubtless to the time when He laid the foundations of the Earth in the waters of the mighty Deep. Then, as regards light, He simply said—"Let there be light," and there was light instantaneously. The true Christian rejoices in the *Omnipotent Power* as well as in the *Infinite Love* of God; the thought strengthens his faith and enables him, in his own weakness, to feel the support of the Everlasting Arms. He realizes that all things are his, for he is Christ's and Christ is God's—*1 Cor. iii. 22, 23*. The field of Nature is opened up to him as his possession, as Cowper beautifully sings—

> "His are the mountains and the valleys His,
> And the resplendent rivers. His to enjoy
> With a propriety that none can feel,
> But who, with filial confidence inspired,
> Can lift to heaven an unpresumptuous eye,
> And smiling say—' My Father made them all.' "*

I confess that I cannot imagine how any human being, in his proper senses, can believe that the Sun is stationary when, with his own eyes, he sees it revolving around the heavens, nor how he can believe that the Earth, on which he stands, is whirling with the speed of lightning around the Sun, when he feels not the slightest motion. I can only account for the delusion, as having been introduced by Satan into the minds of certain men, who could inoculate those of others with the poison, his object being to make it appear that God

---

* "The Task," Book V.

is a liar, and to befool the human race, which he so much abhors.   Still I by no means think that all who hold the Pythagorean fable are not Christians, for I believe that there are good men even among Astronomers, who are not aware of the source from which their theories spring, and who do not abet the infidelity to which they tend, and whose lives are better than their philosophy.   And, if the heart be right with God, we may be sure that the mistakes of science will not shut the door of grace.   But we must remember that there is a "full reward"—*2 John i. 8*—for some, who, as richly-laden galleys, shall enter the Port of Peace— *2 Pet. i. 11*—and that there is a salvation for others, who, like those who escape from a burning house, are saved "so as by fire"—*1 Cor. iii. 15.*

We thus see that the Nebular Hypothesis is a mere myth of the imagination, utterly unworthy of acceptance by any serious thinker, as being totally opposed to Scripture, Reason, and Fact.

Let us now proceed to consider the three before-mentioned alleged proofs of the world's globularity.

SECTION 2.

THE CIRCUMNAVIGATION OF THE EARTH.

Circumnavigation is a loud-sounding term, something like Homer's celebrated *polufloisboio thalassēs,** but it simply means "sailing round."   Thus a yachts-

---

* "Iliad," 1, v 34.

man can leave Ryde in the morning, and, after a few
hours, according to the state of the weather, arrive
at Ryde again, by circumnavigating or sailing round the
Isle of Wight. So a man can circumnavigate the world
from any outlying port in the extreme South, say, for
example, Hobart, and return to the same port again,
always premising that the sailing must be either from
East to West, or from West to East. If you look at a
Mercator's map of the world, or even at a pasteboard
globe, you will at once see the impossibility of a ship
circumnavigating the Earth from North to South, or
from South to North, owing to the position of the
Continents, and the great barriers of ice both in the
Northern and Southern regions. But such circular
sailing no more proves the world to be a globe than an
equilateral triangle. The sailing round the world would,
of course, take very much longer, but, in principle, it
is exactly the same as that of the yachtsman circumnavigating the Isle of Wight. Let me give a simple
illustration. A boy wants to sail his iron toy boat by
a magnet, so he gets a basin, in the middle of which he
places a soap-dish, or anything else which he may think
suitable to represent the Earth, and then fills the basin
with water to display the sea. He puts in his boat and
draws it by the magnet round his little world. But the
boat never passes over the rim to sail *under* the basin,
as if that were globular, instead of being simply *circular*.
So is it in this world of ours; from the extreme South
we can sail from East to West or from West to East
around it, but we cannot sail from North to South or
from South to North, for we cannot break through
intervening lands, nor pass the impenetrable ramparts

of ice and rocks which enclose the great Southern Circumference. Hobart is in the Latitude called by Geographers 40° S., and, if we sail thence in a Southward direction, our voyage would at last be stopped by impassable barriers of ice. Even Keith, in his famous " Treatise on the use of the Globes," acknowledges that the circumnavigation of the Earth, as hitherto accomplished, does not prove it to be a sphere : thus he says—

" Since that time (Magellan, 1519-1523), the circumnavigation of the globe has been performed at different times, by Sir Francis Drake, Lord Anson, Captain Cook, &c. . The voyages of the circumnavigators have been frequently adduced to prove that the Earth is a sphere ; but, when we reflect that all the circumnavigators sailed westward round the globe (and not northward and southward, round it), they might have performed the same voyages had the Earth been in the form of a drum or cylinder."*

The farthest Southern Latitude yet reached is about 78°, and the written accounts of those who have sailed in Antarctic Seas, plainly describe the horrors of that inhospitable region. It may be well to give a few extracts from such.   In his " Voyage to the South " Vasco de Gama remarks—

" The waves rose like mountains in height; ships are heaved up to the clouds, and apparently precipitated to the bed of the ocean.   The winds are piercing cold, and so boisterous that the pilot's voice can be scarcely heard, while a dismal and almost continual darkness adds greatly to the danger."

---

* Keith's "Treatise on the use of the Globes," p. 43, a new edition condensed and improved, by Thomas Atkinson, M.A., Simpkin, Marshall & Co., Stationers' Hall Court. London.

Captain Sir James Clarke Ross, R.N., writes as follows in his " Antarctic Voyages "—

" The sea quickly rising to a fearful height, breaking over the loftiest bergs. . . . Our ships were enveloped in an ocean of rolling fragments of ice, as hard as floating rocks of granite, which were dashing against them with so much violence that their masts quivered as if they would fall at every successive blow. The rudders were destroyed, and nearly torn from their stern-posts. . . . . Hour passed away after hour without the least mitigation of the awful circumstances in which we were placed."

In his " Exploring Expedition," Commander Wilkes, U.S.A., writes—

" The general health of the crew is decidedly affected. We feel ourselves obliged to report that in our opinion a few more days of such exposure, as they have already undergone, would reduce the number of the crew by sickness to such an extent as to hazard the safety of the ships, and the loss of all on board."

Such scenes of rigour and desolation are unknown in the Northern regions, in the same degrees of Latitude as those to which the above extracts refer in the Southern seas. In the Arctic there is a Spring and Summer, however brief, where Nature asserts her right of birth and loveliness. On this point Wrangell writes as follows—

" Countless herds of reindeer, elks, black bears, foxes, sable and grey squirrels fill the upland forests; stone foxes and wolves roam over the low ground; enormous flights of swans, geese, and ducks arrive in spring, and seek deserts where they may moult, and build their nests in safety. Eagles, gulls, and owls pursue their prey along the sea-coast; ptarmigan run in troops among the bushes; little snipes are busy among the brooks and in the morasses; the social crows seek the neighbourhood of man's habitations; and when the sun shines in spring, one may sometimes even hear the cheerful note of the finch, and in autumn that of the thrush."

I have given the above extracts from competent authorities, in order to show the vast difference which exists in the same number of degrees of Latitude between the Arctic and Antarctic regions, with regard to life and vegetation. The reason of the great disparity of the climate in these two regions cannot be better expressed than in the words of Parallax—

"Thus it is a well ascertained fact that the constant sun-light of the North develops with the utmost rapidity numerous forms of vegetable life, and furnishes subsistence for millions of living creatures. But in the South, where the sunlight never dwells or lingers about a central region, but rapidly sweeps over sea and land, to complete in twenty-four hours the great circle of the Southern circumference, it has not time to excite and stimulate the surface, and, therefore, in comparatively low Southern latitudes, everything wears an aspect of desolation."*

A glance at the Map, at the beginning of this book, will show that the parallels of latitude, instead of *converging* towards the South, as Astronomers and Geographers tell us they do, gradually *expand* from the North centre towards the boundaries of the great

---

* "Zetetic Astronomy; Earth not a Globe," pp. 116, 117, by Parallax, published by Day & Son, 17 Paternoster Square, London. I regret to say that this splendid work has for some time been out of print, and a new edition is very greatly required—meanwhile, perhaps, a stray copy might be procured by applying to Mr. John Williams, Secretary of the Universal Zetetic Society, 54 Bourne Street, Netherfield, Notts. The last price which I heard was paid for the work was £1. The original cost was 7/6.

Southern circumference. Within the last seventy years there has been quite a mania for expeditions to the North Pole, while the poor South has been shamefully neglected. Is this because it is so very far away from us, or because it is secretly feared by our Astronomical friends that there may be *no South Pole at all*, so that all their fond hopes of the Earth being a Globular Planet would be " at one fell swoop " dispelled,

> "And like the baseless fabric of a vision,
> Leave not a wrack behind "?

The result of the Challenger's prolonged cruise, as has been stated, of 70,000 miles, did not do much to raise their expectations, for, like a discouraged deerhound, that had lost the quarry, she did not discover a passage to the supposed other side of the world, through the ice-bound waters of the South. Should, however, our Astronomers consider the problem of a South Pole to be still unsolved, I would advise them, with the assistance of their good friend, the Government, to fit out another " Challenger," and endeavour "to break the record" of former explorers. At the same time I confess that I have a strong conviction that their steamer would be no more able to circumnavigate the world, by forcing a passage through the mighty ramparts of the South, than for a balloonist to steer his course through the Bands of Orion.*

---

* Since the above was written I have been glad to learn that a British Antarctic Expedition, assisted by the Government, is now in progress; also that another has been promoted by Germany, both being expected to sail from their respective countries in the ensuing summer.

SECTION 8.

THE APPEARANCE AND DISAPPEARANCE OF SHIPS AT SEA.

The Astronomical argument is as follows—

The hull of a ship, being larger than the masts, should at a distance be first visible in approaching the shore, but it is not, the masts being first seen. Again, in sailing from the shore, the hull, for the above reason, should be last seen, but it is not, for the masts are—therefore the sea must be globular.

The late Professor Huxley gave us a tit-bit of Astronomic reasoning on the above alleged proof, which is so very *recherché* that it might be gilt-framed and placed in the hall of the Royal Society. It is as follows—

"We *assume* the convexity of water, because we have no other way to explain the appearance and disappearance of ships at sea."

We *assume*, therefore water is convex! Surely this celebrated Scientist should have known that no real *proof* can be drawn from mere *assumption*. The argument may be *Huxleyan*, but it is certainly not *Baconian*, and, as he acknowledged that he had no other explanation to offer for the convexity of water, we must just take it for what it is worth, which is simply—Nothing.

Some years ago the late Mr. R. A. Proctor, a well-known writer and lecturer on Astronomy, wrote two articles in "Knowledge" on the above subject, called

"Pretty proof of the Earth's Rotundity." But alas! for the "pretty proof," as it was soon found to be no proof at all, and would never have been brought forward to prove the supposed convexity of water from the appearance and disappearance of ships at sea, had Astronomers been aware of the *true* law of Perspective. This law at the horizon requires the eye of the observer to see the *higher* part of an object before he can see the *lower*. The horizon, or the line where the sea and the sky seem to meet, *is always on a level with the eye*, no matter how high the observer may be above the water's surface. This is evident even from a balloon, as the following extract from the "London Journal" of July, 1857, will show—

"The chief peculiarity of the view from a balloon, at a considerable elevation, was the altitude of the horizon, which remained practically on a level with the eye, at an elevation of two miles, causing the surface of the Earth to appear *concave* instead of *convex*, and to *recede* during the rapidity of ascent, while the horizon and the balloon seemed to be stationary."

Mr. Glaisher writes in a like manner as to his experience in a balloon—

"The horizon always appears on a level with the eye."*

Mr. Elliot, an American Æronaut, gives a similar testimony in a letter from Baltimore—

"I don't know if I ever hinted heretofore that the æronaut may well be the most sceptical man about the rotundity of the Earth. Philosophy impresses the truth upon us, but the view of the Earth from the elevation is that of a vast *terrestrial basin*, the deeper part of which is that directly under one's feet. As

---

* Mr. Glaisher's Report in the "Leisure Hour" of 21st May, 1864.

we ascend, the Earth seems to recede, actually to sink away, while the horizon gradually, and gracefully lifts, a diversified slope stretching away further and further to the line that at the highest elevation seems to close with the sky. Thus, upon a clear day, the æronaut feels as if suspended at about an equal distance between the vast blue oceanic concave above and the equally expanded basin below."

This law of Perspective meets us on every hand; and cannot be gainsaid. If, on a straight road, we observe a row of lamps, which are all of the same size, we shall find that, from our standpoint, their height will gradually diminish as we look toward the farther end; but, if we ourselves approach to that end, the nearer we get to it, the higher proportionately will the lamps appear. Again, if, on a straight line, we look at a frozen lake from a certain distance, we shall observe people who appear to be skating on their *knees*, but, if we approach sufficiently near, we shall see them performing graceful motions on their *feet*. Farther, if we look through a straight tunnel, we shall notice that the roof and the roadway below converge to a point of light at the end. It is the same law which makes the hills sink to the horizon, as the observer recedes, which explains how the ship's hull disappears in the offing. I would also remark that when the sea is undisturbed by waves, the hull can be restored to sight by the aid of a good telescope long after it has disappeared from the naked eye, thus proving that the ship had not gone down behind the watery hill of a convex globe, but is still sailing on the *level* of a *Plane* sea.

We are generally treated in Astronomical books with a diagram, illustrative of Proctor's " Pretty proof "—

three ships on the arc of a circle one being near the
top, and one toward each end of the arc. I have one
before me now on p. 69 of the well-known work—
" Joyce's Scientific Dialogues," published by Milner
and Co., Limited, London. I got it lately in order to
refresh my memory with some of the curiosities of
Modern Science, whilst writing this book. The curve
of the arc measures three inches, and, if it were continued, the whole circle would be about eight inches,
representing the presumed circumference of the world
equal to 25,000 miles at the Equator. The length of each
ship is three-eighths of an inch, so that, by the rule of
simple proportion, each ship would be about 1,171 miles
long ! Why are such absurd diagrams given, if not to
deceive the eye and warp the judgment of the unsus-
pecting reader ? In closing my remarks on this " Pretty
proof of the Earth's Rotundity," I beg to subjoin the
following questions asked by " Zetetes " in his article
on " Ships at Sea," in the October, 1893, Number of
" The Earth (not a Globe) Review."*

" In the diagrams of ships at sea, given in Astronomical
works, Why are the ships placed near the top and not under?
Why is the first ship not placed *on the top*, why near the top,
and always *to go up* first, and then to go down afterwards?

" Has any object in Nature ever been seen to rise perspec-
tively as it recedes, and then, remaining at the same altitude,
to *descend?* By whom? When? Where? Is not the observer
always on *the top* of the Earth? If not, why not? If the Earth
were a globe, would not the horizon be a tangent to the sphere
at the point of observation? If so, ought not a ship begin to
descend at once as soon as it leaves the observer? Why does a

---

* John Williams, 54 Bourne Street, Netherfield, Notts.

vessel not suit its behaviour to the globular theory? Is it
because it is only a theory? Why do Astronomers violate the
law of Perspective when they make diagrams of ships at sea?
And now, when the tricks of the so-called Astronomical
'Science' are exposed, why should not all our readers believe
the plain truth, that the Earth and sea form one vast out-
stretched and circular plane?"

SECTION 4.

THE EARTH'S SHADOW IN A LUNAR ECLIPSE.

The Moon has been a sad trouble to our Modern
Astronomers, as she has so often belied their theories;
but, being determined to make use of her somehow,
they assert that the globularity of the world is proved by
the shadow of the Earth passing over her in a round
form during a Lunar Eclipse.

Before entering into this subject, it may be as well
to say a few words respecting Eclipses. Many people,
when they find that an Eclipse takes place at the time
predicted, are apt to think what a wonderful science
Modern Astronomy must be that can foretell such events
so exactly. But the truth is that the recurrence of
Eclipses are mere matters of calculation from those
which have happened at certain times before, and it is
known by experience that such will take place at certain
times again. The Chaldeans calculated them thousands
of years ago, and Aristarchus and Ptolemy could predict

them as well as Newton or La Place. Mrs. Somerville in her " Physical Sciences," p. 46, remarks—

" No particular theory is required to calculate Eclipses, and the calculations may be made with equal accuracy, *independent of every theory.*"

I remember a good story respecting a man who had been summoned to give evidence in a certain trial. He did not appear but a friend came in his stead. " Why," asked the Judge, " does Mr. Blank not appear? " " My Lord," replied the man, " I could give your Lordship a dozen reasons why he could not come." " Let us have them, then," said the Judge. " In the first place, my Lord, my friend is dead." " That will do," said his Lordship, " you can keep your eleven other reasons to yourself." So the Earth having been proved by experiment to have no curvature, and is declared by God to be " founded upon the seas and established upon the floods," that fact ought, as a matter of course, to be a sufficient reason why it is not a wandering Planet, and, therefore, that it would be as impossible for its shadow to cause an Eclipse of the Moon, as for that dead man to give evidence in a Court of Law. Still, perhaps, it may be useful and interesting to make a few remarks respecting this alleged proof, as they will show some of the great mistakes which our Modern Astronomers have made.

According to the Newtonian theory, it is necessary in a Lunar Eclipse, for the Sun to be on the opposite side of the supposed globular Earth, so that the Earth's shadow may thus in passing be cast upon the Moon. But, as Lunar Eclipses have occurred when both the

Sun and the Moon were above the horizon, it stands to reason that, in such circumstances, it would be absolutely impossible for the shadow of the Earth to have been the cause of the Eclipse of the Moon.

During an Eclipse of the Moon its surface has repeatedly been seen during the whole time it lasted, thus clearly proving that its Eclipse could not have been caused by the shadow of the Earth. I quote the following illustration of the fact from what took place at Collumpton, Devonshire, on 19th March, 1848—

"The appearances were as usual till twenty minutes past nine; at that period, and for the space of the next hour, instead of an Eclipse, or the shadow (umbra) of the Earth being the cause of the total obscurity of the Moon, the whole phase of that body became very quickly and most beautifully *illuminated*, and assumed the appearance of the glowing heat of fire from the furnace rather than tinged with a deep red. . . . The *whole disc* of the Moon being as *perfect with light* as if there had been *no Eclipse whatever*. . . . The Moon positively gave good light from its disc during the total Eclipse."*

Again, the Earth, with a supposed diameter of 8,000 miles, is said to revolve round the Sun, with the velocity of about 1,100 miles per minute; the Moon being reckoned to have a diameter of 2,200 miles, and to go round the Earth at the rate of 180 miles per minute, thus, according to calculation, the Eclipse of the Moon, by the shadow of the Earth passing it, should not take four minutes, whereas the usual time occupied by a Lunar Eclipse is generally about two hours, and it has been known to have been extended to four.

---

* " Philosophical Magazine," No. 220, for August, 1848.

Parallax sums up the matter as follows, and quotes several instances to show that the opinion has lately gained ground among Astronomers of note, that there are *non-luminous* bodies in the heavens which may cause an Eclipse of the Moon—

"We have seen that during a Lunar Eclipse the Moon's self-luminous surface is covered by a semi-transparent 'something'; that this 'something' is a definite mass, because it has a distinct and circular outline, as seen during its first and last contact with the Moon. As a Solar Eclipse occurs from the Moon passing before the Sun, so, from the evidence above collected, it is evident that a Lunar Eclipse arises from a similar cause. A body, semi-transparent and well defined, passing before the Moon; or between the Moon's surface and the observer on the surface of the Earth.

"That many such bodies exist in the firmament is almost a matter of certainty, and that one such as that which eclipses the Moon exists at no great distance above the Earth's surface, is a matter admitted by many of the leading Astronomers of the day."*

It is thus clearly evident that there is not the shadow of a proof that the shadow of the Earth is the cause of a Lunar Eclipse, and therefore no argument can be drawn from this alleged proof that the Earth is a globular Planet.

I doubt not that many of my Readers know the famous passage in the Æneid—

> *Facilis descensus Averni,*
> *Sed revocare gradus superasque evadere ad auras,*
> *Hic labor, hoc opus est.*

---

* " Zetetic Astronomy," pp. 148, 149.

It is true that Virgil did not write as an Astronomer, but as a Poet, yet the thought has occurred to me that the above lines, with a small parenthetical addition, might be suitably employed to show the impossibility of our World careering round the Sun, and might, perhaps, be read with renewed appreciation by some of our repentant Astronomers, thus—

" It is easy to descend to the lower regions,
But (for the Earth) to retrace its steps and ascend to the upper skies,
There is the difficulty—this is the task."

CHAPTER IV.

REMARKS ON SOME OTHER ALLEGED PROOFS OF
THE WORLD'S GLOBULARITY.

SECTION		PAGE
1.	VARIABILITY OF PENDULUM VIBRATIONS	85
2.	SUPPOSED MANIFESTATION OF THE ROTATION OF THE EARTH	86
3.	RAILWAY AND EARTH'S CENTRIFUGAL FORCE	89
4.	DECLINATION OF THE POLE STAR	90
5.	MOTION OF STARS NORTH AND SOUTH	91
6.	THE PLANET NEPTUNE	93

AFTER the collapse of the three strongest alleged proofs for the globularity of the world, treated in the previous Chapter, it seems to me to be almost unnecessary to examine those of less importance, but, as some of my Readers may, perhaps, like to know at least what they are, I beg to name the following list.

Loss of time on sailing westward—Sphericity from semi-fluidity—Degrees of Longitude—Spherical Excess —Theodolite Tangent—Tangential Horizon—Station and Distance—Great Circle sailing—Continued Daylight in the extreme South—Analogy in favour of Rotundity— Deflection of falling bodies—Difference of Solar and

Sidereal time—Station and Retro-gradation of Planets
—Transmission of Light—Precession of the Equinoxes
—Variability of Pendulum vibrations—Supposed mani-
festations of the Rotation of the Earth—Railways and
the Earth's Centrifugal force—Declination of the Pole
Star—Motion of Stars North and South—The Planet
Neptune.

It would take up too much time and occupy more
space in this volume than can be spared, to enter into
a detailed examination of all these alleged proofs, most
of which are of a technical character, but, should any
of my Readers care to see them fairly discussed, and,
I may add, fully refuted, in a masterly manner, I beg
to refer them to the able work of Parallax, " Zetetic
Astronomy, Earth not a Globe," already mentioned.
However, in order to show somewhat of their nature, I
purpose making a few remarks on the last half dozen
of those named, and from these alleged proofs may be
learned the worthlessness of them all, as far as *real
evidence* is concerned. Some of them are ingenious, and
show that our Astronomical friends have had their wits
sharpened by the desire to devise *some* reasons for
upholding their theory that the Earth is a Planet, but
all their arrows fall short of the mark, being " turned
aside like a deceitful bow "—*Psa. lxxviii. 57.*

The following tit-bit from Professor Airy is worth
quoting, as showing, *in the absence of proof*, how fond
our Astronomers are of *Theory, Supposition, and
Assumption.*

" Newton was the first person who made calculations of the
figure of the Earth, in the *theory* of gravitation. He took the
following *supposition* as the only one to which his *theory* could

be applied. He *assumed* the Earth to be a fluid. This fluid he *assumed* to be equally dense in every part. . . . For trial of his *theory* he *supposed* the fluid Earth to be a spheroid. In this manner he *inferred* that the form of the Earth would be a spheroid in which the length of the shorter is to the length of the longer or equatorial diameter in the proportion of 229 to 230."*

The following tit-bit is a choice specimen of occult reasoning, taken from Sir Norman Lockyer's work on "Astronomy"—

"You have *to take it as proved* that the Earth moves."

Here is another from Sir John Herschel—

"*We shall take for granted* from the outset the Copernican system of the world."

These gentlemen do not condescend to give even one single proof that their system is true, and might with as much folly have said—"We shall take for granted that the Moon is made of green cheese." One more tit-bit I copy from the pen of that redoubtable champion of Modern Astronomy, the late Mr. R. A. Proctor, as it is such a good illustration of the "Doctrine of Assumption," so frequently set forth in this "most exact" School of Science—

"We find that the Earth is not flat, but a globe, not fixed, but in very rapid motion; not much larger than the Moon, and far smaller than the Sun, and the greater number of the stars."

"We find"! indeed, but *quo warranto*, by what authority? Where is the proof of the finding? In courts of Law the prisoner is not condemned till he

---

* Professor Airy's Six Lectures on Modern Astronomy, 4th Ed., p. 194.

has been *proved* guilty, so neither, in the courts of Common Sense, can the Earth be adjudged guilty of revolving round the Sun, till it has been *proved* to have committed that preposterous offence.

We see, from the extract before given from Professor Airy's Lectures, that even he acknowledges that Newton's theory of the globularity of the Earth is only *supposition* and *assumption*, and yet by Modern Astronomers it is paraded about as if it had been a true deduction from exact experiment. The only "exactness" which Modern Astronomy appears to possess is its "inexactness," for it differs *toto cælo* from the Astronomy of the Word of God and the facts of Nature.

SECTION 1.

VARIABILITY OF PENDULUM VIBRATIONS.

The Pendulum was summoned into court to be a witness for the spheroidity of the World, and its revolution round an imaginary axis. The length of a Pendulum, vibrating seconds at the Equator, was found to be 39.027 inches, while at 79° 49' 58" N, it was 39.197 inches. The Earth being thus *assumed* to be a globe, it is argued that it must have "a centre of attraction of gravitation," and, as the Pendulum falls more rapidly at the North Pole than at the Equator, the radius must thus be shorter, so it is said that the Earth is a sphere flattened at the Poles. But all this

is beside the mark, for the very first element of proof
is wanting, namely, that the Earth is a globe at all.

It is a well ascertained fact that heat expands while
cold contracts most metals, and it was at last acknowledged that variations of temperature are quite sufficient
to cause variations in the vibrations of the Pendulum.
Mr. Bailey, in Vol. 7 of Memoirs of the Royal Society,
says that

"the vibrations of a pendulum are powerfully affected in
many places by local attraction of the substratum on which
it is swung, or by *some other influence* at present unknown to
us, and the effect of which far exceeds the errors of observation."

General Sabine himself relates, that

"Captain Foster was furnished with two invariable Pendulums of precisely the same form and construction as those
which had been employed by Captain Kayter and myself. Both
Pendulums were vibrated at all the stations, but, from *some
cause* which Mr. Bailey *was unable to explain*, the observations
of one of them was so *discordant* at South Shetland as *to require*
their rejection."*

The Pendulum declines, therefore, to stand sponsor
for the supposed Rotation of the Earth.

————

SECTION 2.

SUPPOSED MANIFESTATION OF THE ROTATION
OF THE EARTH.

In 1851 M. Foucault made a strong effort, by means
of the Pendulum, to prove the Rotation of the Earth

———

* "Figure of the Earth," by Johannes Von Gumpach; 2nd Edition, pp. 229-244.

round its imaginary axis, and the attempt was for a while hailed with delight by the Scientific world. The following extract, from an article respecting it, appeared in the Literary Gazette of the day.

"Suppose the Pendulum already described to be set moving *in a vertical plane from North to South;* the place in which it vibrates to ordinary observation, would appear to be stationary. M. Foucault, however, has succeeded in showing that this is not the case, but that the plane itself is slowly moving round the fixed point as a centre in a direction contrary to the Earth's rotation, i.e., with the apparent heavens, from East to West. His experiments have since been repeated in the hall of the Observatory, under the superintendence of M. Arago, and fully confirmed. If a point be attached to the weight of a Pendulum by a long and fine wire, capable of *turning in all directions,* and nearly in contact with the floor of a room, the line which this point appears to trace on the ground, and which may be easily followed by a chalk mark, will be found to be slowly, but visibly and continually moving round like the hand of a dial."

Many were the experiments made in the Pantheon and other halls of science to test the truth of this wonderful experiment, but the indignant Pendulum would not lend itself to lure men into the belief of a Rotating Earth, for its vibrations were most variable, and even sometimes entirely contrary to what the Newtonians said they ought to be, so that this marvellous experiment, which was to convince the public at sight, that the world is a Rotating Planet, had to be abandoned with disgust. But how could it be otherwise? If the Earth rotates at the rate of 1,000 miles per hour at the

Equator, and in the same space of time goes 65,000 miles on its journey round the Sun, how could any Pendulum, under such disadvantageous circumstances be ever expected to beat equal vibrations? It would be an impossibility. Hence no proof can be adduced from the Pendulum that the Earth is a spheroid rotating on an imaginary axis. *Punch* could not miss the opportunity of having a joke at the expense of this rotating *fiasco*, with which I shall close my remarks of the supposed manifestation of the rotation of the Earth.

" To the Editor of *Punch*,

    " Sir,

       " Allow me to call your serious and polite attention to the extraordinary phenomenon demonstrating the rotation of the Earth, which I at the present moment experience, and you yourself or anybody else, I have not the slightest doubt, would be satisfied of under similar circumstances. Some sceptical individuals may doubt that the Earth's motion is visible, but I say, from personal observation, it is a positive fact. I don't care about latitude or longitude, or a vibratory pendulum, revolving round the line of a tangent on a spherical surface, nor axes, nor apsides, nor anything of the sort. That is all rubbish. All I know is that I see the ceiling of this coffee-room going round. I perceive this distinctly with the naked eye—only my sight has been sharpened by a slight stimu-lant. I write after my sixth go of brandy and water, whereof witness my hand.

                               " SWIGGINS.

" Goose and Gridiron, May 5, 1851.

    " P.S.—Why do two waiters come when I only call one? "

SECTION 8.

RAILWAYS AND EARTH'S CENTRIFUGAL FORCE.

A Newtonian says—

"Another proof of the diurnal motion of the Earth, has been made manifest since the introduction of railways. On railways running due North and South in the Northern hemisphere, it is found that there is a greater tendency in the carriages to run off the line to the right than to the left of a person proceeding from the North to the South, or from the South to the North in the Northern hemisphere. But this is the case in all parts of the world on lines of railway so placed whether they are long or short."

It would be difficult to beat this piece of impertinent bounce. It is not an argument, but simple *assertion* and *assumption*, and does not really deserve an answer. Practical railway men treat such a statement as that above made with contempt, because they know that it never has been found true in experience. Well may Astronomers call the axis round which the Earth is said to rotate "imaginary," as it has no existence in fact.

That the Earth has no rotation has been frequently shown by the firing of a cannon loaded with ball, fixed firmly in the ground, in an exactly vertical position. It has been found that, after the cannon has been fired by a slow match, the ball on an average took fourteen seconds to ascend and fourteen seconds to descend, and that it generally fell within two feet of the cannon, indeed, in some instances, it actually returned to the

cannon's mouth. Now, if the Earth, as stated by
Astronomers themselves, moves from West to East, and
rotates in the latitude of England, at the rate of 600
miles per hour, it being estimated at 1,000 at the Equator,
the ball should, by their calculations, have fallen more
than a mile and a half behind the cannon, instead of
which it fell close to it, thus clearly proving that there
is no rotatory motion in the Earth whatever.

SECTION 4.

THE DECLINATION OF THE POLE STAR.

Our Modern Astronomers have ransacked Creation
—the Heavens, Earth, and Sea, to discover some *real*
proof that this world of ours is a Planet, but have been
as unsuccessful as were the prophets of Baal to bring
down fire on Carmel—*1 Kings xviii. 23—28*. One of
the many *alleged* proofs they have offered, is the
Declination of the Pole Star, as the traveller journeys
from the North towards the Equator. They seem to be
unaware that this Declination is caused simply by the
law of Perspective, which makes an object appear lower
the further we recede from it, as has been already
explained in the disappearance of ships at sea after their
quitting the shore, or of mountains when we leave them
behind. The angle under which an object is seen
diminishes the farther we recede from that object, until,
at a certain point, the line of sight, and the apparently
uprising surface of the Earth upon or over which it

stands, will converge to the angle which constitutes the vanishing point, beyond which the object is invisible. The horizon is always a *straight* line wherever it may be seen, whether from the level of the sea, or from a balloon three miles high in the air, a certain proof that the Earth is a Plane and not a Planet.

SECTION 5.

THE MOTION OF STARS NORTH AND SOUTH.

It has been asserted, as another supposed proof of the rotundity of the Earth, that, as the Great Bear and other constellations sweep around the Northern Polar Star, so the Southern Cross and other stars circle round a small star in the South, called Sigma Octantis. This, however, is only *assertion*, not proof, and even if it were true, would not affect the question as regards the shape of the Earth. From every meridian at the Equator can be seen the Pole Star, the Great Bear and many other stars in the Northern region, but cannot be seen from the Equator the Southern Cross or the Sigma Octantis, which ought to be visible there if there were a South Pole. Sir James Clarke Ross did not see the Southern Cross till he was 8° South of the Equator,* and, in their scientific voyage to Brazil in 1817—1820, MM. Von Spix and Carl Von Martins wrote as follows—

"On the 14th June, in Latitude 14° S., we beheld for *the*

----
* "South Sea Voyages," Vol. *i*, p. 119.

first time, the glorious constellation of the Southern heavens, the Cross, which to navigators is a token of peace, and, according to its position, indicates the hours of the night. We had long wished for the constellation, as a guide to the other hemisphere, we therefore felt inexpressible pleasure when we perceived it in the resplendent firmament."

Again, Humboldt says—

"We saw distinctly, *for the first time,* the Cross of the South on the nights of the 4th and 5th of July, in the 16th degree of Latitude. It was strongly inclined, and appeared from time to time among the clouds. . . . The pleasure of discerning the Southern Cross was warmly shared in by such of the crew as had been in the Colony."

Were there such a thing as a South Pole why is it that the Southern Cross is not visible at the Equator? The nearest approach to that ever recorded was that of Sir James Clarke Ross in 8° S., and in Longitude 30° W. Again, it would be seen far above the horizon, like the Great Bear round the Pole Star, whereas, when Humboldt saw it in Latitude 16° S., it was "strongly inclined," which means that it was rising in the East, and joining with the other stars in the great movement round the Northern heavens.

It is evident, therefore, that the world is no more a Globular Planet than a shilling is, and that a South Pole is only an unproved assumption of our Modern Astronomers.

SECTION 6.

THE PLANET NEPTUNE.

When I was a young man, about half a century ago, I had read a good deal concerning Astronomy and Geology, and, although a Poet, one of a class usually allowed to have considerable scope for imagination, I could never credit the Munchausen fables taught about the stars and rocks. I confess, however, that my scepticism regarding Modern Astronomy was, for a short time, somewhat shaken, when I heard that Dr. Galle of Berlin had discovered a Planet, whose existence had some time previously been independently predicted by M. Le Verrier and the late Professor Adams of Cambridge.

It seems that, for some time, perturbations had been observed in the Planet Uranus, and these Astronomers thought that they must have been occasioned by some planet beyond Uranus, and made their calculations accordingly. The whole scientific world was elated, and pæans of triumph sounded in all directions at the appearance of this newly found planet. And I must say I was not surprised, for sadly did our Astronomers need some peg on which to hang a proof of the rotundity of the world. But, unfortunately for them, it was not long before this supposed proof died a natural death, as it was soon ascertained that Neptune, the lately discovered planet, *did not at all answer* to any of the calculations made respecting it, as the following extract from *The Times* of 18th September, 1848, will show—

"Paris, September 15, 1848.

"The only sittings of the Academy of late in which there was anything worth recording, and even this was not of a practical character, were those of the 29th ult. and the 11th inst. On the former day M. Rabinet made a communication respecting the planet Neptune, which has generally been called M. Le Verrier's planet, the discovery of it having, as it has been said, been made by him, by theoretical deductions which astonished and delighted the scientific public. What M. Le Verrier had inferred, from the action in other planets, of some body which ought to exist was verified—at least so it was said at the time, by actual vision. Neptune was actually seen by other Astronomers, and the honours of the Theorist obtained additional lustre. But it appears from a communication of M. Rabinet, that this is not the planet of M. Le Verrier. He had placed the planet at a distance from the Sun equal to thirty-six times the limit of the terrestrial orbit—Neptune revolves at a distance equal to thirty times of these limits, which makes a difference of nearly *two hundred million of leagues!* M. Le Verrier had assigned to his planet a body equal to thirty-eight times that of the Earth, Neptune has only one-third of the volume! M. Le Verrier had stated the revolution of his planet round the Sun to take place in two hundred and seventeen years, Neptune performs its revolution in one hundred and sixty-six years! Thus, then, Neptune is not M. Le Verrier's planet, and all his theory as regards that planet falls to the ground. M. Le Verrier may find another planet, but it will not answer the calculations which he had made for Neptune."

Thus we see that the supposed prediction respecting

the planet Neptune, instead of being a proof of the truth of Modern Astronomy, has only been instrumental in driving another big nail into its coffin. But even if Le Verrier's calculations had been right, while they might possibly have propped up for a little longer the tottering fabric of this "science falsely so called," they could not avert its ultimate fall. They afford no proof of the world's globularity, for there is no necessary connection whatever between the size and revolution of a Planet, and the figure and stability of the Earth.

CHAPTER V.

THE WORLD CIRCULAR BUT NOT GLOBULAR;
HAS IMMOVABLE FOUNDATIONS, THEREFORE
NOT A PLANET.

SECTION   PAGE

1. RELATIVE PROPORTION OF LAND AND WATER -   96

2. THE COMPASS A PROOF THAT THE EARTH IS NOT
A PLANET   -   -   -   -   -   -   98

3. DANGERS OF NAVIGATION IN SOUTHERN SEAS,
CAUSED BY THE THEORY THAT THE WORLD
IS GLOBULAR   -   -   -   -   -   102

4. THE SUPPOSED REVOLUTION OF THE EARTH
ROUND THE SUN PROVED TO BE UNTRUE   108

5. THE EARTH STRETCHED OUT UPON THE WATERS,
WHICH HAVE AN IMPASSABLE CIRCUMFERENCE   111

6. THE EARTH PROVED TO HAVE IMMOVABLE
FOUNDATIONS   -   -   117

SECTION 1.

THE RELATIVE PROPORTION OF LAND AND WATER.

WHEN I call the World Circular, I mean to convey
the idea that it is Circular as a basin, but not Globular
as a ball, the two adjectives having entirely distinctive
meanings. Again, when I speak of the Earth or dry

land as being Horizontal, I do so relatively not absolutely, as its mountains at once refute the supposition of its being a *perfect* Plane. Mount Everest, the highest part of the Himalayan range, is 29,000 feet, or about five and a half miles, above the level of the sea, but this is a mere trifle in comparison with the vast extent of the Earth. It is estimated that that portion of the Earth constituting the Continents of Europe, Asia, and Africa is about 10,800 miles in breadth, and that the length of North and South America is about 8,200 miles, besides which there is the large, but much smaller Continent of Australia, and islands innumerable, of great and small degree. The average height of the whole land above sea level is considered to be about 1,000 feet.

The whole surface of the world is reckoned to be about two hundred million square miles, of which three-tenths is stated to be land and seven-tenths water.* Some authorities estimate the land to be one-fourth, and others only one-fifth in proportion to the expanse of the water. The greatest depth of any ocean as yet sounded is found to be in the Pacific, where in some places it is over four thousand fathoms, which is a little more than four and a half miles, from which it would appear that the irregularities of the sea are not so great as those of the land. It has been supposed, indeed, that, for the most part, the great ocean beds are flat, as may be seen from the following quotation from Professor W. B. Carpenter's work, "The Deep Sea and its contents"—

"Nothing seems to have struck the 'Challenger's' surveyors

---

* "The Library Atlas," William Collins, Sons & Co., Limited; Glasgow, London, and Edinburgh.

more than the extraordinary flatness (except in the neighbourhood of land) of that depressed portion of the Earth's crust
which forms *the floor of the ocean area.*"

This comparative flatness of the vast ocean beds
will account for the calm, regular flow of the immense
currents of the Great Deep to be referred to afterwards,
and proves beyond doubt that the Earth is not a
Planetary Globe. It is also noteworthy that the oceans
become shallower in the vicinity of the Southern Circumference, where the soundings of the " Erebus " and
" Terror " varied from 400 to only 200 fathoms.* From
this it would appear that the waters of the Great Deep
are contained in a vast circular rocky basin, and confirms
the Scriptural statement that the Earth " is founded upon
the seas and established upon the floods "—*Psa. xxiv. 2.*

SECTION 2.

THE COMPASS A PROOF THAT THE EARTH IS NOT A PLANET.

Our Modern Astronomers have strained every nerve
to make people believe that the Earth is a Globular
Planet. Of the many proofs which may be given that
it is not, one of the simplest and best, after those derived
from Scripture and the incontrovertible fact of the levelness of the sea, is obtained from the Mariner's Compass.
Had the Astronomers, or their disciples, only consulted
it, they would soon have been convinced, from the
following reasons, that the Earth is not a Planet but a

---

* "Imperial Gazetteer," article "Antarctic," p. 165.

Plane. The needle of this most important instrument is *straight*, its two ends pointing North and South at the same time, consequently *the meridians must be straight lines* also; whereas, on a Globe, they are *semi-circles*. Even at the Equator the needle *points straight*, which would be impossible, were that the mid-way of a vast convex Globe, as, in such case, the one end would dip towards the North, and the other be pointed towards the sky. Again, the navigator, when he goes to sea, takes his observations, and relies on the Compass to guide him as to the direction in which he wishes to proceed; he does not provide himself with the model of a Globe, which, if the world were a Globe, would surely be the safest plan for him to adopt, but he takes flat maps or charts. Thus, *in practice*, he sails his ship as if the sea were *horizontal*, though *in theory* he had been erroneously taught that it is *convex*.

I shall not enter into a discussion respecting the deviation or declination of the Compass in certain places, especially in very high latitudes, the cause of which has not yet been satisfactorily explained.

The late Astronomer Royal, Sir George B. Airy, says in his treatise on Magnetism—

"On the whole we must express our opinion that the general cause of the Earth's magnetism still remains one of the mysteries of cosmical physics."

Professor Newmayer remarks—

"That without an examination and survey of the magnetic properties of the Antarctic regions, it was utterly hopeless to strive with any prospects of success at the advancement of the theory of the Earth's magnetism."

I do not expect, however, that such examination, which,

indeed, should have been made long ago, will do much
to clear up the mystery of the magnet.

The introduction of the Compass into Europe is of
comparatively recent date; most probably the first
application of it there was made by Marcus Paulus, a
Venetian, who had travelled in China, and brought back
the invention from that country in 1260. What confirms
this conjecture is, as stated under the article " Compass "
in the Encylopædia Britannica—

"That at first they used the Compass in the same manner
as the Chinese still do, i.e., they let it float on a little piece of
cork, instead of on a pivot. It is added that their Emperor
Chiningus, a celebrated Astrologer, had a knowledge of it
1,120 years before Christ."

The Phœnicians, in their long voyages to Carthage
and the Cassiterides, must doubtless have known its use,
as also the Israelites in the time of Solomon, when they
made their three-year expeditions to and from Tarshish
and Ophir.* Moderns, who deem themselves " so very
advanced " in science, are, in many things, mere *parvenus*
to the Ancients.

Our Astronomers, as also all who are acquainted with
the use of the Compass, know that, when undisturbed,
its needle always points to the NORTH. Now if, as they
tell us, the Earth is continuously turning round its
imaginary axis, twenty-four thousand miles every day,
as well as travelling around the Sun upwards of five
hundred and sixty millions of miles every year, it follows,
as a matter of course, that the needle would point out
the NORTH *as being in every part of the circuit of the
heavens*, during the time occupied by the Earth in its

---

* 1 Kings x. 11, 22; 2 Chron. x. 21.

supposed revolutions; so that, in this case, the Magnetic Pole, instead of being *a specific point*, would be a *vast circle*.

But the NORTH is that particular locality which is situate immediately under the Pole or North Star, and does not leave its habitat. The Compass, in being carried round with the world, while its needle would still point to the NORTH, would consequently cease to be of any service whatever in showing the true direction by land or sea; its occupation, like Othello's, would be gone, for the NORTH will not change its position to suit the whims of Modern Astronomers. Under the Pole Star its place was fixed by God before the creation of Adam —there it is now—and there it will remain "till the heavens be no more "—*Job xiv. 12*, and "the Earth also and the works that are therein shall be burned up "— *2 Pet. iii. 10*.

Notwithstanding this our Astronomers still persist in teaching the Earth's axial motion, and its revolution round the Sun, theories which, if true, would, for the reasons above given, result in the utter obliteration of *all locality*, North, South, East, and West, and the engulfment of all the distinctive landmarks of nature in one universal chaos. To such I would exclaim with Jacob—" O my soul, enter not thou into their secret " —*Gen. xlix. 6*. Alas! for poor Astronomic Science! To what depths of folly does it descend when it rejects the Word of God for fables. The fact of the Compass needle always pointing to the NORTH, like the fact of water invariably finding its own level, conclusively proves that the Earth is stationary—a veritable *Terra Firma*, and not a revolving Planet.

SECTION 3.

DANGERS OF NAVIGATION IN SOUTHERN SEAS, CAUSED BY THE THEORY THAT THE WORLD IS GLOBULAR.

Modern Astronomers have caused great danger to shipping in Southern Seas, by inducing the Nautical Authorities to frame their tables of Navigation on the assumption that the world is Globular. If we look at any globe we see that its circumference is always greater at the middle than at any other part. The circumference of the world at the Equator is estimated by our Astronomers as being about 25,000 statute. miles, and consequently longitudes *decrease continuously* from that line to what they call the North and South Poles. But, upon the principle, as taught by Scripture and common observation, that the world is not a Planet, but consists of vast masses of land stretched out upon level seas, the NORTH being the *centre* of the system, it is evident that the degrees of longitude will *gradually increase* in width the whole way from the North centre to the icy boundary of the great Southern Circumference. In consequence of the difference between the actual extent of longitudes and that allowed for them by the Nautical Authorities, which difference, at the latitude of the Cape of Good Hope, has been estimated to amount to a great number of miles, many Ship-masters have lost their reckoning, and many vessels have been wrecked.

Parallax, in his able work "Zetetic Astronomy," previously mentioned, has gone fully into this matter, but the whole is too long for quotation here, so I shall confine myself only to a few of the more important particulars—

"In laying the Atlantic cable from the *Great Eastern* steamer in 1866 the distance from Valencia, on the South-Western coast of Ireland, to Trinity Bay, in Newfoundland, was found to be 1,665 miles. The longitude of Valencia is 10° 30' W., and of Trinity Bay 53° 30' W. The difference of longitude between the two places being 43°, and the whole distance round the earth being divided into 360°. Hence, if 43° be found to be 1,665 nautical or 1942 statute miles, 360° will be 13,939 nautical or 16,262 statute miles; then taking the proportion of radius to circumference, we have 2,200 nautical or 2,556 statute miles as the actual distance from Valencia in Ireland to the Polar centre of the earth's surface." p. 91.

The above reckoning was corroborated almost exactly by Mr. Gould, Coast Surveyor to the United States Government, who ascertained—

"the difference of longitude between Heart's Content station, Newfoundland, and that at Valencia, or in other words, between the extreme points of the Atlantic cable—to be 2 hours, 51 minutes, 56.5 seconds."*

"The Sun passes over the earth, and returns to the same point in twenty-four hours. If in 2 hours, 51 minutes, 56.5 seconds, it passes from the meridian of the Valencia end of the cable to that of the termination at Heart's Content, a distance of 1,942 statute miles, how far will it travel in twenty-four hours? On making the calculation, the answer is 16,265

---

* *Liverpool Mercury*, 8th January, 1867.

statute miles. The result is only three miles greater distance than that obtained by the first process." p. 92.

Let us now look at a Southern Longitude—

" In the Australian Almanac for 1871, page 126,* the distance from Auckland (New Zealand) to Sydney is given as 1,315 miles nautical measure, which is equal to 1,534 statute miles. At page 118 of the Australian Almanac for 1859, Captain Sloper, H.M.S. *Acheron*, communicates the latitude of Auckland as 36° 50' 05" S. and longitude 174° 51' 40" E.; latitude of Sydney 33° 51' 45" S., and longitude 151° 16' 15" E. The difference in longitude or time distance, is 23° 34' 25", calculating as in the case of Valencia to Newfoundland, we find that 23° 34' 25" represents 1,534 statute miles, 360° will give 23,400 statute miles as the circumference of the earth at the latitude of Sydney, Auckland, and the Cape of Good Hope. Hence the radius or distance from the centre of the north to the above places is, in round numbers, 3,720 miles. Calculating in the same way, we find that from Sydney to the Cape of Good Hope is fully 8,600 statute miles." pp. 93, 94.

As regards Longitudes still farther South Parallax writes as follows—

" Having seen that the diameter of the Earth's surface— taking the distance from Auckland in New Zealand, to Sydney, and thence to the Cape of Good Hope, as a *datum arc*—is 7,440 statute miles; we may inquire how far it is from any of the above places to the great belt of ice which surrounds the Southern oceans. Although large ice islands and icebergs are often met with a few degrees beyond Cape Horn, what may be called the solid, immovable ramparts of ice seem to be as far south as 78 degrees. In a paper read by Mr. Locke before the

---

* Published by Gordon & Gotch, London, Sydney, and Melbourne.

Royal Dublin Society, on Friday evening, November 19th, 1860, and printed in the Journal of that Society, a map is given representing Antarctic discoveries, on which is traced a 'proposed exploration route,' by Captain Maury, U.S.A.; and in the third paragraph it is said: 'I request attention to the diagram No. 1, representing an approximate tracing of the supposed Antarctic continent, and showing the steamer track, about twelve days from Port Philip, the chief naval station of the Austral seas, to some available landing point, bight or ravine, under the shadow of the precipitous coast.' The steamer's track is given on this map in a dotted line, curving eastwards from 150 degrees to 180 degrees longitude, and from Port Philip to 78 degrees south latitude. If we take the chord of such an arc, we shall find that the direct distance from Port Philip to 78 degrees south would be about nine days' sail, or ten days' from Sydney. No ordinary steamer would sail in such latitudes more than 150 miles a day; hence ten times 150 would be 1,500 miles; which added to the previous ascertained radius at Sydney, would make the total radius of the earth, from the northern centre to the farthest known southern circumference, to be 5,224 statute miles. Thus, from purely practical data, setting all theories aside, it is ascertained that the diameter of the earth, from the Ross Mountains, or from the volcanic mountains of which Mount Erebus is the chief, to the same radius distance on the opposite side of the northern centre, is more than 10,400 miles; and the circumference, 32,800 statute miles." pp. 97, 98.

In consequence of the difference between fact and theory, as exemplified by the actual extent of longitudes in Southern seas greatly exceeding the calculations made by Official Authorities, which are based on the supposition that the world is globular, instead of horizontal.

many valuable lives and vessels have been sacrificed. Ship-captains, who have been educated in the globular theory, know not how to account for their getting so much out of their course in Southern latitudes, and generally put it down to currents; but this reason is futile, for although currents may exist, they do not usually run in *opposite directions*, and vessels are frequently wrecked, whether sailing East or West. Even such an astute navigator as Sir James Clarke Ross, R.N., remarks in his " South Sea Voyages "—

" We found ourselves every day from twelve to sixteen miles by observation in advance of our reckoning."—Vol. I., p. 96.

" By our observations at noon we found ourselves fifty-eight miles to the eastward of our reckoning in two days." p. 27.

As proof that much danger to life and property arises from this great nautical mistake respecting the extent of longitudes in Southern seas, I beg to subjoin the following testimony from independent sources—

" In the Southern hemisphere navigators to India have often fancied themselves east of the Cape when still west, and have been driven ashore on the African coast, which, according to their reckoning, lay behind them. This misfortune happened to a fine frigate the *Challenger* in 1845."*

" How came Her Majesty's ship *Conqueror* to be lost? How have so many other noble vessels, perfectly manned, *perfectly navigated*, been wrecked in calm weather, not only in a dark night, or in a fog, but in broad daylight and sunshine—in the former case upon the coasts, in the latter upon sunken rocks—from being ' out of reckoning,' under circumstances which until now have baffled every satisfactory explanation."†

---

* " Tour through Creation," by Rev. Thomas Milner, M.A.
† " Figure of the Earth," p. 206, by Von Gumpach.

"Assuredly there are many shipwrecks from alleged errors of reckoning, which may arise from a somewhat false idea of the general form and measurement of the Earth's surface; such a subject, therefore, ought to be candidly and boldly discussed." *

So long as our Nautical Authorities continue under the mesmerism of Modern Astronomers, we may expect but little, if any, change in the Laws of Navigation, and, as for the Astronomers, judging from the past, there does not seem much chance of amendment. Still, it is not impossible that even from among them, some brave spirits may arise, who, for the sake of our common humanity, will break the bonds of theory by grasping the sword of fact. I would respectfully and earnestly suggest that the Government itself should take up the matter, and appoint a competent Committee who would thoroughly investigate the subject, as to whether the world is Globular or Horizontal. If the men of that Committee are honest, and willing to determine the question by their appeal to facts, corroborated by actual demonstration, as well as by Scripture, I have not the slightest doubt that the result of their verdict would be—that the Earth is a *Terra Firma*, stretched out on the horizontal waters of the Great Deep. The Government could then give instructions to the Nautical Authorities at the Board of Trade, to amend their Laws of Navigation accordingly, just as in 1862, the Houses of Lords and Commons issued an Order that all Railways were to be constructed on a *Datum Horizontal line* without allowing one inch for curvature.

---

* *The Builder*, 20th September 1862.

SECTION 4.

THE SUPPOSED REVOLUTION OF THE EARTH
AROUND THE SUN PROVED TO BE UNTRUE.

Mr. Laing, on page 122 of "Modern Science and Modern Thought," tells us that

"The distance of the Earth from the Sun being 93 million miles, and its orbit an ellipse nearly circular, it follows that in Mid-Winter, in round numbers, it is 186 million miles distant from the spot where it was in Mid-Summer."

Such revolution of the Earth is altogether fabulous. If it were true there would, by observation, be discovered a difference in the relative position of the stars, but there is not. This fact was one of Tycho Brahe's chief objections against the theory of a revolving Earth. Experiments were tried in his day at intervals of six months to test if there was any difference, but, after the keenest scrutiny, none was found, thus proving the Earth to be stationary. Tycho Brahe was not only a great Astronomer, but an honest man, and dared, in spite of all opposition, to speak what he believed to be true. Would that we had a few more like him now; in such case there would soon be a change in Astronomic and Geographic text-books, as far as regards the figure of the world.

Mr. Laing attempts an explanation, as follows—

"Their (the stars) distance is so vastly greater than 186 million miles, that a change of basis to this extent makes no change perceptible to the most refined instruments in their bearing as seen from the Earth."

Nil Dicit, his explanation is simply—nothing. The presumed measurements of a few, apparently the nearest, stars, have been made on an *entirely erroneous basis*, and are, therefore, not of the slightest value. Tycho's objection against the revolution of the Earth is known to be as valid now, as when he proved its truth more than 300 years ago, and the subterfuge used to evade it is utterly futile.

Our Modern Astronomers were at first of opinion that the Sun was the *Centre* of the Universe, but in later years, as has been already observed, most, if not all of those whose ideas respecting the infinite have become very considerably enlarged, now think the Sun to be a subsidiary itself, although still the Baal or Lord of the Solar system. They still consider the Earth to be a mere satellite of the Sun, and to revolve around it at the rate of eighteen miles per second! Dear Reader, do you feel the motion? I trow not, for if you did, you would not so quietly be reading my book. I doubt not you have been, like myself, on a railway platform when an express train rushed wildly past at the rate of sixty-five miles per hour, when the concussion of the air almost knocked you down. But how much more terrible would be the shock of the Earth's calculated motion of *sixty-five thousand miles* per hour, one thousand times faster than the speed of the railway express. Astronomers try to evade the argument that persons would be killed thereby, by saying that, as the air goes around with the Sun, the shock would not be felt, but this will not meet the facts of the case, for thousands of people travel from

East to West, which is directly contrary to the course which Astronomers say the Earth takes—from West to East—so that such travellers would have to bear the whole force of the concussion. Happily, however, no deaths, resulting from such a catastrophe, have as yet been recorded in the columns of *The Times* or *Telegraph*, so that it would decidedly seem that the tremendous revolution of the Earth, whirling round the Sun, were a mere phantom of the Astronomic brain. What about

> " The lazy-pacing cloud,
> That floats upon the bosom of the air? "

According to the dictum of science, it should, with the speed of lightning, follow the atmosphere of the Earth round the Sun, but it moves as slowly as

> " The boy, with satchel on his back,
> Creeping like snail unwillingly to school."

What about the lark which, at early morn, soars aloft, trilling its lays of luscious melody? Why was it not swept away in the tumultuous atmosphere? But it still continues singing, in happy ignorance of any commotion in the heavens. Who has not noticed, on a calm Summer day, the thistle-down floating listlessly in the air, and the smoke ascending, straight as an arrow, from the peasant's cottage? Would not such light things as thistle-down and smoke have to obey the impulse and go with the Earth also? But they do not. I am sure that neither Mr. Coxwell and his companion, nor, indeed, any other æronauts, would ever have ventured into the car of a balloon, if they thought they would run the risk of being carried round the Sun by the resistless force of the atmosphere accompanying the Earth. Yet such, according to the law of science, would undoubtedly be the case with respect to the balloon, but, whether the bodies of the unfortunate æronauts would continue to be carried round the Sun, like Ixion on the wheel, or whether, becoming melted by the heat, like the wax on the wings of Icarus, they would fall into the gulf below, is a question which I am not sufficiently learned to decide, and prefer leaving it for discussion at an early meeting of the Royal Astronomical Society.

It is evident, therefore, from the above reasons, that there is no revolution of the Earth around the Sun.

SECTION 5.

THE EARTH STRETCHED UPON THE WATERS, WHICH HAVE AN IMPASSABLE CIRCUMFERENCE.

If the Reader will kindly look at the Map at the beginning of this book, he will see that the centre of this world is at that part which our Astronomers call the North Pole, around which, at no very great distance, the Continents of Europe, Asia, and North America commence their far-extending masses amid vast oceans towards the great icy barriers of the Southern Circumference, which no human being has ever yet passed.

According to the teaching of the Bible, the Earth is STRETCHED OUT UPON THE WATERS—*leruqo he arets ol he-mim*—*Psa. cxxxvi. 6. Leruqo* comes from the verb *reqo*, to stretch out, extend, or expand, hence the noun *reqio*, the firmament, or the stretched out expanse of the heavens. There is no idea whatever of globularity in the word, it simply means "stretched out" or "spread abroad." This we may see by the following quotations— "They did beat into *thin plates* the gold "—*veriqou at pehhe hezehheb—Exod. xxxix. 3.* Again—"He that spread abroad the Earth and that which cometh out of it "— *Isa. xlii. 5.* Speaking of the greatness of God, Zophar, the Temanite, said to Job among other similitudes—"the measure thereof is longer than the Earth and broader than the Sea "—*Job xi. 9,* and Jehovah asks Job the question—"Hast thou considered the breadth of the Earth?"—*Job xxxviii. 18.* There is no spheroidity in measures of *length* and *breadth*.

Farther, this stretching out the Earth upon the waters was done by God alone—"that stretcheth out the Earth by Myself "—*reqo he arets meati—Isa. xliv. 24.* The Earth is no fortuitous concourse of atoms, as some suppose, nor an off-shoot from the Sun, as thought by others, nor even metamorphosed from that "wonderful stone," with the mythic account of which, Lord Kelvin, when Professor Thomson, astonished the weak nerves of a Glasgow audience some years ago. That was, indeed, a most "wonderful stone," shot from some ruptured body in the heavens, containing germs which, in the course of untold millions of years, were evolved into varying forms of life and usefulness, until at last the "wonderful stone" became this beautiful world of ours! With this marvellous stone the image of the great goddess Diana, which, it was said, fell down from Jupiter, was nothing whatever in comparison. Let us hear the Word of God—" I am JEHOVAH that maketh all things ; that stretcheth out the heavens alone, that spreadeth abroad the earth by Myself; that frustrateth the tokens of the liars, and maketh diviners mad ; that turneth wise men backward, and maketh their know-ledge foolish "—*Isa. xliv. 24, 25.*

The Earth, being thus "stretched upon the waters," has, of course, waters *under* it; so we read that the Israelites were commanded as follows—

" Thou shalt not make unto thee any graven image, or any likeness of any thing that is in the Earth beneath, or that is in *the waters under the* Earth "—*Exod. xx. 4;* and again—" Thou shalt not make thee any graven image, or any likeness of any thing that is in Heaven above, or on the Earth beneath, or that is in *the waters beneath the Earth* "—*Deut. v. 8.*

No waters could possibly exist under a revolving Planet—but waters do exist under the Earth—therefore the Earth is not a revolving Planet.

In *Isaiah xl. 22* God is poetically described as sitting upon or over (*ol*) "the circle of the Earth." The Hebrew word there used for circle is *hhoog*, a circle or circumference, *not a globe*, and the Greek word used to translate it in the same passage in the Septuagint is *guros*, a circle, not *sphaira*, a sphere. The fact is that no word for " globe " or " sphere " occurs in the Bible from beginning to end. Again, in *Proverbs viii. 27*, we read, *be-hhegoo hhoog ol peni tehoom*, " when He set a circle upon the face of the deep," referring to the impassable ice barriers of the great Southern Circum-ference. This is corroborated by *Job xxvi. 10*—" He hath described a circumference upon the face of the

8

waters, unto the boundary of light with darkness ";
or, as Dr. Young translates it—" a limit hath He placed
on the waters, unto the boundary of light with darkness."
The word here used for " boundary " or " limit " is
hhoog, the same as described as " circle " or " circumference," as previously noted.

Before leaving this subject of the Circumference,
there is one other passage in the Authorised Version of
the Bible to which I would like to refer, as it has been
made a pretext for believing the theory of the Earth
whirling round the Sun. It is as follows—" He
stretcheth out· the North over the empty place, and
hangeth the Earth upon nothing "—*Job xxvi. 7.* The
Hebrew is—*neteh tsephoon ol tehoo tehleh avets ol
belimeh*, the proper translation of which is—" He
spreadeth out the North over the desolate place (the
abyss of waters), and supporteth the Earth upon
fastenings." I am much surprised that not only the
translators of the Authorised and Revised Versions, but
such a distinguished scholar as the late Dr. Robert
Young, could have made such a strange mistake, as to
say that God " hangeth the Earth upon nothing," which
is neither a proper rendering nor common sense ; besides
which it distinctly contradicts the Word of God which,
in so many other places, declares that *the Earth rests
upon Foundations.* There must be a support for any
thing that hangs, and our Modern Astronomers were not
long in taking advantage of the above mistranslation by
saying that, as it was impossible for such a heavy mass
as the Earth to stand by itself, the passage must mean
that it whirls round the Sun by the force of Gravitation.
But a little examination of two words in the original

will soon put matters straight. Shakespeare says,
   " The Earth hath bubbles, as the water hath,'
and the theory of the world rushing round the Sun,
impelled by the hypothetic law of Gravitation, is one of
the biggest that ever required pricking.

The Hebrew word *teleh* means to hang, suspend, or
support by *actual contact*. Thus, to give a few instances—

   " Shall hang thee upon a tree "—*Gen. xl. 19.*

   " On the willows, in the midst thereof we hanged up our
harps "—*Psa. cxxxvii. 2.*

   " Will men take a pin of it to hang any vessel thereon?"
—*Ezek. xv. 3.*

But *belimeh*, wrongly translated " nothing," is the
crucial word. Our translators appear to have derived
it from the noun *blee*, signifying consumption or desolation, and the pronoun *meh*, who, which, what, but the
meaning " nothing," drawn from these words, seems to
be very far-fetched. Hebrew is a very ancient language,
in all probability the most ancient of any, and this being
the only place in the Bible where the word *belimeh*
occurs, it is, of course, difficult to test the meaning. I
have myself, however, not the slightest doubt, that
Parkhurst is right in deriving the noun *belimeh* from
the verb *belem*, to confine, restrain, or hold in, so used
in *Psa. xxxii. 9*, and that *belimeh* simply means
" fastenings," or " supports," and this interpretation
exactly agrees with what JEHOVAH asked Job a little
farther on—" Whereupon are the foundations (*ademeh*,
sockets) made to sink, or who laid the corner-stone
thereof? "—*Job xxxviii. 6.* But, while I consider Parkhurst to be correct as to the *rendering* of the word
belimeh, I believe him to be wrong as to the strange

application of it which he makes when he says—

"What can this mean but the columns of light and spirit, between which the Earth is suspended (comp. *1 Sam. ii. 8*), and which, like the two reins of a bridle, *hold* (if I may be allowed the expression) the mighty steed within its circular course."[*]

That Parkhurst, from the "Record of his Life," was an excellent man, there is every reason to believe, and that he was a profound scholar we know, but he was a Hutchinsonian, and held peculiar views as to the Earth's movements by means of conflicting ethers, which he drags in on every possible occasion. I cannot here enter into his theory, which I consider to be quite untenable, but would refer any who might wish to examine it to an able work by Mr. J. A. Macdonald, "The Principia and the Bible; a Critique and an Argument."[†] Bagster's "Analytical Hebrew and Chaldee Lexicon" also gives the meaning of the verb *belem*, "to bind, to bridle," and I am informed, on reliable authority, that Breslau also derives *belimeh* from *belem* to fasten, but I have not his Lexicon at hand to verify the fact myself.

It is, therefore, evident from the above examination, that the real meaning of *belimeh* in *Job xxvi. 7* is that God supports the Earth upon fastenings, or, in other words, upon "foundations," the truth of which will be fully confirmed in the following Section, in which it will be seen that the Earth is not only *stretched out* upon the waters which have an impassable circumference, but that it has *Immovable Foundations*, therefore IT CANNOT BE A PLANET.

---

[*] Parkhurst's Hebrew Lexicon, p. 65, 8th Edition ; C. & J. Rivington, London.
[†] Judd & Glass, New Bridge Street, London.

SECTION 6.

THE EARTH PROVED TO HAVE IMMOVABLE FOUNDATIONS.

" The pillars of the Earth are the Lord's, and He hath set the Earth upon them "—*1 Sam. ii. 8.*

" The foundations of the world were discovered at the rebuke of JEHOVAH "—*2 Sam. xxii. 16, and Psa. xviii. 15.*

" Where wast thou when I laid the foundations of the Earth? Declare if thou hast understanding. Who determined the measures thereof if thou knowest? or who stretched the line upon it? Whereupon were the sockets made to sink? or who laid the corner-stone thereof? "—*Job xxxviii. 4—6.*

" He hath founded (*yesedeh*) it upon the seas, and established (*yebooneneh*) it upon the floods "—*Psa. xxiv. 2.*

" The world also is established that it cannot be moved "—*Psa. xciii. 1 and xcvi. 10.*

" Of old hast Thou laid the foundation of the Earth "—*Psa. cii. 25.*

" He founded the Earth upon its bases that it cannot be moved for ever "—*Psa. civ. 5.*

Thou hast established (*kunenet*) the Earth and it abideth " (*vetomed*)—*Psa. cxix. 90.*

" JEHOVAH by wisdom founded (*yesed*) the Earth "—*Pro. iii. 19.*

" When He gave the sea its bound, that it should not transgress His commandment, when He appointed the foundations of the Earth "—*Pro. viii. 29.*

" For the windows on high are open, and the foundations of the Earth do shake "—*Isa. xxiv. 18.*

"Have ye not understood from the foundations (*musdut*) of the Earth?"—*Isa. xl. 21.*

"Yea, mine hand hath laid the foundation of the Earth"—*Isa. xlviii. 13.*

"If Heaven above can be measured, and the foundations of the Earth searched out beneath, then will I also cast off all the seed of Israel for all that they have done, saith JEHOVAH"—*Jer. xxxi. 37.*

"Hear, O ye mountains, JEHOVAH's controversy, and ye enduring foundations of the Earth"—*Mic. vi. 2.*

"I will utter things which have been kept secret from the foundation (*katabolē*) of the world"—*Matt. xiii. 35.* The word used in this passage for foundation means literally "a casting down," see *Heb. xi. 11.* Parkhurst in his Greek and English Lexicon, p. 299,* writes as follows—

"If *katabolē* in this expression be understood strictly in this sense, it will seem parallel to the Hebrew *yesed, founding* or *laying a foundation,* and the whole phrase *katabolē tou kosmou* to the Hebrew *arets yesed, laying the foundations of the Earth,* which is several times used in the Old Testament," &c.

"Inherit the Kingdom prepared for you, *pro katabolē kosmou,* before the foundation of the world"—*Matt. xxv. 34.*

"The blood of all the prophets which was shed from the foundation of the world"—*Luke xi. 50.*

"For Thou lovedst Me (*pro*) before the foundation of the world"—*John xvii. 24.*

"Even as He chose us in Him before the foundation of the world"—*Eph. i. 4.*

"Thou, Lord, in the beginning hast laid the foundation of the Earth"—*Heb. i. 10.*

"Who was fore-ordained, indeed, before the foundation of the world"—*1 Pet. i. 20.*

---

* Edition, 1851, Longman & Co., London.

"Whose names are not written in the Book of Life of the Lamb, slain from the foundation of the world"—*Rev. xiii. 8.*

"And they that dwell on the Earth shall wonder, they whose names were not written in the Book of Life from the foundation of the world"—*Rev. xvii. 8.*

There is, however, one question which the enquirer still may ask—Granting that the Earth has foundations, *to what* are these foundations fixed, for there is no *stability* in water by which the Earth could be firmly held? To this I answer—the Bible does not say that the Earth was fixed *to* the waters or seas, but that it was founded (*ol*) *upon* or *over* them, which we know from other Scriptures previously mentioned to be positively true—"the waters UNDER the Earth"— *Exod. xx. 4; Deut. v. 8.* What difficulty would there be for God, who made the strong firmament of the Heavens above, and with whom all things are possible —*Mar. ix. 23*, except to "deny Himself"—*2 Tim. ii. 13*, to form such a vast basin of impregnable rocks as would contain the whole waters of the Great Deep? Is it not written He hath "bound the waters in a garment? Who hath established all the ends of the earth?"— *Pro. xxx. 4.* Upon such a basin the foundations of the mountains could be settled, and the hills which were of old—*Pro. viii. 25.* "The pillars of the Earth are JEHOVAH's, and He hath set the world upon them" —*1 Sam. ii. 8, Job ix. 6.* The mountains, and other lands, which have been already discovered in various parts of the farthest known Southern Seas, may in all probability, form the beginning of those impassable barriers which girdle the mighty basin of the world's location, designated by Job as—"a circumference upon the face of

the waters, unto the boundary of light with darkness "—
Job xxvi. 10.

One more question may still be asked—By what
means could this stupendous basin of rocks be upheld?
I reply at once—by THE FIAT OF GOD, "upholding all
things by the Word of His Power "—*Heb. i. 3.* Thought
utterly fails in attempting to solve the problem of God's
Omnipotence. It becomes lost, like a little child in a
pathless forest. "Canst thou by searching find out
God? Canst thou find out the Almighty unto perfec-
tion? It is high as Heaven what canst thou do?
Deeper than Sheol, what canst thou know "—*Job xi. 7, 8.*
In depths such as this, the only right way for us is, in
humility of heart, like the poor lacemaker,

> "Who knows, and knows no more, her Bible true,
> A truth the brilliant Frenchman never knew,"*

to believe what God—"who cannot lie "—*Tit. i. 2*—
declares to be true, that the Earth is "founded upon
the seas, and established upon the floods "—*Psa. xxiv. 2.*
Our ignorance will, then, through His teaching, be
changed to knowledge, and our faith become a citadel
of strength.

I am quite aware of the argument of *Accommodation,*
used by some, especially by scientific parsons, I presume
as a sort of soporific to their conscience, that, of course,
God knew that the world goes round the Sun, but
states in the Bible, that the Sun goes round it, in
deference to the ignorance of men who daily see it
apparently so revolving. Such prevarication as this
appears to me to be nothing less than making a liar

---

* Cowper's "Truth."

of Him of whom it is written—" It is impossible for God to lie "—*Heb. vi. 18*, and requires to be treated with the contempt that it deserves. What a travesty would such be in the character of the Holy God, in thus lending Himself to such a Jesuitical and such a useless deception!

Dear Reader, do not let us make any mistake in a matter of such deep importance as this. We cannot serve two masters—we cannot believe that the Bible and Modern Astronomy are both true, for the teaching of the one is diametrically opposed to that of the other. A writer in " The Earth and its Evidences," of October, 1888, truly remarks—

" The attempt to harmonize the Mosaic and the modern or professional system of the universe, is plainly to attempt the communion of light with darkness. How often has failure waited on such incongruous unions! But still some there are who never seem to recognize the hopelessness of the task."

Even the infidel Thomas Paine clearly saw this years ago when he wrote in " The Age of Reason "—

" The two beliefs cannot be held together in the same mind, he who *thinks* he can believe both, *has thought very little of either*."

As God so distinctly declares that of old He laid the foundations of the Earth—*Psa. cii. 25*, do not let us be so sinful and foolish as to say that He did not. Only shame and confusion of face can be expected to follow those, who defiantly reject the revealed Word of the Living God for the contradictory theories of dying men.

CHAPTER VI.

THE HORIZONTALITY OF LAND AND WATER PROVED.

SECTION   PAGE

1. RAILWAYS   - - -   - -   122

2. RIVERS   -   126

3. CANALS   -   127

4. SUBMARINE CABLES   134

5. THE LIGHT OF LIGHTHOUSES SEEN AT A DISTANCE   135

SECTION 1.

RAILWAYS.

OUR Modern Astronomers tell us that the world, consisting of land and water, forms a Globe bulging out a little at the Equator, somewhat in the shape of an orange. Geographers follow suit, and, in illustration of the theory, have manufactured a · pasteboard globe, on which are marked the principal places in the world, with a North and South Pole, parallels of Latitude and Longitude, &c., &c. I have beside me now Keith's well-known "Treatise on the use of the Globes," which, I am sure, would try the patience and the brains of any ordinary mortal who may attempt to master its pages. Astronomers have also favoured us with a Globe of the

Heavens, made, like a dress-coat, to order, in the most approved style of fashion, though the fact is that the Heavens are no more a Globe than the Earth is, for it is written that God—" Stretcheth out the Heavens as a curtain, and spreadeth them out as a tent to dwell in " —*Isa. xl. 22; Zech. xii. 1*. The firmament, as already shown, is called in Hebrew *reqio*, a stretched out expanse, and Job is asked the question—" Canst thou with Him (God) spread out the sky, which is strong as a molten mirror ? "—*Job xxxvii. 18*. But, as we are now dealing with things that are Terrestrial we shall leave those that are Celestial for the present.

Rational people believe Salisbury Plain to be a *Plane,* and Lake Windermere to be *horizontal*, but our Astronomers say that this is all a mistake, that we must not trust our eyes, when we see these or other such places, as being horizontal, but that we should believe what they tell us, that Salisbury Plain, Lake Windermere, as also all other plains, lakes, and places upon the Earth, as well as the vast Pacific and all other oceans, are only parts of a great Globe, and, therefore, must have a CURVE; besides which, *mirabile dictu*, that all rush together round the Sun at the rate of 65,000 miles per hour ! They give their law for this fancied curvature, based on the world being 25,000 miles in circumference at the Equator, as being 8 inches for the first mile, 2 feet 8 inches for the second, 6 feet for the third, and so on, the rule being to square the number of miles between the observer and the object, then multiply that square by 8 inches and divide by 12 to bring it into feet, the quotient being the supposed curvature. Unfortunately, however, for Astronomers this theory does not

agree with fact, for this rule of curvature has been found
to be utterly fallacious both on land and water. All
houses have to be built on level ground, but no allowance
whatever is made for the curvature of the Earth, and
all compasses point North and South at the same time
even at the Equator, which incontestably proves that the
sea is horizontal, and, therefore, that the world is not
globular, for if it were, one end of the magnet would
then dip towards the North and the other point to the
Heavens.

Seeing, doubtless, the absurdity of the Astronomic
law of curvature, and the difficulties to which, if
attempted to be carried out in practice, it would lead,
the Houses of Lords and Commons, in the Session of
1862, made the following Order with regard to Railway
operations—

"The section shall be drawn to the same *horizontal* scale
as the plan, and to a vertical scale of not less than one inch to
every one hundred feet, and shall show the surface of the
ground marked in the plan, the intended level of the proposed
work, the height of every embankment, and the depth of every
cutting, and *a datum horizontal line, which shall be the same
through the whole length of the work;* or any branch thereof
respectively, and shall be referred to some fixed point. . . .
near either of the termini. (See line D.D. fig. 2)."*

Besides the above Government Order for the construction of Railways on *a datum horizontal line,* we are
informed in " Theoretic Astronomy," p. 47, as follows—

"On the Royal Observatory wall at Greenwich is a brass
plate, which states that a certain horizontal mark is 154 feet

---

* Vacher & Sons, Broad Sanctuary, Tothill Street, London.

above mean water at Greenwich, and 155.7 feet above mean water at Liverpool."

Here our Astronomers publicly acknowledge that the difference of the level of the water between Greenwich and Liverpool is only one foot seven inches, while, by their theoretic law of curvature, reckoning the direct distance as 180 miles, the difference of level between these two places should be over four miles! They thus completely stultify their own law of curvature, and expose themselves to ridicule by thus upholding a theory so contrary to ascertained fact.

In proof of the Astronomic supposed curvature not being allowed for in the construction of Railways, let me cite the case of the well-known London and North-Western Railway between London and Liverpool, which forms a straight line between these two places of 180 miles. The highest point, about midway, is at the station of Birmingham, which is 240 feet above the level of the sea at London and Liverpool. If we suppose the Earth to be a globe, the chord of the arc between London and Liverpool, according to Astronomic theory, would be at Birmingham 5,400 feet above sea level, added to which the actual height of the station at Birmingham (240 feet), when we would have the theoretic height there of 5,640 feet, which would be more than a thousand feet above Ben Nevis, the loftiest mountain in Great Britain, which everyone who has been at Birmingham knows not to be the case. Thus it is clear that this Astronomic law of curvature fails in actual practice. In a long line, like that of the Great Pacific Railway, extending across North America, the supposed curvature would, of course, be proportionately great, extending to many miles in height, but not one inch was allowed by the engineers for curvature during the whole course of the construction of that vast line of Railway. And, if we think of it, how could it be otherwise? All Railway metals *must*, of necessity, be *straight*, for how could any engine or carriage run with safety on a *convex* surface?

SECTION 2.

RIVERS.

Let us look at the case of Rivers. In the grand language of Scripture it is said of God—" Thou didst cleave the Earth with rivers "—*Hab. iii. 9*, every one of which, large or small, a nameless brook or the mighty Amazon, flows DOWNWARDS, as it is written—" All rivers run into the sea "—*Ecc. i. 7*. Whoever heard of a river in any part of its course flowing UPHILL? Yet this it would require to do were the Earth a Globe. Rivers, like the Mississippi, which flow from the North southwards towards the Equator, would need, according to Modern Astronomic theory, to run UPWARDS, as the Earth at the Equator is said to bulge out considerably more, or, in other words, is *higher* than at any other part. Thus the Mississippi, in its immense course of over 3,000 miles, would have to *ascend 11 miles* before it reached the Gulf of Mexico! Whereas it is described as

" a rapid desolating torrent, its violent floods from the melting of the snow in the higher latitudes, sweeping away whole forests."*

Again, in one portion of its long route, the great river Nile flows for a thousand miles with a fall of only one foot, which, of course, would be a sheer impossibility, were the Astronomic curvature a reality. Yet this curvature is still acknowledged to be an essential part of Modern Astronomic Science, as taught in this tinsel age. Well might even Ovid exclaim—

> "*Prob Superi! quantum mortalia pectora cœcœ*
> *Noctis habent.*"

Heavens! what thick darkness pervades mortal breasts, and Jeremiah might repeat his wail of sorrowful reproach—

"A wonderful and horrible thing is come to pass in the land, the prophets prophesy falsely and the priests bear rule by their means, and my people love to have it so, and what will ye do in the end thereof?"—*Jer. v. 31.*

———

SECTION 8.

CANALS.

We shall now take evidence of the non-curvature of the Earth from Canals, and it may be well to commence with the Bedford Canal, as that some years ago attracted a good deal of attention among Scientific men.

The late Mr. John Hampden, of Swindon, Wilts, a

---

* "Imperial Gazeteer," article "Mississippi," Blackie & Son, Glasgow, Edinburgh, and London.

great opponent of the Copernican theory of the Earth,
offered to wager £500 that the water of the Bedford
Canal was perfectly level, and, after some considerable
time had elapsed, the challenge was accepted by Professor
Alfred Russell Wallace of London. These gentlemen,
accompanied by their friends, the late Mr. William
Carpenter, then of Lewisham, afterwards of Baltimore,
Mr. W. B. Coulcher of Downham Market, and Mr. J. H.
Walsh, Editor of *The Field*, who held the stakes,
accordingly met at the Bedford Canal on 5th March, 1870,
to decide the question. It was originally intended to test
experiments similar to those which had been made by
Parallax several years before, but, unfortunately, this
plan was, at the last moment abandoned, and another
mode of trial adopted, the effect of which Mr. Hampden
did not understand ; in consequence of which, much to
his disgust, he believed he was done out of the wager.
Parallax, when he heard the decision, was assured
from his own former experiments on the Canal, that
there must have been something wrong in carrying out
the test of 5th March, and accordingly went down soon
afterwards to the Bedford Canal to make still further
proof of the water being level. He gives the following
account of an experiment then made by himself, on pp.
21, 22 of his excellent work, previously mentioned—
" Zetetic Astronomy—Earth not a Globe "—

" Although the experiments already described and many
similar ones, have been tried and often repeated, first in 1838,
afterwards in 1844, in 1849, in 1856, and in 1862, the Author
was induced in 1870 to visit the scene of his former labours,
and to make some other (one or more) experiments of so simple a
character, that no error of complicated instruments, or process

of surveying could possibly be involved. He left London (for Downham Market Station), on Tuesday morning, April 5, 1870, and arrived at the Old Bedford Sluice Bridge about two miles from the station, at twelve o'clock. The atmosphere was remarkably clear, and the sun was shining brightly on and against the western face of the bridge. On the right hand side of the arch, a large notice board was affixed (a table of tolls, &c., for the navigation of the Canal). The lower edge of this board was 6 feet 6 inches above the water as shown at B figure 12.

FIG. 12.

"A train of several empty turf boats had just entered the Canal from the river Ouse, and was about proceeding to Romsey in Huntingdonshire. An arrangement was made with the 'Captain' to place the shallowest boat the last in the train; on the lowest part of the stern of the boat a good telescope was fixed, the elevation being exactly 18 inches from the water. The sun was shining strongly against the white notice-board, the air was exceedingly still and clear, and the surface of the water smooth as a molten mirror, so that everything was extremely favourable for observation. At 1.15 p.m. the train of boats started for Welney. As the boat receded the notice-board was kept in view, and was plainly visible to the naked eye for several miles; but, through the telescope it was distinctly seen throughout the whole distance of six miles. But, on reaching Welney Bridge, a very shallow boat was procured, and so fixed that the telescope was brought to within 8 inches of the surface of the water; and still the bottom of the notice-board was clearly visible. The elevation of the telescope being

Q

8 inches, the line of sight would touch the horizon, if convexity exists, at the distance of one statute mile; the square of the remaining five miles, multiplied by 8 inches, gives a curvature of 16 feet 8 inches, so that the bottom of the notice-board— 6 feet 6 inches above the water—should have been 10 feet 2 inches *below the horizon*, as shown in fig. 13 "—

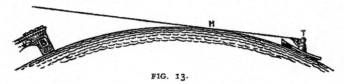

FIG. 13.

As it may perhaps be possible that some persons may still imagine water to be globular, from the decision having been given against Mr. Hampden, I beg to sub-join the following summary of the case by Parallax, who thoroughly investigated it at the time of occurrence, from which it will be seen that the mishap arose, *not from the convexity of the water* of the Canal, but from *the instrument* by which it was measured *having been improperly adjusted.*

"On the 5th of March, 1870, a party, consisting of Messrs. John Hampden, of Swindon, Wilts, Alfred Wallace, of London, William Carpenter, of Lewisham, M. W. B. Coulcher, of Down-ham Market, and J. H. Walsh, Editor of *The Field* newspaper, assembled on the northern bank of the 'Old Bedford Canal,' to repeat experiments similar to those described in figs. 2, 3, 4, and 5 on pages 11 to 14 of this work. But, from causes which need not be referred to here, they abandoned their original intention, and substituted the following. On the western face of the Old Bedford Bridge, at Salter's Lode, a signal was placed at an elevation of 13 feet 4 inches above the water in the

Canal; at the distance of three miles a signal post, with a disc
12 inches in diameter on the top, was so fixed that ' the *centre* of
the disc was 13 feet 4 inches above the water line '; and at the
distance of another three miles (or six miles altogether), on
the eastern side of the Welney Bridge, another signal was
placed '3 inches above the top rail of the bridge, and 13 feet
4 inches above the water-line.'* This arrangement is represented in the following diagram, fig. 94.

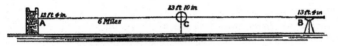

FIG. 94.

" A, the signal on the Old Bedford Bridge; B, the telescope
on Welney Bridge; and C, the centre signal post, three miles
from each end. The object-glass of the telescope was 4½ inches
diameter; hence, the centre, or true eye-line, was 2¼ inches
higher than the top of the signal B, and 3¾ inches *below* the
top of the signal-disc at C. On directing the telescope, 'with
a power of 50,' towards the signal A, the centre of which was
2¼ inches *below* the centre of the telescope, it was seen to be
below it; but the disc on the centre pole, the top of which
was, *to begin with*, 3¾ inches *above* the centre, or line of sight,
from the telescope, was seen to stand considerably *higher* than
the signal A. From which, three of the gentlemen immediately,
but most unwarrantably, concluded that the elevation of the
disc in the field of view of the telescope was owing to a rise
in the water of the Canal, showing convexity! whereas it was
nothing more than simply the upward divergence (of that
which was *already* 3¾ inches *above* the line of sight), produced

* Report by Messrs. Carpenter & Coulcher, published in *The Field*,
of March 26th, 1870.

by the magnifying power of the telescope, as shown in the experiment with the lens, on page 267, fig. 92.

"Why did they omit to consider the fact that 3¾ inches excess of altitude would be made by a magnifying power of 50, to appear to stand considerably above the eye-line, and that a mere hair's-breadth of dip—an amount which could not be detected—towards the distant signal would by magnifying, diverging, or dilating all above it, make it appear to be lifted up for several feet? Why did they not take care that the *top* of the centre disc was *in a line* with the telescope and the distant signal A? Why, also, was the centre of the object-glass fixed 2¼ inches *higher* than the centre of the object of observation at the other end? There was no difficulty in placing the *centre* of the telescope, the *top* of the middle disc, and the *centre* of the farthest signal mark at the *same altitude*, and therefore in a straight line. For their own sake as gentlemen, as well as for the sake of the cause they had undertaken to champion, it is unfortunate that they acted so unwisely; that they so foolishly laid themselves open to charges of unfairness in fixing the signals. Had they already seen enough to prove that the surface of the water was horizontal, and therefore instinctively felt a desire to do their best to delay as long as they could the day of general denunciation of their cherished doctrine of the Earth's rotundity? Such questions are perfectly fair in relation to conduct so unjust and one-sided. It is evident that their anxiety to defend a doctrine which had been challenged by others overcame their desire for 'truth without fear of consequences'; and they eagerly seized upon the veriest shadow of evidence to support themselves. In the whole history of invention, a more hasty, ill-conceived, illogical conclusion was never drawn; and it is well for civilization that such procedure is almost universally denounced. It is scarcely possible to draw a favourable conclusion as to their motives in departing from their first intention. Why did they not confine themselves to the repetition of the experiments, an account of which I had long previously published to the world, and to test which the expedition was first arranged? That of sending out a boat for a distance of six miles, and watching its progress from a fixed point with a good telescope, would have completely satisfied them as to the true form of the surface of the water; and as no irregularity in altitude of signals, nor peculiarities of instruments, could have influenced the result, all engaged must at once have submitted to the simple truth as developed by the simplest possible experiment. That men should cling to complication, and prefer it to simplicity of action, is difficult to understand, except on the principle as it was said of old, 'some love darkness better than light.' It is certain that many are ever ready to contend almost to death for their mere opinions, who have little or no regard for actual truth, however important in its bearings or sacred in its character."*

I shall now refer to the Suez Canal, the construction of which some years ago caused such a commotion in the Political world. Many are fond of speaking of this canal as a marvellous triumph of Modern Science, so it may be well to remind such, that the feat of joining the Mediterranean and Red Seas by means of a Canal, for the purpose of commercial navigation, had been accomplished by the Ancients long, long before. Neco, the Pharoah-Nechoh of *2 Kings xxiii. 29—35*, an Egyptian monarch who reigned 617—681 B.C., was the first to begin the Canal, which, after beng used for centuries, was at last overwhelmed by the sands of the desert in 767 A.D.†

---

* " Zetetic Astronomy," pp. 268-271.
† " Egypt, Past and Present," by W. H. Davenport Adams; pp. 55, 365, 366. T. Nelson & Sons, London, Edinburgh, and New York.

The distance between the Red Sea at Suez and the Mediterranean Sea is 100 statute miles, the *datum* line of the Canal being 26 feet* below the level of the Mediterranean, and is continued *horizontally* the whole way from sea to sea, there not being a single lock on the Canal, the surface of the water being parallel with the datum line. It is thus clear that there is no curvature or globularity for the whole hundred miles between the Mediterranean and the Red Sea; had there been, according to the Astronomic theory, the middle of the Canal would have been 1,666 feet *higher* than at either end, whereas the Canal is perfectly horizontal for the whole distance.

The Great Canal of China, said to be 700 miles in length, was made without regard to any allowance for supposed curvature, as the Chinese believe the Earth to be a Stationary Plane. I may also add that no allowance was made for it in the North Sea Canal, or in the Manchester Ship Canal, both recently constructed, thus clearly proving that there is no globularity in Earth or Sea, so that the world cannot possibly be a Planet.

SECTION 4.

SUBMARINE CABLES.

Let us now pass on to the Atlantic Submarine Cable, which stretches its huge length between Valencia on the west coast of Ireland and Trinity Bay in Newfoundland,

---

* Its depth has since then been increased to 28 feet.

a distance of 1,665 nautical or 1,942 statute miles. Surely, if convexity in water is to be discovered anywhere, it would be found in such a long distance as this, but it is simply a case of *non est inventus*, for the very good reason that there is no curvature to be found at all. It must, like a bank-note forger, have absconded. The greatest depth of the Atlantic was sounded at about one-third of the distance from Newfoundland, 2,424 fathoms; the next deepest part, 2,400 fathoms, was about one-third of the way from Valencia, while in the middle it was less than 1,600 fathoms, at which place, according to Astronomic calculation, it should have been about 119 statute miles *higher* than at either end! Facts, it is said, are " stubborn things," and it is thus evident that there is no curvature in the Atlantic, and as, according to the law of nature, water everywhere finds its own level, it is proved that it has no globularity throughout the oceans of the whole world.*

SECTION 5.

THE LIGHT OF LIGHTHOUSES SEEN AT GREAT DISTANCES.

I confess that it appears to me to be almost as unnecessary, as gilding gold or painting the lily, to give further evidence that the Earth is not a Planet, still, as some people are fond of having assurance made doubly sure, piling an Ossa upon a Pelion, I shall add another proof

---

* See paper respecting the Atlantic Cable published by the Admiralty, 8th October, 1869.

to the fact that there is no curvature in the sea, from the Light of Lighthouses seen at great distances.

A glance at "The Lighthouses of the World,"* will show at what great distances some of their lights are visible, which would be utterly impossible were the sea convex, as our Modern Astronomers pretend it to be. I shall name a few instances—

The Cordonan light on the Gironde, on the west coast of France, has an altitude of 207 feet, and is visible 31 statute miles. If we make the usual Astronomic allowance for the supposed curvature of water, it should be quite invisible, as it would, allowing for the height of the spectator, be about 210 feet *below the horizon.*

The Madras light is 132 feet high, and can be seen 28 statute miles, but, reckoning the Astronomic convexity, and allowing for spectator's height, it could not be seen, as it would be *below the horizon* at least 220 feet.

The following extracts I copy from an excellent pamphlet, lately received, called "Zetetic Cosmogony," written by Mr. Thomas Winship, Durban, Natal†—

"Another and an unconscious witness to the horizontality of water is Mr. Smith of Cape Point, as the following shows:

"'A LIGHT FROM AFAR.

"'To the Editor of the *Cape Times.*

"'Sir, at nine o'clock this evening, the Danger Point Light was distinctly visible to the naked eye, from the homestead at Cape Point, (about 150 feet above sea level); this being the first occasion, since the erection of the Danger Point Lighthouse, on which the flashes of light had been noticed by myself. The

---

* R. H. Laurie, 35 Minories, London.
† T. L. Cullingworth, 40 Field Street, Durhan, Natal; John Williams, 54 Bourne Street, Netherfield, Notts.

light must be most powerful to be seen from a distance of over fifty miles in a clear night. I think half a minute interval between three quick flashes.

> " ' I am, &c.,
>
> " ' A. E. SMITH.'

"According to this, therefore, if the world be a globe, *the light should have been 1,666 feet below Mr. Smith's line of sight.*" p. 59.

"But, says someone, there is no allowance made for refraction in any of the foregoing calculations. That is quite true, but constitutes no valid objection, in the light of the following extract from the ' Encyclopædia Britannica,' article ' Levelling.' ' We suppose the visual rays to be a straight line, whereas, on account of the unequal densities of the air at different distances from the earth, the rays of light are incurvated by refraction. The effect of this is to lessen the difference between the true and apparent levels, but in such an extremely variable and uncertain manner, that if any constant or fixed allowance be made for it in formula or tables, it will often lead to a greater error than what it was intended to obviate. For, though the refraction may at a mean compensate for about one-seventh of the curvature of the Earth, it sometimes exceeds one-fifth, and at other times does not amount to one-fifteenth. We have, therefore, made no allowance for refraction in the foregoing formulæ.' " p. 62.

"The distances which ' Signals at Sea ' can be seen prove imcontestably that the Earth is a motionless Plane.

"*Pearson's Weekly* of the 29th December, 1894, says— ' Evidently we have not got to the bottom of the matter yet. In August, 1890, the C Manœuvre Fleet signalled with Search Light to colliers 70 miles away. . . . The information comes from Mr. F. T. Jane the Artist, who was on board at the time.

According to the Astronomers *these vessels should have been 3,200 feet below the horizon*, allowing for a height of 40 feet on the signalling vessel, and 26 feet on the colliers!!!'"

I may add that the *Daily Mail* of 10th November, 1899, gives the representation of a Search-light at Kimberley which is stated to have been visible at a distance of 115 miles! This, of course, would be impossible if the Earth were a Globular Planet.

I could very easily add many more proofs to similar effect, but I forbear; the fact is I am embarrassed with the riches of evidence that the Earth is not a Planet, and my difficulty in writing this book has not arisen from any lack of matter, but as to how I may best select and condense it, so that it may be of most use to my Readers, without omitting anything of real importance.

In closing this Chapter I cannot help remarking to what opposite extremes Inconsistency leads, and what sad havoc it makes with Truth. Here we have on the one hand our Government making a Resolution or Order respecting the construction of Railways on a *datum horizontal line*, on the principle that the Earth is a *Stationary Plane*, and, on the other hand, subsidising the Astronomical Society and Board Schools which teach that it is a *Whirling Ball*. I wish some honest M.P., who sees the absurdity of such procedure, and possesses the ability to propose the remedy, would have the courage to bring the matter before Parliament; I am sure he would well deserve the thanks of the Nation. So long as our Astronomers are abetted by the Government, so long, I fear, they will utter their discordant notes, and flaunt their rags of false science before the gaping multitude with a pride " that might make angels weep." No wonder that the Chinese, who possessed the light of what is called Civilization, when our own country was steeped in heathen darkness, should consider us to be barbarians now for believing that the world rushes round the Sun. In this matter they at least have common sense upon their side, while we, as a nation, have abandoned ours, and bow the knee to Baal.

CHAPTER VII.

THE SUN, MOON AND STARS ACCORDING TO MODERN ASTRONOMY.

SECTION   PAGE

1. THE SUN   -   -   -   140

2. THE MOON   -   -   147

3. THE STARS -   -   152

SECTION 1.

THE SUN.

It is truly painful to contemplate the results of Modern Astronomy—its rejection of the Word of God with respect to the revolution of the Sun, and its consequent tendency towards infidelity—its abandonment of reason, and its denial of the proper use of our senses as to the observation of actual facts—its brazen effrontery in teaching without proof the most ridiculous fallacies —fill the minds of the thoughtful and devout with real sorrow, knowing that so many have been already beguiled, and so many are still being beguiled under its baneful influence.

Herschel, perhaps, in one sense, as much as Newton

himself, tried to make fools of us when he wrote the following tit-bit—

"In the disorder of our senses we transfer in idea the motion of the Earth to the Sun, and the stillness of the Sun to the Earth!"

which statement virtually means—Do not believe your own common senses, but take our theories for granted: if you do not feel any motion in the Earth, *imagine* that you do; and if you see the Sun circling in the heavens, *suppose* that it is the Earth which does so! Truly it was his own senses which were disordered when he taught that it is the Earth and not the Sun that moves. The absurdities of Modern Astronomy are nowhere more apparent than in the theories respecting the Sun, to a few of which I now beg to refer.

It is by the presumed distance of the Sun from the Earth that Astronomers make their calculations. Thus, as Mr. R. A. Proctor states in "The Sun"—

"The determination of the Sun's distance is not only an important problem of general Astronomy, but it may be regarded as THE VERY FOUNDATION OF ALL OUR RESEARCHES."

As previously stated Astronomers have differed so very much respecting its distance, even from three to one hundred and four millions of miles, that, as a matter of necessity, their calculations MUST be radically wrong. Besides, when these were first made, the Sun, according to their theory, was *stationary*, now they acknowledge that *it moves*, and, since its creation, *has always been moving*, so that their computations cannot possibly be correct. However, for the present, they have settled among themselves, the distance of the Sun from the

Earth to be between ninety-one and ninety-two millions
of miles. Its size is computed to be about twelve
hundred and forty thousand times larger than our world;
its diameter being estimated at eight hundred and fifty
to eight hundred and eighty-two thousand miles, and its
entire cubic space at six hundred and eighty-six thousand
and eighteen billions, nine hundred and sixty-eight
thousand millions of miles!!! *Credite posteri!* will
posterity believe that their forefathers could ever have
been so foolish as to accept such ridiculous fancies as
facts? And yet this is what grey-haired *savants* call
Truth, and gushing Journalists who, I am inclined to
believe, do not personally know much about the matter,
write fulsome articles to bolster up the delusion.

One of the fables which our Astronomers seem to
delight in telling us, is that the distance between the
Earth and the Sun is so great, that it would take an
express train, going at the rate of sixty miles per hour,
one hundred and seventy-three years to reach it, at which
wonderful news I doubt not that Dominie Sampson,
could he hear it, would exclaim with special emphasis
—*Pro-di-gi-ous!* What would be thought of a man who
wanted to light his dining-room with a lamp 1,240,000
times larger than the room itself? Would not his friends
think him only fit for a lunatic asylum? Yet such a
preposterous act, with respect to the lighting of this
world, if not attributed by some Astronomers to their
own deity "Natural Law," is palmed upon the JEHOVAH
of Hosts, who is "wonderful in counsel and excellent in
working"—*Isa. xxviii. 29.* He doeth all things well,
proportioning the means to the end which He has in
view.

It appears to me that Modern Astronomy, like Roman Catholicism, is an attempt to revive Pagan superstition. The former, for temples has observatories, and the latter for the Pantheon has the Vatican; for Baal the Astronomers have Newton, and for Astarte, the Queen of Heaven, the Roman Catholics have the Virgin Mary. I have lately been strengthened in the conviction that the adoration of the Virgin Mary is only a continuation of the worship of Astarte or Astaroth, by an admirable Lecture delivered by the late Rev. G. W. Straten, Rector of Aylston, Leicester, to which I beg to refer my Readers, as also to that very excellent and learned work, "The Two Babylons," written by the late Rev. A. H. Hislop of Arbroath, both of which may be obtained as mentioned below.* The Bible order of the heavens has been completely subverted by our Astronomers; instead of the Sun revolving round the world, the world is declared to revolve round it, as a mere Planet of little note in Astronomic esteem, although the Blessed Son of God gave His own heart's blood for its redemption. Angels desire to look into that wondrous sacrifice, which Scientists like Huxley and Darwin regard only with cynical scorn, because of their ignorance of that in which the highest and truest science consists.

The Greek heathen philosopher Pythagoras brought the Sun worship with him from Egypt, where he had resided for a considerable time, and had been initiated into its mysteries by the Priests. His system of Astronomy lingered for a while, till it was supplanted by that of Ptolemy, and for many centuries seems to

* S. W. Partridge & Co., Paternoster Row, London.

have been forgotten, till Copernicus drew the fabled
phœnix from its ashes. By Newton and his followers it
has been skillfully adapted to suit the depraved taste of
modern idolatry, for idolatry is far from being extin-
guished in Christendom, and still flourishes, in various
forms, in this degenerate age under assumed names.

The Sun has spots. Fabricius, nearly three hundred
years ago, was the first among Modern Astronomers to
note them, although they were known to the Chaldeans
in early ages. Since his time many Astronomers have
made them their special study; one in particular is said
to have observed them for thirty years every day on
which the Sun was visible. They appear and disappear,
and it is yet not really known what they are, but, the
chief deduction drawn from them is, that the Sun turns
upon an axis in about twenty-four days. Some of the
spots observed on the *photosphere*, or disc of the Sun,
are whiter than iron at a white heat, and come and go
so rapidly, that they are called *faculæ* or torches. The
edge of the disc is called the *chromatmosphere*, or the
" sierra," or, as one has expressed it, " a quivering fringe
of fire."

As it might, perhaps, be thought that, in describing the
wonders of the Sun, I am acting the part of a Munchausen
myself, I think it will be safer for me to quote a passage
or two from the works of Modern Astronomers themselves,
who, if sometimes considered prone to exalt their own
importance, should not, as a matter of politeness, be
supposed guilty of exaggerating the marvels of their own
idol.

Sir Robert Ball says—

" Unparalleled in its lustre, the planet Venus is unexampled in the intensity of the pull with which it seeks to make the Earth swerve from its revolution around the Sun. I have calculated the magnitude of this force, and when expressed in tons the figures that are required baffle our power of comprehension. The tons in the attraction, or rather, I ought to say, in the disturbing force, of Venus are comparable with the miles in star distances. The force is indeed 130,000,000,000,000 tons " !*

Miss Giberne writes as follows—

"It sounds to us both grand and startling to hear of jets of liquid lava from Mount Vesuvius, ten thousand feet in height, or to read of a river of lava from a volcano in Iceland pouring in one unbroken stream for fifty miles.

"But what shall be thought of the long flames mounting to a height of fifty or a hundred thousand miles above the edge of the Sun? What shall be thought of a tongue of fire long enough to fold three or four times round our solid Earth? What shall be thought of the awful rush of burning gases sometimes seen, borne along at the rate of one or two or even three hundred miles in a single second across the Sun's surface? What shall be thought of the huge dark rents in this mighty fiery ocean, rents commonly from fifty to one hundred thousand miles across, if not seldom more?

"Fifty thousand miles! a mere speck scarcely visible without a telescope; yet large enough to hold seven Earths like ours flung in together. The largest spot measured was so enormous that eighteen Earths might have been arranged in a row across the breadth of it, like huge boulders of rocks in a mountain cavern, and to have filled up the entire hole about one hundred Earths would have been needed."†

* "The cause of the Glacial Age," pp. 73, 74; Kegan Paul, Trübner & Co., London.
† "Sun, Moon and Stars," pp. 19, 20; Seeley & Co., 38 Great Russell Street, London.

Now all this, as the Yankee would say, is "very tall talk," but it amounts to nothing, because it is only *assumption*, and should at least teach the votaries of Modern Astronomy not to give statements as facts, till they have first been proved to be true—" If any man think that he knoweth anything, he knoweth nothing yet as he ought to know "—*1 Cor. viii. 2.* The fact is that in this time-state our knowledge is very imperfect: *blepomen gar arti di' esoptron en ainugmati,* "for we see as yet through a mirror obscurely," or, as in a riddle—*1 Cor. xiii. 12.* In the Great Beyond " we shall see face to face, and *fully know* even as we are *fully known.*"*

Even such an enthusiastic writer as Miss Giberne confesses—

"We do not know with any certainty whether the Sun is through and through one mass of glowing molten heat, or whether he may have a solid or even a cool body within the blazing covering. Some have thought the one and some the other. We only know that he is a mighty furnace of heat and flame, beyond anything that we can possibly imagine in our quiet little earth." †

Our talented Authoress must surely, in describing our Earth as " quiet," have had in her mind the teaching of the Bible, where it says—" Behold all the Earth sitteth still and is at rest "—*Zech. i. 11,* a very different state from that which our Astronomers teach, namely, that it is rushing round the Sun at the rate of sixty-five thousand miles per hour, one thousand times faster than an Express Railway train.

---

* Epiginōskō.
† "Sun, Moon and Stars," p. 18.

SECTION 2.

THE MOON.

Although the Moon is so silvery white, she is the *bête noir* of our Modern Astronomers, as, in various ways, she refuses to act as, according to their theories, she ought to do. Being the orb nearest the Earth, they have taken special pains to map her out with so-called mountains and seas, as if she had been one of its continents, though they are bound to confess that it is only " the eye of a practised Astronomer " that is able to discriminate between the one and the other. She has also been photographed, at least after a certain fashion, as explained by Sir Robert Ball in a note on p. 62 of his " Story of the Heavens "—

" The photographs were taken by Mr. Nasmyth from models carefully constructed by him to illustrate the features of the Moon. This is no doubt a somewhat imaginary sketch."

I have not the least doubt of it myself, but it answers the Astronomic purpose for which it was so systematically prepared—the gulling of the people.

It is now, however, said to be discovered that the Moon has neither water nor atmosphere, so that not even the famous " Man in the Moon " could reside there, and the once celebrated Crisian Sea is now, alas! *vox et prœterea nihil.* Yet notwithstanding this acknowledged want of water and atmosphere, the Author of the article " Moon," in " The Dictionary of Arts and Sciences," writes as specifically regarding its supposed inhabitants, as if he had obtained his information direct from themselves on the spot, thus—

"As the Moon illuminates the Earth by a reflex light, so does the Earth the Moon; but the other phenomena will be different for the most part.

"1. The Earth will be visible to but a little more than one-half of the Lunar inhabitants.

"2. To those who see it, the Earth will appear fixed, or at least to have no circular motion, but only that which results from the Moon's libration.

"3. Those who live in the middle of the Moon's visible hemisphere see the Earth directly over their heads.

"4. To those who live in the extremity of that hemisphere, the Earth seems always nearly in the horizon, but not exactly there, by reason of the libration.

"5. The Earth in the course of a month would have all the same phases as the Moon has. Thus the Lunarians, when the Moon is at E. in the middle of their night, see the Earth as full or shining with a full face; at C. and G. it is dichotomised or half light and half dark; at A. it is wholly dark or new; and at the part between these it is gibbous.

"6. The Earth appears variegated with spots of different magnitudes and colours arising from the continents, islands, oceans, seas, clouds, &c.

"7. These spots will appear constantly revolving about the Earth's axis, by which the Lunarians will determine the Earth's diurnal motion in the same way as we do that of the Sun."

From the above interesting tit-bit of Astronomic intelligence, we learn that the Moon is inhabited, and that the Earth is a Planet! That is, *in the writer's imagination*, for no proof whatever is tendered that such is the case. It is a pity he did not carry his observations a little farther, by telling us what sort of beings the Lunarians are, who can manage to exist without water and atmosphere. Perhaps they may be like Newtonians, who conceive theories without reason, and draw deductions without proof.

As the Moon is allowed by our Astronomers to be " very considerably smaller than the Earth," she ought, like the Earth, in accordance with Newton's wonderful law of Gravitation, to revolve around the Sun, as they say the Earth does from West to East, but, like a self-willed maiden, she takes her own way, and revolves round the Earth from East to West. Besides, it was considered to be her province to control the tides, but such great difficulties have arisen in that direction, that many Astronomers are now seeking for some other causes to explain the working of their regular flux and reflux in the grand economy of nature.

In writing of the Moon, Miss Giberne remarks—

" Her diameter is about two-sevenths of the Earth's diameter, her entire surface is about two twenty-sevenths of the Earth's surface, her size is about two ninety-ninths of the Earth's size, and her whole weight is about one-eightieth of the Earth's weight."*

The Moon's distance from the Earth is said, by our Astronomers to be 240,000 miles. It certainly would be passing strange that He who is as infinite in His Wisdom as in His Love, should place this luminary, which was expressly made to light the world at night, at such an enormous distance from it as this, and I am sure that

* " The Sun, Moon and Stars," p. 150.

their calculation is utterly erroneous, even as that of
their fancied distance of the Sun. Some Zetetics have
estimated the distance of the Moon from the Earth, to
be about one thousand times less than that supposed by
our Astronomers, that is only about 240 miles, and this
undoubtedly appears to me far more probable than their
preposterous calculation of 240,000 miles.

If our Modern Astronomers do not deny God, they
at least appear by their writings to ignore His Power,
Wisdom, and Superintendence. They despise the true
science of the Bible, and substitute for it the false
theories of their own wayward fancy. They do not seem
to be aware that the works of God's creation are all
made according to number, weight, and measure—that
order, adaptation, and usefulness are combined in every
part of the universe. Man is " fearfully and wonderfully
made "—*Psa. cxxxix. 14.* The eye of a fly is as admirably designed, as the mechanism of the Sun in the
Heavens—

" For He (God) looketh to the ends of the earth, and seeth
under the whole heaven, when He maketh a weight for the
wind; yea, He maketh the waters by measure, when He made a
decree for the rain, a way for the lightning of the thunder "—
Job xxviii. 24—26.

" Who hath measured the waters in the hollow of His hand,
and meted out heaven with the span, and comprehended the
dust of the earth in a measure, and weighed the mountains in
scales, and the hills in a balance? Who hath directed the spirit
of JEHOVAH, or being His counsellor hath taught Him? "—
Isa. xl. 12, 13.

Our Astronomers also state that the Moon receives
her light from the Sun, which is an unwarrantable

mistake, for Scripture tells us—"God made two great luminaries, the greater luminary to rule the day, and the lesser luminary to rule the night "—*Gen. i. 16.* The Hebrew word here used for luminary is *maur*, a noun of instrument, from *aur* light, thus showing that the Moon, as well as the Sun, is *an independent light-giver*, each imparting its own light irrespective of the other.

We often see the Sun and the Moon at the same time in the heavens, the Sun rising in the East, and the Moon setting in the West. Now, were the Newtonian theory true that the Moon receives her light from the Sun, and, were it possible for a *sphere*, as the Moon is said to be, to act as a *reflector* at all, the Moon, thus facing the Sun, ought to grow *brighter*, instead of which, as Hamlet's ghost said of the glow-worm as the matin drew nigh—

"It 'gins to pale its ineffectual fire."

Having already shown from Scripture that the Moon does not receive her light from the Sun, before closing this Chapter, I shall add a few thoughts from Reason and Fact, to prove that she possesses a light of her own, totally different from that of the Sun.

The light which is reflected must necessarily be of the *same character* as that which causes the reflection, but the light of the Moon is *altogether different* from the light of the Sun, therefore the light of the Moon is not reflected from the Sun. The Sun's light is red and hot, the Moon's pale and cold—the Sun's dries and preserves certain kinds of fish and fruit, such as cod and grapes, for the table, but the Moon's turns such to putrefaction —the Sun's will often put out a coal fire, while the Moon's will cause it to burn more brightly—the rays of the

Sun, focussed through a burning-glass, will set wood on fire, and even fuse metals, while the rays of the Moon, concentrated to the strongest power, do not exhibit the very slightest signs of heat. I have myself long thought that the light of the Moon is *Electric*, but, be that as it may, even a Board School child can perceive that its light is totally unlike that of the Sun.

———

SECTION 8.

THE STARS.

The Stars are in Scripture associated with the Moon in their rule of the night—" the Moon and the Stars to rule by night "—*Psa. cxxxvi. 9.* They are called—" Stars of light "—*Psa. cxlviii. 3,* from which it would certainly appear that they have an independent, and not a borrowed light. They have a variety of colours. Humboldt says—

" By the aid of the telescope have been discovered in the starry vault in the celestial fields which light traverses, as in the corallas of our flowering plants, and in the metallic oxides, almost every gradation of prismatic colour between the two extremes of refrangibility. . . . In a cluster near the Southern Cross—red, green, blue, and bluish green—appear in large telescopes, like gems of many colours, like a superb piece of fancy jewellery."

Note also the following Scriptural passages respecting their light-giving power—

" For the Stars of heaven and the constellations thereof will not give *their light;* the Sun shall be darkened in his going forth, and the Moon shall not cause *her light* to shine "— *Isa. xiii. 10.*

" The sun and the moon are darkened, and the stars withdraw *their shining* "—*Joel ii. 10.*

" Thus saith Jehovah, which giveth the sun for a light by day, and the ordinances of the moon and of the stars *for a light by night* "—*Jer. xxxi. 35.*

Our Modern Astronomers imagine the Stars to be immense worlds or suns, some of them many thousands of times larger than our own, and at an enormous distance. Sir Robert Ball, in his " Cause of an Ice-Age," p. 77, says of Sirius—that it is " a million times as distant from us as the Sun "—that is, that it is ninety-two millions of millions of miles from the Earth ! It is thought that Stars are in a more or less advanced state of development, and that probably some of them may be already inhabited by beings suited to their spheres. Their distance from us they calculate to be so immense, that, according to Sir William Herschel, the light from some of them will take a thousand years to reach this world of ours ! Just fancy the Almighty and All-wise God making a star to give light to this world which would take a thousand years to show its first glimmer there ! It was not thus He acted on the first day of the Adamic Creation, when He said—" Let there be light, and there was light "— *Gen. i. 3.*

We have neither in Scripture, nor in nature, the least hint of any world except our own and the invisible one beyond, and we have no other means of information on the subject. The best telescopes have failed to show any signs of any inhabitant in any star or planet.

Some years ago it was fancied that canals were seen in the Planet Mars, and that, therefore, presumably, it would be inhabited, but they have since vanished like a morning dream.

Sir David Brewster argued from ANALOGY that the Stars and Planets must be inhabited, because the Earth is. But this argument is a *petitio principii*, a mere begging of the question, for it must first be proved that the Earth is a *heavenly body*, which never has been, and never can be proven. There is a great difference, indeed, between Heavenly bodies, and the body of this Earth, notwithstanding the revelations of the spectroscope. They are particularly contrasted in Scripture, thus—

"There are heavenly bodies and earthly bodies, but of one kind, indeed, is the glory of the heavenly, and of another kind is the glory of the earthly "—*1 Cor. xv. 40.*

Thus, this presumed argument for a Plurality of worlds from ANALOGY is not worth one single straw. Yet, nevertheless, Dr. Henderson boldly reproduces the argument in his "Treatise on Astronomy," for the especial benefit of Mr. Verdant Green—

"The great probability is that every Star is a SUN, far surpassing ours in magnitude and splendour; they all shine by their own native light. . . . What a most powerful SUN must that little Star Vega be, when it is 53,937 times larger than our Sun. . . . The Stars being thus *supposed* to be suns, it is *extremely probable* that they are the centres of *other systems of worlds* round which may revolve a numerous retinue of planets and satellites. *Therefore* (*sic*) there must be a plurality *of suns* and *a plurality of worlds.*"

How wonderful is this argument of *analogical supposition*, but, unfortunately for Modern Astronomers, it lacks the support of *Truth,* therefore its conclusion cannot bring conviction to the thoughtful mind.

No revolving body, so far as we know, was ever made for the permanent residence of any rational being. A few minutes afford quite sufficient sensation to the occupant of a seat in the showman's merry-go-round or Great Wheel; no one would like to spend a night in either. The Stars, which Byron so felicitously styled, " the poetry of Heaven," although not designed for human habitation, are most useful, not only for giving light and showing us our position by night, but, in all probability, are of service in the economy of nature in a manner of which we little dream. Did not JEHOVAH ask Job— " Canst thou bind the sweet influences of Pleiades ? "— *Job xxxviii. 31.* One Star was especially used to guide the Wise Men of the East to the birthplace of our Blessed Saviour. They are splendid lamps, placed in the canopy of the sky, to give light, instruction, and blessing to this world of ours, and we may be positively certain that, like the lamps of a city, they are very much smaller than the place they were made to illumine.

Instead of the enormous distances attributed to the Stars by Modern Astronomers, they cannot, from the position assigned to them by God, as light-givers to the Earth, be very far away. Parallax was of opinion

" that all the visible luminaries of the firmament are contained within a vertical distance of 1,000 statute miles."*

> " What ! will not one world content thee, atom,
> But thou must create more ; yes, world on world
> In thy imagination? Where is thy warrant?

---

* " Zetetic Astronomy," p. 104.

And canst thou prove it from the Word of Truth?
Must we believe because thou sayest it
Without a greater proof?
Make good thy other sayings, then we may
Afford thee credit such as thou deserv'st;
But the Word of God says no such thing;
And this we credit far beyond thy word.
Consider this one well, and thou wilt want
No other *earthly* world, but only heaven." *

The following forcible remarks by Mr. William Bathgate, bearing upon this subject, are well worthy of attentive consideration.

" Astronomers, and scientific men generally, strenuously oppose any comparison between their theories and the Bible, knowing that they cannot be reconciled. Of what use is it for them to say that their magnificent ideas of innumerable suns and worlds show forth the glory of God, if they cause men to have less respect for the Bible? Revelation and nature cannot disagree: if they seem to do so, man is to blame for it. Sir Horace Walpole became an infidel, because he could not reconcile Christianity with the plurality of worlds, and Modern discoveries in Astronomy and Geology with a divine revelation; and the infidel Thomas Paine, and a host of other persons have based their strongest arguments upon the assumption that the Copernican theory is true, which system has been a strong fort with the infidels for many generations. Do the heavens set forth the glory of Newton, or do they declare the glory of God? In the Bible we are led to believe that the sun, moon, and stars are subservient to the earth; that in consequence of events having taken place on the earth, these heavenly bodies were darkened; that God took five times as long to make the

---

* Lander's " David and Goliath," p. 49.

earth as He did the heavenly bodies. Who has a right to say that God, in giving to man an account of His creation, as contained in the First Chapter of Genesis, misrepresented the order and nature of the facts to suit man's capacity? As if man could not have understood them as easily from the Word of God as he does from the mouths of the Astronomers?

"Who ever heard of a person, after constructing some intricate piece of workmanship, explaining the order and nature of its mechanism entirely different from the truth to suit the capacity of his hearers?

"What had the earth to revolve round before the sun was made, if we are to believe the Newtonian theory?

"The Bishop of Peterborough says—'I have no fear whatever that the Bible will be found in the long run to contain more science than all the theories of philosophers put together'; and there is no doubt that when the earth is generally believed to be a plane, the Bible will be respected more than ever, since it will be found to be *literally true* when speaking of the Creation, and infidelity will lose its strongest hold against Christianity."*

Our Astronomers confess that no *human being* could ever dwell in the Stars or Planets, the constitution of which is entirely opposed to the requirements of our nature. If inhabited at all, their occupants must of necessity be of a different order of creation from ourselves. The Bible gives not the slightest hint of such, and respecting such we have no other means of knowledge, while speculation is useless. It is enough for us to know that we live in the only world recognized in the Scriptures, with the exception, of course, of *tēn*

---

* "The Shape of the Earth," by William Bathgate; John Parker, Green Lane, Stoneycroft, Liverpool.

oikoumenēn tēn mellousan, the world that is to come, to
which all believers in the Lord Jesus Christ, redeemed
through His vicarious Sacrifice, will go after they have
left this *nun estin*, the world that now is.   This world
was made by Christ—The Word of God—*John i. 1—3*,
and a glorious world it was till lost through the entrance
of sin, but, according to promise, it will be restored again
to more than its pristine loveliness.   Our Lord, in the
depth of His immeasurable Love, gave Himself " for the
life of the world "—*John vi. 51*, and the Apostle Peter
points to the times *apokatastaseōs pantōn*, " of the restoration of all things, which God hath spoken by the mouth
of all His holy prophets since the world began "—
Acts iii. 21, and, as Dryden sang—

> " 'Twas great to speak a world from nought;
>   'Tis greater to redeem."

I would also remark, while on this subject, that the
only places in the Bible, where the word "world" is
used in the plural, "worlds," are in *Heb. i. 2 and xi. 3*,
in each of which the word has been mistranslated
" worlds " instead of " ages "—thus—" God having of old
time spoken unto the fathers in the prophets by divers
portions and in divers manners, hath in the end of these
days spoken to us in His Son, through whom also *tous
aiōnas epoiēsen*, He made *the ages* "—*Heb. i. 1, 2*.—" By
faith we understand *katērtisthai tous aiōnas*, that *the
ages* were fitted together by the Word of God "—
Heb. xi. 3.   Thus there is no such thing as " The
Plurality of worlds," in the Astronomic sense of the term,
ever mentioned in the Scriptures.

We are told in the Bible, that some of the Stars will

fall upon the Earth to hurt, though not to destroy it, but its *destruction* would be inevitable were they of such enormous magnitude as our Astronomers declare them to be. Thus we read—

"There fell from heaven a great Star, burning as a torch, and it fell upon the third part of the Earth, and upon the fountains of waters"—*Rev. viii. 10.* And again,

"The Stars of heaven fell unto the Earth, as a fig-tree casteth her unripe figs, when she is shaken of a mighty wind" —*Rev. vi. 13.*

I ask any sensible man which account concerning the stars is the safer to believe—that of the infallible Word of God, or the mere theories of erring men? I may, perhaps, be thought very narrow-minded in thus depriving the Astronomers of their many fanciful worlds, but I do not think that I can be justly called so, considering the broadness of my views as expressed in "Hades and Beyond," but I have long been an advocate for Truth "according to the Scriptures," having for that sacrificed much, and, so long as I have them upon my side, I fear not what men may think or say.

The constellations, or groups of Stars, are called "fixed," because they do not change in their relative position to each other, but this is a misleading definition, for they, like the others, all circle in faultless order round the heavens—"The Stars, *in their courses*, fought against Sisera"—*Jud. v. 20.* As already stated the Stars are for service to the Earth, with different degrees of size and brilliancy, for them—"God hath divided unto all the people under the whole heaven"—*Deut. iv. 19.* They are all numbered and named by God, who "telleth

the number of the Stars; He giveth them all their
names "—*Psa. cxlvii. 4.*

The distance attributed to the few Stars, which our
Astronomers have attempted to measure, is extravagant
beyond belief; in proof of which I give the following
quotation from Miss Giberne's " Sun, Moon, and Stars,"
pp. 91, 92.

"Alpha Centauri, the second Star which was attempted
with success, is the nearest of all whose distance we know.

"You have heard how far the Sun is from the Earth. The
distance of Alpha Centauri is two hundred and twenty-five
thousand times as much.

"Can you picture to yourself that vast reach of space—a
line ninety-one millions of miles long repeated over and over
again two hundred and twenty-five thousand times.

"But Alpha Centauri is one of the very nearest. The first
Star whose distance was measured, 61 Cygni, is five hundred
thousand times as far as the Sun, and the brilliant Sirius is
nearly one million times as far as the Sun. Others utterly refuse
to show the smallest change of position."

The Modern Astronomer is so fond of expatiating
upon the glories of his starry worlds, that he thinks but
little of his own, like the cloud-soaring eagle,

" Seeming to wonder that a world so dim
Should not have been more beautiful for him."

His mind has become so engrossed with the inconceivable
magnitude of Sirius, Vega, and other Stars, that he calls
the world in which he lives " an atom of a world," though
that " atom of a world," according to his own showing, is
25,000 miles in circumference, quite large enough for
all the purposes for which it is required, and the chief

of these purposes is, that by the works of God's Creation, as well as by the Revelation of His Word, as taught by the Holy Spirit, we may know Him as the only true God, and Jesus Christ whom He hath sent, for this is Life Eternal—*John xvii. 3.*

The Modern Astronomer appears to be deficient in the very first principle necessary for useful enquiry— Common Sense.

" Like the Chaldean he would watch the stars,"

but he lacks the standpoint of the Chaldean—a stationary Earth, for that, according to him, revolves around the Sun at the rate of eighteen miles per second; and how could it be possible for him to measure anything, especially such a circling body as a Star, with accuracy, if handicapped by such a cannon-ball motion as that? If he would only take the trouble to *think seriously,* instead of indulging in wild speculation, he would soon see the absurdity of his theoretic calculations.

To a thoughtful man the contemplation of the starry heavens is truly solemn, when he knows that they, as well as the familiar Earth from which he gazes on them, shall all pass away, " as a tale that is told." Such, it would appear, was in the mind of the Psalmist when he exclaimed—

"Of old hast Thou laid the foundations of the Earth, and the Heavens are the work of Thy hands. They shall perish, but Thou shalt endure; yea, all of them shall wax old like a garment; as a vesture shalt Thou change them, and they shall be changed; but Thou art the same, and Thy years shall have no end. The children of Thy servants shall continue, and their seed shall be established before Thee "—*Psa. cii. 25—28.*

So also, is the coming dissolution of the Heavens, proclaimed by the Prophet Isaiah—

" The host of heaven shall be dissolved, and the heavens shall be rolled together as a scroll, and all their host shall fall away as the leaf falleth from off the vine, and as a fading leaf of the fig-tree "—*Isa. xxxiv. 4.*

And the inspired Author of the Epistle to the Hebrews, quoting from the prophet Haggai, sums up the matter as follows—

" Yet once more will I make to tremble not the Earth only but also the Heavens. And this word, yet once more, signifieth the removing of those things that are shaken, as of things that have been made, that those things which are not shaken may remain. Wherefore, receiving a Kingdom that cannot be shaken, let us have grace, whereby we may offer service well-pleasing to God, with reverence and awe, for our God is a consuming fire."—*Heb. xii. 26—29.*

CHAPTER VIII.

THE SUN ACCORDING TO THE SCRIPTURES.

Section		Page
1.	Light comes out of Darkness - -	163
2.	Zetetic measurements respecting the distance and diameter of the Sun -	167
3.	Some particulars respecting the Sun - -	174
4.	Scriptural proof of the Rising and Setting of the Sun - · - -	180

SECTION 1.

LIGHT COMES OUT OF DARKNESS.

It is good to pass from fiction to fact—to have, instead of a rotten plank, a strong bridge on which to cross the stream—in lieu of panting in the foggy atmosphere of impossible Theory, to breathe the pure air of heavenly Truth. Let us now, therefore, endeavour to learn something of what the Bible tells us concerning the Sun.

"And God said, let there be luminaries (light-givers) in the firmament of the heavens, to divide the day from the night, and let them be for signs and for seasons, and for days and for years; and let them be for light in the firmament of the

heavens, to give light upon the Earth, and it was so. And God
made two great luminaries, the greater luminary to rule the
day, and the lesser luminary to rule the night, the Stars also;
and God set them in the firmament of the heavens to give light
upon the Earth, and to rule over the day and over the night,
and to divide between the light and between the darkness, and
God saw that it was good, and the evening and the morning
were the fourth day "—*Gen. i. 14—19.*

"Ah!" says the Sceptic, "what a bungling performance must this have been, not to make the Sun till
the *fourth* day; the world must have been left in
darkness for three days." Be not so fast with your
criticism, Mr. Sceptic; there was light *before* the Sun's
formation, as there is light without it now, and will be
hereafter. On the very first day of the Adamic
Creation—" God said, Let there be light, and there
was light "—*Gen. i. 3,* the record of which, as Longinus
remarked, is one of the finest instances of the sublime.

Light, strictly speaking, is a *formation,* not an *original
creation.* God said—" I *form* (*yutser*) the light, *and I
create* (*ve-bera*) darkness "—*Isa. xlv. 7.* Great have been
the differences of opinion as to light among Scientists,
some advocating the corpuscular and others the undula-
tory theory. Had they gone to the Book, which they so
much neglect, they would have learned long ago, strange
as it may seem to them, that Light is born out of the
womb of Darkness. Darkness is not a negation—a mere
absence of light—but a substance of various degrees of
density. Thus we are told that at the beginning
" Darkness was upon the face of the Deep "—*Gen. i. 2,*
and that " God divided between the light and between
the darkness, and God called the light day, and the

darkness He called night, and there is an evening, and there is a morning—one day "—*Gen. i. 4, 5*.

Thus we find that in the mysterious order of what is generally called Nature, but which, to speak more correctly, is the Providence of God, light sprang out of darkness, a beautiful illustration of which truth, the Apostle Paul, doubtless with reference to this very fact, gives us in spiritual things—" For God, *Ho eipōn ek skotous phōs lampsai*, who commanded *light to shine out of darkness*, hath shined in our hearts, to give the light of the knowledge of Himself in the face of Jesus Christ " —*2 Cor. iv. 6* Again, *ēte qar poti skotos nun de phōs en Kurio hōs tekna phōtos peripateite*, " for at one time ye were darkness, but now are ye light in the Lord, walk as children of light "—*Eph. v. 8 ;* and the Psalmist says —" Unto the upright there ariseth light in the darkness " —*Psa. cxii. 4*.

The darkness, out of which light is evolved, is of various degrees of density ; sometimes it is so gross or thick as to resemble that over the land of Egypt, recorded in *Exodus x. 21*, the darkness, " that might be felt " as if by groping. Again—" Moses drew near unto the *thick darkness*, where God was "—*Exod. xx. 21*. Milton writes of " darkness visible," that is, where nothing but darkness itself can be seen, an experience, which, perhaps, some of my Readers may have known, as, on one special occasion, I have myself. Thus, it is evident that the opinion entertained by most, that darkness is merely the privation of light, is erroneous. As light comes out of darkness it proves that darkness must be a veritable entity or substance. This may be marvellous to us, but all God's works are marvellous, and I do not

know that it is more so than that water is composed of
certain portions of oxygen and hydrogen gases. The
truth is that the marvels of Creation are inexplicable.
We see results, but as to the "why" and the "how,"
they are to us hidden as the writing in a sealed letter.
We must have faith to believe that everything which
God does is done in the best manner possible, and we
should, as Parnell tells us,

> "Know that God is Just,
> And, where we can't unriddle, learn to trust."

He is the wisest who knows his Bible best, and lives in
accordance with its teaching.   There is more *real* science
to be found in the Bible, particularly in Genesis, Job,
Psalms, Proverbs, Ecclesiastes, Isaiah, and Ezekiel, than
in all the Universities and Observatories in the world.
Grand nuggets of true knowledge are embedded there,
but they are required to be sought for in a reverent spirit,
for "God resisteth the proud but giveth grace unto the
humble"—*James iv. 6.*   Our Lord said—"I thank Thee,
O Father, Lord of heaven and earth, because Thou hast
hid these things from the wise and understanding, and
hast revealed them unto babes, even so, Father, for so
it seemeth good in Thy sight "—*Matt. xi. 25, 26.*

Parkhurst held strongly the procession of light out
of darkness; indeed, in one sense, it might be called
the basis of his system of the circulation of the celestial
fluids, which, as he thought, caused the revolution of
the world.   I am afraid, however, that, in his zeal to
uphold his theory, he sometimes got an esoteric meaning
from certain Hebrew words to harmonize with it, which
other good lexicographers do not appear to have found.

Still, in my opinion, his system, although I cannot approve of it, is superior to Newton's; he held that there is a plenum in the heavens, which Newton, on account of his fancied law of Gravitation, rejected, and he had a reverence for the Word of God which Newton, in his theory of the universe, deliberately ignored. Parkhurst's able exponent, Macdonald, in his work, "The Principia and the Bible," previously quoted, has some important remarks on light, especially in Chapter II. of Part II., to which I would refer any of my Readers who may be interested in that important subject.

SECTION 2.

ZETETIC MEASUREMENTS RESPECTING THE DISTANCE AND DIAMETER OF THE SUN.

Zetetics, who, as the name implies, seek only to know the truth as to God's wonderful works of Creation, although somewhat differing as regards the exact distance of the Sun from the Earth, are all agreed that it is comparatively near. Those now most in the front consider it to be under or about three thousand miles, and they utterly repudiate the estimate of Modern Astronomers—92,000,000 miles!—as being contrary to all reason. The Sun was made to give light and heat to the Earth, and what a wasted expenditure of both would there be at such an enormous distance. The idea is too absurd to be attributed to any human Architect, much less to the All-wise Creator of the Universe. It may be interesting to some of our Astronomical friends, for me to mention briefly how these Zetetic measurements have been taken, as they might then, perhaps, make some practical experiments. themselves, and thus be convinced that the extravagant distances, calculated on the theory of a Planetary Earth, are altogether erroneous.

Dr. Rowbotham's (Parallax) experiment was very simple; I shall give it in his own words, as described in "Zetetic Astronomy," pp. 102—104—

"The illustration given above (that of measurements by plane trigonometry), have referred to a fixed object; but the Sun is not fixed, and, therefore, a modification of the process, but involving the same principle, must be adopted. Instead of the simple triangle and plumb line represented in fig. 57, an instrument with a graduated arc must be employed; and two observers, one at each end of a North and South base line, must at the same moment observe the under edge of the Sun as it passes the meridian; when, from the difference of the angle observed, and the known length of the base line, the actual distance of the Sun may be calculated. The following case will fully illustrate this operation, as well as its result and importance. (Taken 13th July, 1870.)

"The distance of London Bridge to the sea-coast at Brighton, in a straight line, is 50 statute miles. On a given day at 12 o'clock, the altitude of the Sun from near the water at London Bridge, was found to be 61 degrees of an arc, and, at the same moment of time, the altitude from the sea-coast at Brighton was observed to be 64 degrees of an arc, as shown by fig. 58. The base line from L to B, 50 *measured* miles, the angle at L 61 degrees, and the angle at B 64 degrees. In addition to the method by calculation, the distance of the

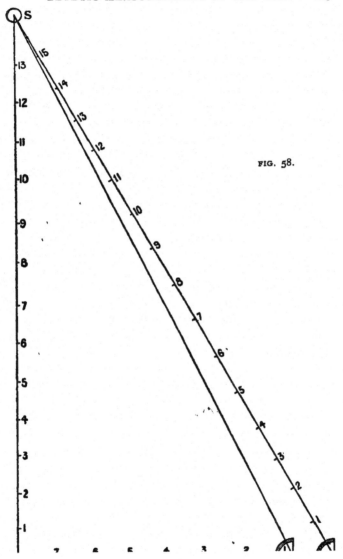

FIG. 58.

under edge of the Sun may be ascertained from these elements
by the method called 'construction.' The diagram, fig. 58,
is, in the above case, 'constructed,' that is, the base line
from L to B represents 50 statute miles, and the line L, S, is
drawn at an angle of 61 degrees, and the line B, S, is
drawn at an angle of 64 degrees. Both lines are produced
until they bisect or cross each other at the point S. Then,
with a pair of compasses, measure the length of the base line
B, L, and see how many times the same length may be found in
the line L, S, or B, S. It will be found to be sixteen times, or
sixteen times 50 miles, equal to 800 statute miles. Then
measure in the same way the vertical line D, S, and it will be
found to be 700 miles. Hence it is demonstrable that the distance of the Sun over that point of the Earth to which it is
vertical is only 700 statute miles."

Another method of measurement was adopted by the
late Mr. John Hampden, in a Pamphlet mentioned
below,* from which I quote as follows—

"The Sun travels from east to west on the equator, just
15 miles a minute, or 900 miles in the 60 minutes, and it
enlarges or diminishes its orbit just 15 miles every day, or
900 miles every 60 days.

"And again, precisely the same figures must be employed
to define the width of the twelve or fifteen meridians of longitude from North to South as are used to describe the daily
enlargement of the Sun's orbit from one parallel of latitude to
the next, and the next, occupying 90 days—that is, it increases
by 11½ from 7½ and 15 up to 1,350 and 157½." pp. 40, 41. . . .

"The Sun's altitude, at all seasons, is only 900 miles, or
just equal to a meridian of longitude on the Equator. In the
June or Northern Solstice it is vertical at 1,350 miles from the

---

* "A Dialogue on the Elementary Principles of Physical Cosmogony"; Civil
Service Printing & Publishing Co., 8 Salisbury Court, Fleet Street, London.

Equator; in May and July it is vertical at 900 miles, north; in April and August, it is vertical at 450 miles, north; in March and September, it is crossing the line; in February and October, it is vertical at 450 miles, south; in January and November it is vertical at 900 miles, south; and in the Southern or December Solstice it is 1,350 miles from the Equator.

"The diameter of the Sun's Northern or June orbit is just 4,200 miles; that of its Equinoxial orbit is 6,900 miles; and that of its diameter or Southern orbit 9,600 miles; or a difference of 2,700 miles between each " (p. 42).

Mr. Thomas Winship of Durban, Natal, gives his measurement of the Sun's distance as follows—

"When the Sun is on the Equator, and thus has no de-clination, the angle it makes with the Earth and the sea on all distances on that circle is a right angle. At an angular dis-tance of 45 degrees from the Equator, north or south, the distance of the base line from the observer to the Equator is of necessity the same as the Sun's vertical distance from the Earth's Equator. That is to say, in any right-angled triangle, where the angle at the apex of the triangle is 45 degrees, the other angle must of necessity be the same, as these two angles in any such triangle are equal to the right angle, viz., 90 degrees. The angles being equal the sides are of necessity equal; therefore the base line is equal to the vertical. . . .

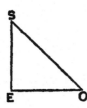

"Let S E O be a right-angled triangle, right-angled at E; S the Sun, E the Equator, and O an observer at 45 degrees north latitude.

"From the figure it is evident that 45 degrees is the angular distance of the Sun at 45 degrees north, and no other angle can be got in actual practice (allowing, of course, for such corrections as height of eye, semi-diameter, &c.); so that the

distance on the surface of the Earth to the Equator—from O
to E, is the same as from the Equator to the Sun in the heavens
—E to S. Multiplying 45 by 60 (60 Geographical miles equal
1 degree), we get 2,700 Geographical miles as the distance from
O to E, and thus from E to S. THE SUN IS, THEREFORE, 2,700
MILES DISTANT FROM THE EARTH. If the Sun were 96,000,000
miles distant from the Earth, our observer at 45 degrees N. or
S. latitude would be that distance from the Equator!!!"*

Another Zetetic, the late Editor of " The Earth (not
a Globe) Review," known as " ZETETES," has written an
able paper on the distance of the Sun, the whole of which
is too long for insertion here, so I must content myself
by quoting only the preliminary part, which, however,
is sufficient to show that " Zetetes " considers the Sun to
be about three thousand miles distant from the Earth.

"But take the time of the vernal and autumnal equinox,
when the Sun is directly over the Equator. We will also take
the Astronomer's assumption that the light of the Sun travels
in straight lines, except just near the surface of the Earth,
when they sometimes allow for what is termed refraction. But
as they have no agreed and definite standard of refraction,
and what they do sometimes allow is only a small figure, we
may at present ignore this for the purpose of simplifying the
problem before us. They cannot reasonably object to our
following their lead here.

"Now it is a well-known property that all the angles of
any triangle are together equal to two right angles, or 180
degrees. If, then, we take any right-angled triangle as A, B, C
having one angle at the base B a right angle, and the other
angle at the base C 45 degrees we know that the angle at the

---

* " Zetetic Cosmogony " pp. 115, 117; T. L. Cullingworth, 40 Field Street,
Durban, Natal ; John Williams, 54 Bourne Street, Netherfield, Notts.

apex A must also be 45 degrees, and the perpendicular B, A, equal to the base line, B, C.

"Now let A represent the Sun's position over the Equator on the 21st of March, and B the place of some spectator on the Equator directly beneath the Sun when on the meridian say of Bordeaux, which is almost that of Greenwich, and lef C represent the town of Bordeaux in France at about 45 degrees N. Lat. Here, then, we have some general data for determining the Sun's distance from the Earth; that is, the line A, B, or the perpendicular height of the Sun above the Equator at B, is equal to the line C, B, or the base line, or distance between Bordeaux and the point B on the Equator.

"Now the Geographers affirm that 1 degree equals 60 geographical or 69½ statute miles. Then multiply 45 degrees by these figures, and we get the distance, according to the Astronomers, that Bordeaux is from the nearest point of the Equator on the same meridian, namely 2,700 geographical miles, or about 3,107 English or statute miles. In round numbers, then, 3,000 miles proximately is the distance of the Sun from the Equator, shown according to the terms of the Astronomers themselves."

With regard to the Diameter of the Sun, the estimates of Modern Astronomers vary from 850,000 to 882,000 miles, thus making a difference between themselves of 32,000 miles! These calculations are so preposterously absurd that they only deserve to be treated with contempt. Mr. Winship of Natal, who is an Expert in nautical matters, asserts that its Diameter is only 32 geographical miles, as will be seen from the following extract from p. 120 of his valuable work, "Zetetic Cosmogony," previously mentioned—

" If the navigator neglects to apply the Sun's semi-diameter to his observation at sea, he is 16 nautical miles (nearly) out in calculating the position his ship is in. A minute of arc on the sextant represents a nautical mile, and, if the semi-diameter be 16 miles, the diameter is, of course, 32 miles. And, as measured by the sextant, the Sun's diameter is 32 minutes of arc, that is 32 nautical miles in diameter. Let him disprove this who can. If ever disproof is attempted, it will be a literary curiosity, well worth framing."

Personally I do not feel competent to decide what is the exact distance and diameter of the Sun, but, from the testimony of Scripture, that that luminary was appointed by God to give light and heat, days and years, signs and seasons to the Earth, as also from the dictates of reason with regard to the fitness of things, I am convinced that it must be comparatively near us, and I consider that the measurements as to its distance by the Zetetics previously referred to, and the diameter allowed for it by Mr. Winship, are THE VERY EXTREME of what might be required for its performance of the purposes for which it was created. We may be positively certain that the vast distance and diameter of the Sun, ascribed to it by Modern Astronomers, is only a wild chimera of the brain, and at complete variance with Scripture, Reason, and Fact.

SECTION 8.

SOME PARTICULARS RESPECTING THE SUN.

Let us now look at the following points—

1. In the beginning darkness was upon the face of the Deep, or vast abyss of waters, in which the Earth,

before the Adamic Creation, was wholly submerged. Afterwards the Spirit of God moved upon the waters, and God said " Let there be light, and there was light."

2. God divided between the light and between the darkness, from which it would seem that, in consequence of this operation, the finer particles were separated from the grosser, and formed by God's fiat into light. The Hebrew for light is *aur*, from the root *ar* to flow, whence we also have *yaur*, a river, so called from its flowing motion.

3. On the Fourth day of Creation God made the Sun, Moon and Stars, which are all independent light-givers, and it appears to me that these were all formed from different combinations of light with some pervading ether, or other product unknown to us, by the Word of God, who is the only perfect Alchemist in the universe.

4. The word *aur*, light, is occasionally used for fire —" a third part shalt thou burn in the *fire*, in the midst of the city "—*Ezek. v. 2*, whence it seems as if fire were a development of light, as exhibited by the Sun, from which, it is said, immense flames, discoverable by the telescope, proceed.

5. Light can be reconverted into darkness—" the light is darkened in the heavens thereof "—*Isa. v. 30*— " The Sun shall be turned into darkness "—*Joel ii. 31*. " Seek Him that maketh the seven Stars (the Pleïades), and Orion, and turneth the shadow of death into the morning, and maketh the day dark with night "— *Amos v. 8*.

6. The light of the Sun and Moon can also be much

increased—" Moreover the light of the Moon shall be as the light of the Sun, and the light of the Sun shall be seven-fold, as the light of seven days, in the day that JEHOVAH bindeth up the hurt of His people, and healeth the stroke of their wound "—*Isa. xxx. 26.* The heat also of the Sun shall be greatly intensified—" And the fourth angel poured out his bowl upon the Sun, and power was given unto him to scorch men with fire, and men were scorched with great heat "—*Rev. xvi. 8, 9.*

7. I have already proved from Scripture that light existed *before* the Sun, and I shall now show that a time shall come when that luminary will not be required at all. Speaking of the restoration of God's ancient people, Israel, Isaiah says—" The Sun shall no more be thy light by day, neither for brightness shall the Moon give light unto thee, but JEHOVAH shall be unto thee an everlasting light, and thy God thy glory "—*Isa. lx. 19.* Again, of the New Jerusalem it is written—" The City hath no need of the Sun, neither of the Moon to shine in it, for the glory of God did lighten it, and the lamp thereof is the Lamb "—*Rev. xxi. 23.* And, concerning the habitation of the Saints in the Grand Hereafter we read—" There shall be no night there, and they need no light of lamp, neither light of Sun, for the Lord God shall give them light, and they shall reign for ever and ever "—*Rev. xxii. 5.*

Thus we see that the Sun is no Baal or Lord of the universe, but only an *Obed* or servant, formed by God to give light and heat to our world, and to regulate its times and seasons as at present constituted, but whose service can be dispensed with when no longer required.

8. God made light on the First day, and what was

then given was quite sufficient for the first three days of Creation, but, on the Fourth day, when vegetable and organic life were introduced, He made the Sun, as also the Moon and Stars, such being necessary for the higher state of existence, for God always admirably adapts the means to the end.

9. In *Genesis i. 16* we read literally—

Ve-yosh	*Alöheim*	*at*	*sheni*	*he-maret*
" And made	God	the substance	two	the luminaries
he-gedlim	*at*	*he-maur*	*he-gedel*	
the great	the substance	the luminary	the greater	
le-memshelet	*he-yum*	*ve-at*	*he-maur*	
for the ruling	the day	and the substance	the luminary	
he-qethen	*le-memshelet*	*he-lileh*	*ve-at*	
the lesser	for the ruling	the night	and the substance	
	he-kukebim			
	the stars.			

From the above passage we may gather that these are all independent bodies of light, concentrated in different chemical combinations or affinities; the Sun red and heat-causing, the Moon pale and cold, and the Stars of a variety of colours. It may be well to note also, that the account of the formation of the Stars occupies only four words in the Hebrew, while that of the Earth and its inhabitants takes a great many more; whereas, were they the vast bodies which our Astronomers represent them to be, we would naturally expect that the relation made concerning them would have been far more fully detailed in the Inspired Record than it is.

How these luminaries are being continuously replenished, we cannot know with certainty, because we are not told by Scripture, but, from whatever source, it is amply sufficient for the purpose, as, after their long course of well nigh six thousand years, their light is still as good as ever. If I might hazard a conjecture, I would suggest that it might possibly be by their absorbing the entities of the plenum of space, as they circle round the heavens. The ways of God are very mysterious to our finite minds, but, by and bye, we shall know how wise and yet how simple they are.

10. The Sun is sometimes eclipsed for a short time, in consequence of the Moon coming between it and the observer on the Earth. Such eclipses, as before mentioned, are quite independent of any particular theory, being calculated from those which have been previously observed. Thus, as Professor Olmsted remarks—

"It is not difficult to form some general notion of the process of calculating Eclipses. It may be easily conceived that, by long-continued observation on the Sun and Moon, the laws of their revolution may be so well understood, that the exact place which they will occupy in the heavens at any future time may be foreseen and laid down in tables of the Sun's and Moon's motions; that we may thus ascertain, by inspecting the tables, the instant when these bodies will be together in the heavens, or be in conjunction."*

"Hippocratus (150 B.C.) constructed tables of the motions of the Sun and Moon; collected accounts of such Eclipses, as had been made by the Egyptians and Chaldeans, and calculated all that were to happen for 600 years to come."†

11. God made the Sun and Moon, not only to give light to the world, but to be for signs and seasons, for

---

* "Mechanism of the Heavens," p. 191.
† "Encyclopædia Londonensis," Vol. 11, p. 402.

days and for years. The Sun is the chronometer of the world, and by it all time is regulated by land and by sea. Through it, by means of Eclipses, Mr. Dimbleby claims to have calculated the very day on which the present *Kosmos*, or ornamented world, began to be formed.* I use the word *Kosmos* in order to distinguish it from *arets*, the Earth which was without form and void, when Darkness was upon the face of the Deep. *When* that unformed Earth was originally created no human being knows, and the guesses of Astronomers and Geologists, as to its possible age, are utterly without value, because they have no data on which to base their calculations.

12. In order to fulfil the purposes for which God made the Sun, it was necessary for it, instead of being stationary, to revolve around the world. By this means it gives light and heat to the Earth in its various parts, besides which, it is for a sign in the calculation of eclipses and other heavenly motions—for regulating the different seasons, Spring, Summer, Autumn, Winter— for days, when man goeth forth to his labour till the evening—and specially to distinguish the Sabbath or Seventh day from the others—and for years to mark particular occurrences, such as the lives of the Patriarchs, the date of the Deluge, the call of Abraham, the Exodus, the Jewish Captivity, the Times of the Gentiles, the birth of Christ, and other notable events which need not be mentioned here.

God, who knows the thoughts and intents of the heart, was, of course, well aware that some would debase themselves by worshipping the Sun, and that others

---

* " All Past Time," pp. 9, 73, 142, by J. B. Dimbleby; E. Nester, 28 Paternoster Row, London.

would imagine it to be the immovable centre of the universe, has been most particular in describing, in the Scriptures, its daily revolution round the world, so that men might be without excuse as regards either their idolatry or their ignorance. Every evening, at various hours, according to the time of the year, and the place in which we are, the Sun seems to us to go down or set, but always re-appears at dawn of day,

> " Arising, when morn beameth on the lea,
> To mock the doctrine of the Sadducee."

In the Arctic region, however, the Sun, for certain days in Summer, does not visibly set at all, but may be seen, during the whole twenty-four hours of the day, performing its regular circle round the heavens, a proof positive that it is only a satellite of the stationary Earth, which cannot, therefore, be a Planet.

SECTION 4.

SCRIPTURAL PROOF OF THE RISING AND SETTING OF THE SUN.

The passages of Scripture respecting the rising and setting of the Sun, are so very numerous that it would occupy too much space to record them all, so I shall only mention a few, which, however, are quite sufficient for the purpose; a complete list can be found, if required, in any good Concordance—

"From the wilderness and this Lebanon, even unto the great river, the river Euphrates, all the land of the Hittites, and unto the

Great Sea, towards *the going down of the Sun*, shall be your border "—*Jos. i.* 4.

" Thus spake Joshua to JEHOVAH, in the day when JEHOVAH delivered up the Amorites before the children of Israel, *Sun, stand thou still* upon Gibeon, and thou, Moon, in the valley of Ajalon. . . . *So the Sun stood still in the midst of heaven, and hasted not to go down about a whole day.* And there was no day like that before it or after it that JEHOVAH hearkened unto the voice of a man, for JEHOVAH fought for Israel "—*Jos. x.* 12-14.

" But let them that love Him (JEHOVAH) be as the Sun when *he goeth forth in his might* "—*Jud. v.* 31.

" And it shall be in the morning, *as soon as the Sun is up*, thou shalt rise early and set upon the city "—*Jud. ix.* 33.

" And the men of the city said unto him *before the sun went down*, what is sweeter than honey, or stronger than a lion? "—*Jud. xiv.* 18.

" So they passed on and went their way, *and the sun went down upon them*, even by Gibeah, which belongeth to Benjamin "— *Jud. xix.* 14.

" David sware, saying, So do God to me and more also, if I taste bread or ought else *till the Sun be down* "—*2 Sam. iii.* 35.

" And Hezekiah said unto Isaiah, what shall be the sign that JEHOVAH will heal me, and that I shall go up to the House of JEHOVAH the third day? And Isaiah said, This shall be the sign unto thee from JEHOVAH, that JEHOVAH will do the thing that He hath spoken—*Shall the shadow* (of the Sun) *go forward ten steps* (degrees) or *go back ten steps?* And Hezekiah answered, It is a light thing for *the shadow to decline ten steps*, nay, *but let the shadow return backward ten steps.* And Isaiah the Prophet cried unto JEHOVAH and He *brought the shadow ten steps backward on which it had gone on the dial of Ahaz* "—*2 Kings xx.* 8-11.

" So *the Sun returned ten degrees*, by which degrees *it was gone down* "—*Isa. xxxviii.* 8.

"In them (the heavens) hath He set a tabernacle for *the Sun,* *which is as a bridegroom coming out of his chamber, and rejoiceth as a* *young man to run his course. His going forth is from the end of the* *heavens, and his circuit unto the end of it*"—*Psa. xix.* 4-6.

"*The Sun also ariseth* (*zeret*) *and the Sun goeth down* (*bu*), *and* *returneth to the place where he arose*"—*Ecc. i.* 5.

"And it came to pass when *the Sun arose,* that God prepared a sultry east wind "—*Jon. iv* 8.

"That ye may be the children of your Father which is in heaven, for *He maketh the Sun to rise* on the evil and on the good, and sendeth rain on the just and on the unjust "—*Matt. v.* 45.

"Let not *the Sun go down* upon your wrath"—*Eph. iv.* 26.

"For *the Sun is no sooner risen* with a burning heat but it withereth the grass "—*Jam. i.* 11.

Such testimony from the Scriptures that the Earth is a *Terra Firma,* and that the Sun rises and sets each day in his journey round the heavens, must be convincing to every unprejudiced mind, and it is really superfluous to add proof from secular sources, with which every country teems, and of which I could quote pages. But what would be the use? If people will not credit what God declares—what common sense teaches—and what their own eyes behold, further arguments would be of no avail, and they must just be left in their ignorance. In the world beyond they will have their sight opened, and deeply will they deplore that they were so sinful and so foolish as to believe a Pagan lie instead of the overwhelming evidence, afforded to them during their sojourn here, of Scripture, Reason, and Fact, that the Earth is not a Planet.

CHAPTER IX.

THE SUN'S PATH AND WORK IN THE HEAVENS.

SECTION   PAGE

1. THE TRUE CAUSE OF DAY AND NIGHT AND THE SEASONS - - - - - - 184

2. THE REASON FOR GAIN AND LOSS OF TIME AT SEA - - - - - 186

3. THE SEASONS OF THE YEAR - - - - - 187

4. THE MIDNIGHT SUN, AND THE ALTERNATION OF SUMMER AND WINTER IN THE NORTHERN CENTRE - - - - - 190

5. THE SUN AND THE ZODIAC - - 195

THERE is no subject, with the exception, of course, of those which are essentially divine, so ennobling to the human mind as the right contemplation of the wonders of the spacious firmament. The atmosphere and the clouds—the rain and the dew—the hurricane and the hail—the thunder and the lightning—teach lessons of love and of thankfulness, of pity and of awe. The majestic Sun, as it travels on its path, the silvery Moon, "walking in brightness," and the variegated Stars, emblazoning, like costly jewels, the mantle of night, draw us from ourselves, and

"Lead from Nature up to Nature's God."

How deeply must the Sweet Singer of Israel have felt this when he exclaimed—

" The heavens declare the glory of God, and the firmament showeth His handiwork. Day unto day uttereth speech, and night unto night teacheth knowledge. There is no speech nor language where their voice is not heard. Their line is gone out through all the earth, and their words unto the end of the world "—*Psa. xix. 1—4.*

SECTION 1.

THE CAUSE OF DAY AND NIGHT AND THE SEASONS.

The Path of the Sun is Concentric, expanding and contracting daily for six months alternately. This is easily proved by fixing a rod, say at noon on the 21st of December, so that, on looking along it, the line of vision will touch the lower edge of the Sun. This line of sight will continue for several days pretty much the same, but, on the ninth or tenth day, it will be found that the rod will have to be moved considerably toward the zenith, in order to touch the lower edge of the Sun, and every day afterwards it will have to be raised till the 22nd of June. Then there will be little change for a few days as before, but day by day afterwards the rod will have to be lowered till the 21st of December, when the Sun is farthest from the Northern Centre, and it is dark there. This expansion and contraction of the Sun's path continues every year, and is termed the Northern and Southern Declination, and should demonstrate to Modern Astronomers the absurdity of calling the World a Planet, as it remains stationary while the Sun continues circling round the heavens.

It has been observed, that both the June and the December paths of the Sun have for centuries been gradually receding from the Northern Centre, which may account for the fact that in Great Britain, as well as in other northern countries, the remains of tropical productions have been found, thus appearing to show that these localities were at one time warmer than they are now. It has also been noticed that the inclemency of the weather in the far Southern latitudes, though still much greater than it is in the same degrees of latitude in the North, seems to be somewhat less than when they were first discovered.

It will thus be seen that, in consequence of this expanding and contracting path of the Sun, as it daily travels round the world, in an inner or outer circle, for six months alternately, as it advances towards or recedes from the Northern Centre, or, as Geographers call it, the North Pole, are produced the various changes in the length of each day and night, morning and evening twilight, the different seasons of the year, Spring, Summer, Autumn, and Winter, and the long periods of alternate light and darkness in the Northern Centre. Such was God's purpose when He first made the Sun, and such was His determination after the whole Earth had been swept by the Noachian Flood, for we read in the Book of books—

"While the Earth remaineth seedtime and harvest, and cold and heat, and summer and winter, and day and night shall not cease "—*Gen. viii. 22.*

SECTION 2.

THE REASON FOR GAIN AND LOSS OF TIME AT SEA.

We often hear it stated that the fact of the mariner gaining or losing a day, in circumnavigating the Earth, is evidence that it is a Globe, whereas, on the contrary, it is a direct proof that it is a Plane. On this point I beg to quote the following terse words of the late Mr. W. Carpenter of Baltimore, from No. 100 of his "One Hundred Proofs that the Earth is not a Globe."*

"The Sun, as it travels over the surface of the Earth, brings 'noon' to all places on the successive meridians which he crosses, his journey being made in a westerly direction, places east of the Sun's position have had their noon, whilst places in the west of the Sun's position have still to get it. Therefore, if we travel easterly, and arrive at the part of the Earth where 'time' is more advanced, the watch has to be 'put on,' or we may be said 'to gain time.' If, on the other hand, we travel westerly, we arrive at places where it is still 'morning,' the watch has to be 'put back,' and it may be said that we 'lose time.' But, if we travel easterly, so as to cross the 180th meridian, there is a loss there of a day, which will neutralize the gain of a whole circumnavigation, and if we travel westerly, and cross the same meridian, we experience the gain of a day, which will compensate for the loss during a complete circumnavigation in that direction. The fact of losing or gaining time in sailing round the world, then, instead

---

* John Williams, 54 Bourne Street, Netherfield, Notts.

of being evidence of the Earth's rotundity, as it is imagined
to be, is, in its practical exemplification, an evident proof
that the Earth is not a Globe."

———

SECTION 8.

THE SEASONS OF THE YEAR.

Our Modern Astronomers have found great difficulty
in accounting for the alternation of day and night, and
the return of the Seasons of the year, so as to be in
keeping with their theory of the world revolving round the
Sun.   They at last hit upon the expedient of supposing
the Earth to rotate upon an imaginary axis once in every
twenty-four hours to explain day and night, and gave it a
peculiar lurch of 23½ degrees, so as to bring in the
Seasons in their course.   It was a clumsy device, and,
of course, utterly fallacious, for, as already shown, the
Earth does not rotate at all, but " is founded upon the
seas and established upon the floods."   Had they left
their vain philosophy, and given heed to the plain
teaching of the Bible, and practical observation, they
would have discovered how simple are the laws of God,
and how unfailing in their action.   He makes no patch-
work, as our Astronomers do, for—" As for God His
way is perfect "—*Psa. xviii. 30.*   In explaining the cause
of the Seasons, I do not think that I can do better for
my Readers than by giving the following extract from

pp. 124, 125 of "Zetetic Cosmogony,"* a particularly able work, lately published by Mr. Thomas Winship of Natal, who, in the first paragraph, quotes Mr. Russell's remarks on that subject, from pp. 16, 17 of "The Wonders of the Sun, Moon, and Stars"—

"'The nearer the Sun gets to the Pole star, the earlier it rises, the higher it reaches at noon, and the later it sets. *This apparent independent motion of the Sun*, therefore, seems to account for longer and shorter days, and the whole phenomena of the seasons, but why the Sun lags as described, or why it moves northerly and southerly at alternate periods, *there is no* apparent evidence.'"

On the above paragraph Mr. Winship remarks as follows—

"On the supposition that the world is a globe rotating against the Sun, and revolving round that luminary, it is impossible to account for what Mr. Russell calls the lagging movement of the Sun. But, on a flat surface, like the world is known to be, there is no assumption needed to account for it. As I have shown the Earth is a stretched-out structure, which diverges from the Central north in all directions toward the south. The Equator, being mid-way between the north centre and the southern circumference, divides the course of the Sun into north and south declinations. The longest circle round the world which the Sun makes, is when it has reached its greatest southern declination. Gradually going northward the circle is contracted. In about three months after the southern extremity of its path has been reached, the Sun makes a circle round the Equator. Still pursuing a northerly course as it

---

* E. L. Cullingworth, 40 Field Street, Durban, Natal; John Williams, 54 Bourne Street, Netherfield, Notts.

goes round and above the world, in another three months the greatest northern declination is reached, when the Sun again begins to go towards the south. In northern latitudes when the Sun is going north, it rises earlier each day, is higher at noon, and sets later; while in southern latitudes, at the same time, the Sun, as a matter of course, rises later; reaches a lesser altitude at noon and sets earlier. In northern latitudes during the southern summer, say from September to December, the Sun rises later each day, is lower at noon, and sets earlier; while in the south he rises earlier, reaches a higher altitude at noon, and sets later each day. This movement round the Earth daily is the cause of the alternation of day and night; while his northern and southern courses produce the Seasons. When the Sun is south of the Equator it is summer in the south and winter in the north, and *vice-versa*. The fact of the alternation of the Seasons flatly contradicts the Newtonian delusion that the Earth revolves in an orbit round the Sun. It is said that summer is caused by the Earth being nearer the Sun, and winter by its being farthest from the Sun. But, if the reader will follow the argument in any text-book, he will see that according to the theory, when the Earth is nearest the Sun there must be summer in both northern and southern latitudes; and in like manner when it is farthest from the Sun it must be winter all over the Earth at the same time, because the whole of the globe-earth would be farthest from the Sun!!! In short it is impossible to account for the recurrence of the Seasons on the assumption that the Earth is globular, and that it revolves in an orbit round the Sun."

SECTION 4.

THE MIDNIGHT SUN, AND THE ALTERNATION OF SUMMER AND WINTER IN THE NORTHERN CENTRE.

In Winter the Northern Centre is darkened, and continues so for some months till the Sun returns again in Summer, and illumines it with its brightness. We have then the phenomenon of " The Midnight Sun," the following vivid account of which appeared in " The Brighton Examiner " of July, 1870. The party referred to consisted of Mr. Campbell, the United States' Minister for Norway, and some other gentlemen who ascended a cliff 1,000 feet high, overlooking the Arctic Ocean—

" It was late but still sunlight. The Arctic Ocean stretched away in silent vastness at our feet, the sound of the waves scarcely reached our airy look-out. Away in the north the huge old Sun swung low along the horizon, like the slow beat of the tall clock in our grandfather's parlour corner. We all stood silently looking at our watches. When both hands stood together at twelve midnight, the full round orb hung trium-phantly above the waves—a bridge of gold running due north spangled the water between us and him. There he shone in silent majesty which knew no setting. We involuntarily took off our hats—no word was said. Combine the most brilliant sunrise you ever saw, and its beauties will pall before the gorgeous colouring which lit up the ocean, heaven, and moun-tains. In half an hour the Sun had swung up perceptibly on its beat, the colours had changed to those of morning. A fresh breeze had rippled over the florid sea; one songster after another piped out of the grove behind us—we had slid into another day."

What a splendid visible proof is the above description of the Sun revolving round a stationary Earth! There, in that high Norwegian latitude, these travellers saw from a lofty cliff, the Sun at Midnight passing in his journey, without having set at all, from one day into another, and proclaiming with effulgent brightness the grand beneficence of God. Thus, as the Poet sings—

> "Th' unwearied Sun from day to day,
> Doth its Creator's power display,
> And publishes in every land
> The work of His Almighty hand."

Had poor Proctor been there I think he would never have written his "Pretty proof of the Earth's rotundity." Facts, such as those above narrated, are too strong to be resisted even by scientific prejudice. It would doubtless teach a useful lesson, as also afford a pleasant holiday, to some of our Astronomic friends, were they to take a trip to "The Land of the Midnight Sun" in one of the steamers advertized for that voyage in the newspapers. I think that they would return wiser than before they went, with less admiration for the hypothesis of Copernicus, with more reverence for the Word of God, and with more respect for common sense.

Respecting this matter the late Mr. Carpenter writes pithily in Nos. 38 and 39 of his "One Hundred Proofs" before-mentioned, which I beg here to subjoin—

"38. When the Sun crosses the Equator in March and

begins to circle round the heavens in north latitude, the inhabitants of high northern latitudes see him skimming round their horizon and forming the break of their long day in a horizontal course, not disappearing again for six months, as he rises higher and higher in the heavens, whilst he makes his twenty-four hours' circle until June, when he begins to descend, and goes on till he disappears beyond the horizon in September. Thus, in the northern regions they have what the traveller calls the 'Midnight Sun' as he sees that luminary at a time when, in the more southern latitudes it is always midnight. If then, for one half the year, we may see for ourselves the Sun making horizontal circles round the heavens, it is presumptive that, for the other half, he is doing the same although beyond the boundary of our vision. This being a proof that the Earth is a plane is a proof that the Earth is not a Globe.

"39. We have abundance of evidence that the Sun moves daily round and over the Earth in circles concentric with the northern regions, over which hangs the North Star; but, since the theory of the Earth being a globe is necessarily connected with the theory of its motion round the Sun in a yearly orbit, it falls to the ground when we bring forward the evidence of which we speak, and, in so doing forms a proof that the Earth is not a Globe."

The foregoing observations, with respect to the path and work of the Sun, apply specially to Northern latitudes; in those of the South, owing to the differing circumstances of position, considerable modifications are, of course, to be expected. In Southern latitudes the particular motion of the Sun appears as yet to be imperfectly known, and further investigation is assuredly required. The South is radiated from the Northern

Centre, from which proceed vast stretches of land and water, especially the latter, which, towards the extremity, have an impenetrable circumference of ice and rocks, described by Job as " the boundary of light with darkness " —*Job xxvi. 10*.

Since the above was written, I have read a very interesting article, " Two Thousand Miles in the Antarctic Ice," in last May No. of the " Windsor Magazine,"* by Dr. Cook, late Surgeon and Ethnologist in the Belgian expedition to the Antarctic Ocean, from which it appears that the Midnight Sun is also seen in that region. The steamer *Belgica* was imbedded in an ice-pack, in Latitude 71°, 22' S., Longitude 84°, 55', W., from 4th March, 1898, to 14th February, 1899, so that the Explorers had thus ample time for observation. The Winter long night of darkness and the Summer long day of light were distinctly marked, though with somewhat of a difference, as regards circumstantial surroundings, from those of the Arctic regions. Thus Dr. Cook, who had himself thrice previously visited the North Polar Seas, and knew by experience what they are, writes respecting the Antarctic as follows—

"I can imagine nothing more desperate than a storm on the edge of the pack. At best it is a dull, cold, and gloomy region, with a high humidity, and constant drizzly fogs. Clear weather is here a rare exception. Storms, with rain, sleet, and snow, is the normal weather condition throughout the entire year." p. 721. Again—

"The *Aurora Australis* was in evidence nearly every night in April, May, July, and August. It was never brilliantly

* Ward, Lock & Co., Limited, Warwick House, Salisbury Court, London.

luminous, or so fantastic in figure as the Aurora Borealis. The weird form was that of an arc, without motion, resting on the South-Western sky. Above and below it were ragged, cloud-like fragments, which changed in form and brilliancy every few seconds. The colour was faintly yellow, and the light emitted was never sufficient to be visibly thrown on the surface snow." p. 732.

It is evident from the foregoing that the Sun, or the Sun's rays, must have a motion over Southern regions which, as far as I am aware, has never hitherto been observed by any explorers there, and I sincerely hope that the Antarctic expeditions lately organized by British and German enterprise, may be able to throw additional light on this important subject. Not only those parts of the ocean to the South of Cape Horn and Australia, but the whole Southern circumference should be carefully examined, as near the barriers of ice as can be safely accomplished. Truth is never afraid of the fullest investigation.

The Sun being visible at Midnight in Antarctic regions during a certain period of the year proves that it has work to do there which has never heretofore been properly recognized, but that does not, in the slightest degree, show the Earth to be a Planet, for it is found, by accurate observation, that the waters of the Antarctic form one complete level with those of the Arctic Ocean, and with all the intervening seas. The Earth is a vast and generally even platform, stretched out upon these waters, for, according to the infallible Word of God, it is " founded upon the seas, and established upon the floods " —*Psa. xxiv. 2.*

SECTION 5.

THE SUN AND THE ZODIAC.

The Zodiac is that vast circle in the heavens, through which the Sun passes in its annual course, or, to speak more correctly, in 365 days, 5 hours, 48 minutes and 48 seconds. The Zodiac has been known so long that its origin is lost in the mist of antiquity. It has been thought by some, and I think with very great probability, that its pictures or signs, with their meaning, were revealed to Adam soon after the Fall. Cassini, in his " History of Astronomy," says—

" It is impossible to doubt that Astronomy was invented from the beginning of the world ; history, profane as well as sacred, testifies to this truth."

The signs of the Zodiac, and other facts regarding the revolution of the Sun in the heavens, were known to the Chaldeans, the earliest and best Astronomers, or Astrologers as they were then called, some hundreds of years before the birth of Moses, as proved by the Accadian tablets recently exhumed, and Sir William Drummond remarks that " the traditions of the Chaldean Astronomers seem the fragments of a mighty system fallen into ruins." There are still extant pictorial records of the Zodiac in the Egyptian temples of Dendera and Esnéh, considered to be about 4,000 years old, and these are supposed to be only copies of others of a still earlier date.

The following are the signs of the Zodiac in the order in which they have always appeared—

    ♈ Aries, the Ram.
    ♉ Taurus, the Bull.
    ♊ Gemini, the Twins.
    ♋ Cancer, the Crab.
    ♌ Leo, the Lion.
    ♍ Virgo, the Virgin.
    ♎ Libra, the Balance or Scales.
    ♏ Scorpio, the Scorpion.
    ♐ Sagittarius, the Archer.
    ♑ Capricornus, the Sea-goat.
    ♒ Aquarius, the Water-carrier.
    ♓ Pisces, the Fishes.

The above signs do not bear any resemblance whatever to the Constellations which they are said to represent; but appear to have been given to declare the grand purposes of God towards man, for the heavens not only set forth the glory of God, but, like a volume unrolled, are intended for the instruction of humanity.

The Rev. Dr. Bullinger, with whom I am happy to have some personal acquaintance, published a few years ago a most interesting work, called "The Witness of the Stars,"* in which he gives an able exposition of the Twelve Signs of the Zodiac, and the thirty-six Constellations with which they are connected. In passing I would remark that there may possibly be a latent allusion to the signs of the Zodiac in *Isaiah xiii. 12,* where we read—"the stars of heaven and the constellations

---

* "Witness of the Stars," Rev. Dr. Bullinger, 25 Connaught Street, London, W.C.

thereof." This book is written on the lines of Ancient and not of Modern Astronomy—for the glory of God and not for the praise of men, and I would strongly recommend its perusal to my Readers. Perhaps a brief reference to some of its teachings may not be unacceptable here. I quote the following from p. 15—

"The word *Zodiac* itself is from the Greek *Zodiakos*, which is not from *zaō* to live, but from a primitive root through the Hebrew *Sodi*, which in Sanscrit means a *way*. Its etymology has no connection with *living creatures*, but denotes a *way* or *step*, and is used of the *way* or path in which the Sun appears to move among the Stars in the course of the year.

"To an observer on the Earth the whole firmament, together with the Sun, appears to revolve in a circle once in twenty-four hours. But the time occupied by the Stars in going round, differs from the time occupied by the Sun. This difference amounts to about one-twelfth part of the whole circle in each month, so that when the circle of the heavens is divided up into twelve parts, the Sun appears to move each month through one of them. This path which the Sun thus makes amongst the Stars is called the *Ecliptic*."

The Apostle Paul had evidently learned the lesson of the Stars when, speaking with regard both to Jews and Gentiles, he says—

"For whosoever shall call upon the name of the Lord shall be saved. How then shall they call on Him in whom they have not believed? And how shall they believe in Him of whom they have not heard? And how shall they hear without a preacher? And how shall they preach except they be sent? . . . . But, I say, Have they not heard? Yea, verily, THEIR SOUND WENT INTO ALL THE EARTH, AND THEIR WORDS UNTO THE END OF THE WORLD."—*Rom. x. 13—15, 18.*

The words in small capitals are taken from *Psalm xix. 4,* which beautiful Psalm in verses 1, 2 testifies that

"The heavens declare the glory of God, and the firmament showeth His handiwork. Day unto day uttereth speech, and night unto night showeth knowledge."

But Paul, in *Romans i. 20,* vindicates the teaching of God by His works—

"For the invisible things of Him from the creation of the world are clearly seen, being understood by the things that are made, even His eternal power and Godhead; so that they are without excuse."

The twelve signs of the Zodiac are twice referred to in the Bible (margin), once in *2 Kings xxiii. 5* and once in *Job xxxviii. 32,* in the latter of which passages the question is asked—" Canst thou bring forth the *Mazzaroth,* (the twelve signs of the Zodiac), in their season ? " The Stars are all numbered and named by God—" not one is lacking "—*Isa. xl. 26.* In Job, which, from the ancient style of the Hebrew, and from its having no reference to the Exodus, is, in all probability, the oldest book in the Bible, a few of the original names of the Constellations are given. Thus in *Job ix. 9* we read—" which maketh Arcturus (*Osh,* the Great Bear), Orion (*Chisel*), and Pleiades (*Chimah,* or the seven stars)." Again, in *Chapter xxxviii. 31,* God asks Job—" Canst thou bind the sweet influences of Pleiades (*Chimah*), or loose the bands of Orion? (*Chisel*) " Also in *Amos v. 8* we read—" *Seek Him* who maketh the seven stars (*Chimah,* the Pleiades) and Orion (*Chisel*)."

The twelve signs or pictures of the Zodiac form a vast circumference in the heavens, and, as proverbially,

a circle has neither beginning nor end, the difficulty is
to find *at which sign* the story of the Stars commences.
Astronomers have for ages begun the circle at Aries, the
Ram, but this unfolds no history. Dr. Bullinger, however, is of opinion, from a representation of part of the
Zodiac, on the roof of the portico of the Old Egyptian
temple of Esnéh in Upper Egypt, that its true beginning
is with Virgo, and its end with Leo. In this very sug-
gestive picture, which is in the form of a parallelogram,
we have on the left a delineation of the Lion, and on
the right that of the Virgin, while *between them* is depicted
the figure of the Sphinx, with the head of a woman and
the body of a lion, with the serpent underneath.

The word " Sphinx " is derived from the Greek word
sphingo, to bind together, and, with the above clue Dr.
Bullinger endeavours to show the conjunction between
the beginning and the end of the wondrous History of
Redemption, unfolding the meaning of the first prophecy
—that the Seed of the Woman would bruise the serpent's
head—*Gen. iii. 15*, and that the Lord Jesus Christ, the
Lion of the tribe of Judah, will be supreme Conqueror at
last over Sin and death. For considerably more than
forty centuries, as, from documents lately discovered, it
is proved to be older than the Great Pyramid, has the
Sphinx lifted her calm, solemn face, gazing on the Lybian
desert, as if peering into the depths of futurity, not far
from the Great Pyramid, that most extraordinary and
enduring work of architecture ever made by man. The
Sphinx has for ages been an inscrutable mystery to the
world, but, if Dr. Bullinger's exposition be correct, its
riddle has been solved at last. Of course all this talk,
respecting the Zodiac and its teachings, will, to the man

of the world, be as " Greek to the gentlemen of the Jury,"
just as the primrose was to Wordsworth's hind—

> "A primrose by the river's brim,
> A yellow primrose was to him,
> And it was nothing more,"

for the mere Cosmopolitan knows not the witness of
the Stars,

> "For ever singing as they shine,
> The hand that made us is Divine."

He has yet to learn the proper meaning of the words
" Creation " and " Revelation," and well would it be for
him to leave the vain babblings of " Science falsely so
called," and accept the pure mathematics of the true.
It was well said by Dr. Carson years ago—" The knowledge of God is the most excellent of all the sciences,"
for, to know Him in Christ is Life Everlasting—
John xvii. 3.

When the Sun first began his journey in the Zodiac,
the Pole Star of the heavens was Alpha in the Constellation Draco. From the peculiar position of the opening
of a certain gallery of the Great Pyramid, which, it is
believed, faced the Pole Star at the time of erection,
some conjecture may perhaps be made as to the age of
this wonderful structure, which was built, on the most
exact astronomical and mathematical lines, by a master-
mind which, in this department has, I think, never yet
been equalled. But the Pole Star of the heavens, round
which the stars now appear to revolve once in every
twenty-four hours, is not Alpha in Draco but Alpha in
Ursa Minor, at some distance from the former position.
This recession of the Pole Star has been very gradual,

amounting only to about 50 seconds in the course of a year.

If the circle of the heavens be divided into twelve, the Sun appears to travel each month through one of these parts or divisions, each of which is about 30 degrees, and is distinguished by a particular representation or picture, the whole of which are called the Twelve Signs of the Zodiac, and through the whole of which the Sun travels in the course of a year. It will thus be seen that the Zodiac has been for well-nigh 6,000 years a continual proof of the revolution of the Sun around the world, so that our Modern Astronomers are positively without excuse in calling the Earth a Planet; and the sooner they honestly confess their error, the better will it be for themselves as well as for others. I shall now conclude this Chapter with the following valuable note from Dr. Bullinger's delightful volume, "The Witness of the Stars," pp. 15, 16.

"Besides these *monthly* differences (between the motion of the Sun and that of the Stars), there is also an *annual* difference; for at the end of twelve months, the Sun does not come back to exactly the same point in the Sign which commenced the year, but is a little behind it. But this difference, though it occurs every year, is so small that it will take 25,579 years for the Sun to complete this vast cycle, which is called *The Precession of the Equinoxes*; i.e., about one degree in every seventy-one years. If the Sun came back to the precise point at which it began the year, each *sign* would correspond always and regularly, exactly with a particular *month*, but owing to the constant regression, the Sun (while it goes through the whole twelve signs every year) commences the year in one sign for only 2,121 years. In point of fact since the Creation the commencement of the year has changed to the extent of nearly three of the signs. When Virgil sings—

"'The White Bull with golden horns opened the year,'

he does not record what took place in his own day. This is another proof of the antiquity of these signs.

"The *Ecliptic*, or path of the Sun, if it could be viewed from immediately beneath the Polar Star, would form a complete and perfect circle, would be concentric with the *Equator*, and all the Stars and the Sun would appear to move in this circle, never rising nor setting. To a person north or south of the *Equator*, the Stars rise and set obliquely; while to a person on the Equator they rise and set perpendicularly, each star being twelve hours above and twelve hours below the horizon.

"The points where the two circles (the Ecliptic and the Equator) intersect each other are called *Equinoctial points*. It is the movement of these points (which are now moving from Aries to Pisces) which gives rise to the term *The Precession of the Equinoxes*."

CHAPTER X.

THE SUN STANDING STILL AND RETURNING BACKWARDS.

SECTION   PAGE

1. THE SUN STANDING STILL OVER GIBEON   -   204

2. THE SUN'S SHADOW TURNING BACK TEN DEGREES
ON THE DIAL OF AHAZ - - - -   210

THESE two miracles are so diametrically opposed to the idea of the world careering round the Sun, that, for the most part, our Modern Astronomers cut the Gordian knot by denying them altogether. Some Christian authors, among whom may be specially mentioned the late Dr. Adam Clarke, while they wished to uphold the miracles, still clung to the theory of a revolving Earth, and have done their best to explain them with that proviso, although, as, indeed, was only to be expected, they have signally failed in their attempt. They would have been wiser, had they treated these miracles in the manner, as adopted with respect to Joshua's, by the late Dr. Gill, who wrote—

"It was a most wonderful and surprising phenomenon to see both luminaries standing still in the midst of heaven. How this is to be reconciled with the Copernican system, or that with this, I shall not enquire."

SECTION 1.

THE SUN STANDING STILL OVER GIBEON.

Dr. Clarke was a good and also a learned man, having the letters LL.D. and F.A.S. tacked to his name, but, unfortunately, he was sadly tarred with the brush of Modern Astronomy. When, in writing his Commentary on the Bible, he came to *Joshua x.*, the famous miracle of the Sun standing still stared him in the face, and he tried hard to explain it on Copernican lines. How he succeeded, or rather how he failed to succeed, may be learned from the following extract from a letter, written by himself at the time, to his particular friend, the Rev. Thomas Roberts of Bath—

"Joshua's sun and moon standing still have kept me going for nearly three weeks. That one Chapter has afforded me more vexation than anything I have ever met with, and even now I am even but about half satisfied with my own solution of all the difficulties, though I am confident that I have removed mountains that were never touched before. Shall I say that I am heartily wearied of my work—so wearied that I have a thousand times wished I had never written a page of it, and I am repeatedly purposing to give it up."*

Let us now look at the miracle itself. After the fall of Jericho and Ai, the Gibeonites, being afraid of their own destruction should they resist, craftily sought to make a covenant of peace with the Israelites, in which they

---

* " Life of Dr. Adam Clarke "; Mason, London.

succeeded.   Adoni-zedec, King of Jerusalem, was so
enraged at the Gibeonites for acting thus, that he con-
federated with four other kings of the Amorites to punish
them severely.   When Joshua heard of this he immediately
left Gilgal with his army, and, by a forced march, all
night, unexpectedly attacked the banded host next day.
A fierce battle ensued, in which God assisted the Israelites
by sending great hailstones upon the Amorites—" There
were more died with hailstones than they whom the
Children of Israel slew with the sword "—*Jos. x. 11.*
Joshua, knowing the immense importance of completely
defeating the Canaanites, and seeing that the day was
nearly done, cried out, doubtless inspired by a divine
afflatus,

Shemesh	*be-Giboun*	*dum*	*ve-yarchh*
" Thou sun	upon Gibeon	stand still	and thou moon

becomeq	*Ajalun*
in the valley of	Ajalon " (*v.* 12).

It is truly grievous to see how good criticism is so
often marred by bad theory.   For example, I have before
me now Calmet's splendid work, " The Dictionary of the
Holy Bible," in which that excellent and learned man
writes as follows—

"By way of shortening criticism it is assumed, 1. that
shemesh signifies *the light* issuing from the Sun, not *the body*
of the Sun itself, as *Exod. xvi. 21, Deut. xxxiii. 14, and
1 Sam. xi. 9, Eccles. xi. 7.*"[*]

And Macdonald, in expounding Parkhurst's theory, says—

"This is suggested in the Hebrew word for *solar light,*

---

[*] Calmet's Dictionary, Vol. III., p. 292; Charles Taylor, Hatton Garden, London, Ed. 1823.

shemesh." Again—" Now it was the *shemesh* and *yareh* which Joshua arrested, ' solar light, and ' lunar light' should be under-stood instead of ' sun' and ' moon,' and the objection in question will instantly disappear."[*]

Thus both Calmet and Parkhurst sought to make it appear that it was only *the light* proceeding from the Sun and Moon which Joshua commanded to stand still, while *the bodies* of these luminaries were not affected at all, so that the Earth might revolve around its axis, and the Moon around the Earth as before! We thus see to what miserable shifts a false science leads.

I have turned up the references given by Calmet, and see nothing whatever in them to justify his assertion, which, I think, would never have been made except by a person determined, at any cost, to uphold the theory of a revolving Earth. Moreover, I have examined every passage in which the word *shemesh* occurs, in one of my best tool-books, " The Englishman's Hebrew and Chaldee Concordance," with the following result. I find that the word *shemesh* is used in the Bible 133 times, in every one of which, with the single exception of *Isaiah liv. 12,* where it is translated " windows," it is applied to the " Sun " simply as the " Sun." There are three other words in Hebrew occasionally used for the Sun, namely, *aur* light, where it is mentioned five times; *hhamah,* from *hham,* hot, warm, six times; and *hheres,* probably from *hheres,* the itch, on account of its heat, three times.

It is thus evident that in the Hebrew Bible, the word *shemesh* is that which is used by far the most frequently

---

[*] " Principia and the Bible," &c., pp. 127, 156.

for the Sun *as a whole*, that is, in its trinity of body, light, and heat, it being ten times to one oftener so used than the other three above-named words put together, and that to limit the meaning of the word *shemesh* only to *the light* proceeding from it, is neither Scriptural, scholarly, nor necessary.

I am exceedingly sorry that these learned men should also in a similar manner have restricted the meaning of the Hebrew word *yarehh* " Moon," as meaning only *the light* of the Moon.   Calmet says,

" Thus *irech* signifies the *light* reflected from the Moon, and not the *body* of the Moon itself; as *Deut. xxxiii. 14; Isa. lx. 20.*"*

but the passages here quoted appear to be totally irrelevant as proof of such a statement.   The fact is, that the word *yarehh*, used for Moon in *Joshua x. 12, 13*, is that which is *commonly applied to it*, in the Old Testament Scriptures.   In looking into the Hebrew Concordance, I see that it occurs twenty-seven times, in all of which it is rendered " Moon " in the common acceptation of the term : *lebneh*, the other Hebrew word for the Moon, being mentioned only thrice.   I have been the more anxious to expose the uncritical criticism of these learned men, in giving a wrong rendering to such important words as " Sun " and " Moon," as so many persons are influenced by great names, and do not take the trouble to investigate for themselves as to the correctness of the statements made.   Besides, how could the " light " stand still, if the " body " emitting it were moving?

Dr. Clarke took the word *dum*, translated " stand

---

* Calmet's Dictionary, Vol. III., p. 292.

still," as his defence for a Copernican Earth, and says in his notes on the passage—

"The terms of the command are worthy of particular note. Joshua does not say to the Sun "stand still," as if he had conceived *him to be running his race round the world*, but 'Be silent' or *inactive*, that is, as I understand it, '*Refrain thy influence*—no longer act upon the Earth to cause it to revolve round its axis.'"

I willingly grant that the word *dum* may be properly translated "be silent," or even be, as the late Lord Cockburn (of Edinburgh) expressed inactivity in another matter, "as quiet as the grave—even as Peebles"; but the Sun showed no sign of inactivity, if, according to Dr. Clarke, it made the huge mass of this world to cease performing its supposed rotation on its axis. The truth is, that the Sun did exactly what Joshua commanded it to do, namely, it "stood still," as narrated in verse 13 —"So the Sun 'stood still' in the midst of heaven, and hasted not to go down about a whole day." Further, the word used for "stood still" in the verse last quoted, is not *dum* but *omed*, "stood still," respecting the meaning of which word there is no difference of opinion whatever, so that the conjectural criticism about *dum* may at once be dismissed as being altogether irrelevant.

The words *bechetse he-shemim*, "in the midst of heaven," would have been more properly translated, "in the partition or division of the heavens," that is, the horizon, for, had the Sun been in the Meridian, there would have been no necessity for such a miracle, nor would it have been then observed, but, when the Sun was near the horizon, about setting, the need of longer

time was great, and the miracle most apparent and oppor-
tune.   Besides, the Moon being over Ajalon, the valley
of oaks, shows that it was about the time of evening.
The miracle was of the utmost value to the Israelites, for
it caused the complete discomfiture of the Amorites, and
led to their further conquests in Canaan.

There is an old rhyme,

*Si Lyra non lyrassit
Lutherus non saltassit,*

" If Lyra had not piped Luther would not have danced,"
and, with respect to this miracle, it may be said—

' Had Newton never lived to dupe mankind,
Clarke never had to Joshua's Sun been blind.'

Other writers, besides the foregoing, have tried to
reconcile this miracle with a revolving Earth, but all in
vain.   The last I have heard of is the Rev. W. W. Howard
of Liverpool, who, in his Lecture on the subject, says—

" My belief is that Joshua and his men, having marched all
night, as the 9th verse tells us, would be tired next morning,
but God caused a great trembling to spread itself among the
foe, and there was an easy victory.   When the war had
pursued the Amorites some distance, hailstones fell upon them,
and did much damage; at the approach to Bethoron the hailstones increased in fury, and Joshua seeing the devastation
produced, and being cognisant of the fatigue of his men,
prayed heaven to let the hurricane go on till total and irreparable
disaster was inflicted."*

This is such a very feeble exposition of the miracle
that I marvel it was ever attempted at all.   Joshua did

* " Joshua commanding the Sun to stand still," &c., to be obtained of the
Author, 47 Heeman Street, Liverpool.

14

not pray for the hurricane to go on, but, inspired by God, said—" Sun, stand thou still over Gibeon and thou, Moon, in the valley of Ajalon," and that prayer was immediately answered, thus proving that day and night are caused by the actual revolution of the Sun, and not by the supposed rotation of the Earth.

SECTION 2.

THE SUN'S SHADOW TURNING BACK TEN DEGREES ON THE DIAL OF AHAZ.

The sun-dial is a very ancient invention, constructed to show the time of the day by the shadow cast upon it by the Sun's revolution round the world. Ahaz, King of Judea, reigned from 726 to 741 B.C., and it is most probable that this dial was called after his name, owing to some enlargement or improvement having been made in it in his reign, as from *2 Kings ix. 13*, it would appear to have been in existence for at least 150 years before, when Jehu was made King over Israel.

Chaldea, I have no doubt, was the birthplace of the dial, as it was of Astronomy, but others believe, as Calmet says in his Dictionary,

"that this invention came from the Phœnicians, and that the first traces of it are discoverable in what Homer says—

> *Nesos tis Suriē kekleisketai (eipon akoneis),*
> *Ortugiēs kathaperthein othi tropoi Helioio.*
>
> *Odyss. xv. v. 402.*

of an island called Syria, lying above Ortygia, where the revolutions of the Sun are observed: i.e., they see the returns of the Sun, the solstices."*

At all events the Dial has been long enough known to make every Modern Astronomer blush for shame, when it is mentioned, as its faithful, though silent, testimony gives daily visible evidence of the revolution of the Sun. This is easily proved. On a fine summer day, take a rod and place it perpendicularly in any quiet spot, a garden for example, where it can catch the rays of the Sun all day, and watch it for about twelve hours. Every quarter of an hour place a small peg at the extremity of the shadow, and you will find that the line described by the shadow is a *curve*. At the beginning of May, in the neighbourhood of London, the curve made in twelve hours will be nearly the half of an ellipse, the greater diameter of which will be about thrice the length of the shorter diameter. If you test this in different places, or in the same place at different times, you will get the data for proving the Sun's particular motion over a stationary Earth.

Sun-dials are of various forms of construction. From the meaning of the Hebrew word *molut*, translated stairs, steps, or degrees, I am inclined to think with Dr. Clarke, that the dial of Ahaz was made for public use, and was raised by steps or degrees which recorded, according to the shadow caused by the Sun, the divisions or hours of the day. In his Commentary on *2 Kings ix. 13*, Dr. Clarke writes as follows—

"*On the top of the stairs.* The *Chaldees*, the *rabbins*, and several interpreters, understood this of the *public sun-dial;*

---

* Calmet's Dictionary, Vol. I., article—"Dial."

which in these ancient times was formed of *steps* like *stairs*, each *step* serving to indicate, by its *shadow*, one hour, or such division of time as was commonly used in that country. This dial was no doubt in the most *public place*, and upon the top of it, or on the *platform* on the top, would be a very proper place to set Jehu, while they blew the trumpets and proclaimed him *King*. The Hebrew *molut* is the same word which is used Chap. xx. 9, to signify the *dial* of Ahaz, and this was probably the very same dial on which that miracle was afterwards wrought; and this dial *molut*, from *olah* to go up, ascend, was most evidently made of *steps*, the *shadows* projected on which, by a gnomon, at the different elevations of the Sun, would serve to show the popular divisions of time."

I do not, however, at all agree with Dr. Clarke, in attributing to *Refraction* the miracle of the Sun's shadow returning ten degrees on the dial of Ahaz. *Refraction* is of so uncertain and unreliable a nature, that even Astronomers themselves generally omit it in their calculations; besides, had such a remarkable instance of it occurred once, it might have happened at other times, but no such phenomenon, as that described by the Scriptures, has ever been seen or heard of either before or after the days of Hezekiah. The Doctor has done all in his power to save the theory of a revolving Earth, in his comments on the Sun's shadow returning ten degrees on the dial of Ahaz, as well as on the Sun and Moon standing still at the command of Joshua; but neither he, nor all the Astronomers of Christendom, can avert from that hapless theory the contempt which it deserves. "The Scripture cannot be broken"—*John x. 35*. The miracles happened just as they were described to have done, and no human reasoning can explain them away.

It is as easy for God, who made the Sun, to cause it to stand still, or to cause its shadow to return backwards, without in any way injuring our stationary Earth, or any of the rolling orbs of heaven. With reverence it may be said respecting these miracles what was spoken regarding an occurrence immeasurably greater—the Resurrection of our gracious Lord—" Blessed are they that have not seen and yet have believed "—*John xx. 29.*

CHAPTER XI.

THE DELUGE: BIBLICAL ACCOUNT.

SECTION   PAGE

1. THE DATE, CAUSE, AND EXTENT OF THE DELUGE   214

2. GOD'S INSTRUCTIONS TO NOAH RESPECTING THE ARK   217

3. SOME OBJECTIONS AGAINST THE DELUGE ANSWERED -   -   219

4. THE EARTH NOT A PLANET, PROVED FROM THE WATERS FINDING THEIR OWN LEVEL ABOVE THE HIGHEST MOUNTAINS - - - -   221

5. THE SUBSIDENCE OF THE WATERS, AND SAFE DEBARKATION OF NOAH AND ALL WITH HIM FROM THE ARK   226

6. THE NOACHIAN COVENANT -   229

7. THE LAST JUDGMENT ON THE EARTH BY FIRE   231

SECTION 1.

THE DATE, CAUSE, AND EXTENT OF THE DELUGE.

IT is well to mark the great precision with which the inspired writers of the Bible choose their words. This is very apparent in the word used for the Deluge in Genesis, *mebul*. There are no less than ten different words for " flood " in the Old Testament, but this is the only one which is ever applied to the Deluge or Flood of Noah, none of the other words being ever used for such a catastrophe at all. This fact confirms the truth of Scripture that *that* was the only Universal Flood which has ever happened since the Adamic Creation, and that such would never occur again.

The Deluge or Flood commenced on the Seventh day or Sabbath, the seventeenth day of Bul, the second month of the Jewish civil year, which corresponds in part with October and in part with November of our Calendar. How do you know this? may some inquirer ask. I reply by the Infallible Word of God which declares—" In the six hundredth year of Noah's life, in the second month, the seventeenth day of the month, the same day were all the fountains of the Great Deep (*tehoom rabah*) broken up, and the windows (*arbat*, floodgates) of heaven were opened "—*Gen. vii. 11.* The date of the year is found in the following manner—

		Year of the World.
Gen. i. 27. Creation of Adam	- -	0
,, *v.* 3. Adam when 130 years old begat Seth		130
,, ,, 6. Seth ,, 105 ,, ,, ,, Enos		235
,, ,, 9. Enos ,, 90 ,, ,, ,, Canaan		325
,, ,, 12. Canaan ,, 70 ,, ,, ,, Mahalaleel		395
,, ,, 15. Mahalaleel ,, 65 ,, ,, ,, Jared		460
,, ,, 18. Jared ,, 162 ,, ,, ,, Enoch		622
,, ,, 21. Enoch ,, 65 ,, ,, ,, Methusalah		687
,, ,, 25. Methusalah 187 ,, ,, ,, Lamech		874
,, ,, 28. Lamech ,, 182 ,, ,, ,, Noah		1056
,, *vii.* 6. Noah was 600 ,, when the Deluge began		1656

1656

I am aware of the discrepancy which exists between some of the dates here given and those of the Samaritan and Septuagint versions, but, after due consideration, I have no doubt that the above, which are taken from the Hebrew text, are correct.

The Deluge was brought upon the world in consequence of the great depravity of the inhabitants;

"God saw that the wickedness of man was great on the earth, and that every imagination of the thought of his heart was only evil continually, and JEHOVAH said, I will destroy man whom I have created from the face of the earth, both man and beast, and the creeping things, and the fowl of the air "— *Gen. vi. 6, 7.*

The illicit connection of *Beni ha Alëihm,* or Sons of God, called also *ha Nephilim,** the fallen ones, with the daughters of men—*Gen. vi. 2—4,* had brought sin to a climax, but God, in His mercy, gave the people one hundred and twenty years for repentance. Noah, a just man, and a preacher of righteousness, found grace in God's sight. He is also called "perfect in his generation," probably because his family had not been mixed up with the Nephilim, and he "walked with God "— *Gen. vi. 9.*

"By faith Noah, being warned of God, of things not seen as yet, moved with fear, prepared an ark to the saving of his house, by the which he condemned the world, and became heir of the righteousness which is by faith "—*Heb. xi. 7.*

---

* As to who the Nephilim are conjectured to have been, I beg to refer my Readers to Chapter IV. of "Hades & Beyond," mentioned on p. 55 of this book.

SECTION 2.

GOD'S INSTRUCTIONS TO NOAH RESPECTING THE ARK.

"God said unto Noah, the end of all flesh is come before Me; for the earth is filled with violence through them, and behold I will destroy them with the earth. Make thee an ark of gopher-wood; rooms (nests) shalt thou make in the ark, and shalt pitch it within and without with pitch. And this is the fashion which thou shalt make it of: the length of the ark shall be three hundred cubits, the breadth of it fifty cubits, and the height of it thirty cubits. A window shalt thou make to the ark, and in a cubit shalt thou finish it above, and the door of the ark shalt thou set in the side thereof; with lower, second, and third *stories* shalt thou make it. And behold I, even I, do bring a flood of waters upon the earth to destroy all flesh wherein is the breath of life from under heaven, and every thing that is in the earth shall die, but with thee will I establish My Covenant, and thou shalt come into the ark, thou and thy sons and thy wife, and thy sons' wives with thee. And of every living thing of all flesh two of every sort shalt thou bring into the ark to keep them alive with thee; they shall be male and female. Of fowls after their kind, and of cattle after their kind, of every creeping thing of the earth after his kind, two of every *sort* shall come unto thee to keep them alive. And take thou unto thee of all food that is eaten, and thou shalt gather it to thee, and it shall be for food for thee and for them. Thus did Noah according to all that God commanded him, so did he "—*Gen. vi. 13—22.*

"And JEHOVAH said unto Noah, Come thou and all thy house into the ark, for thee have I seen righteous before Me in this generation. Of every clean beast thou shalt take to thee by sevens; the male and his female; and of beasts that are not clean by two, the male and his female. Of fowls also of the air by sevens, the male and the female to keep seed alive upon the face of all the earth. For yet seven days, and I will cause it to rain upon the earth forty days and forty nights, and every living substance that I have made will I destroy from off the face of the earth. And Noah did according to all that JEHOVAH commanded him. And Noah was six hundred years old when the flood of waters was upon the earth. And Noah went in, and his sons, and his wife, and his sons' wives with him into the ark because of the waters of the flood. Of clean beasts, and of beasts that are not clean, and of fowls, and of everything that creepeth upon the earth, there went in two and two unto Noah into the ark, the male and the female, as God had commanded Noah. And it came to pass after seven days, that the waters of the flood were upon the earth. In the six hundredth year of Noah's life, in the second month, the seventeenth day of the month, the same day, were all the fountains of the Great Deep broken up, and the windows of heaven were opened, and the rain was upon the earth forty days and forty nights. In the self-same day entered Noah, and Shem, and Ham, and Japheth, the sons of Noah, and Noah's wife, and the three wives of his sons with them into the ark; they, and every beast after his kind, and all the cattle after their kind, and every creeping thing that creepeth upon the earth after his kind, and every fowl after his kind, every bird of every sort. And they went in unto Noah into the ark, two and two of all flesh wherein is the breath of life. And they that went in went in male and female of all flesh, as God had commanded him, and JEHOVAH

shut him in. And the flood was forty days upon the earth,
and the waters increased, and bare up the ark, and it was lift
up above the earth. And the waters prevailed, and were increased greatly upon the earth, and the ark went upon the face
of the waters. And the waters prevailed exceedingly upon the
earth, and all the high hills, that were under the whole heaven,
were covered. Fifteen cubits upward did the waters prevail,
and the mountains were covered. And all flesh died that
moved upon the earth, both of fowl and of cattle, and of beast,
and of every creeping thing that creepeth upon the earth, and
every man; all in whose nostrils was the breath of life, of all
that was in the dry land, died. And every living substance was
destroyed, which was upon the face of the ground, both man
and cattle, and the creeping thing, and the fowl of the heaven,
and they were destroyed from the earth, and Noah only remained
alive, and they that were with him in the ark. And the waters
prevailed upon the earth an hundred and fifty days "—
Gen. vii. 1—24.

SECTION 3.

SOME OBJECTIONS AGAINST THE DELUGE
ANSWERED.

Infidels have long sneered at the Ark, saying that it
was not large enough to hold all the animals, fowls, and
creeping things, with their food for a year; and also that
it was impossible to gather them all together so as to
get them into the Ark. With regard to the first objection that has long since been answered, as the dimensions

of the Ark being known, and, reckoning even by the smaller cubit, it has been geometrically found by Bishop Wilkins,* and other perfectly reliable authorities, to have been amply sufficient for all the purposes required.

With respect to the second objection, there need not be the slightest trouble; the Deluge itself was undoubtedly miraculous, and many of the circumstances attending it were so likewise, and there was no more difficulty in God's collecting the animals and other creatures together to be placed in the Ark, than there was previously when He brought them to Adam to be named—*Gen. ii. 20.*

Other objections against a Universal Deluge have been raised, but, as they are of no *real* value, it is unnecessary to enter into them here; but I would refer any curious Reader to Dr. Clarke's Commentary on Genesis, Chapters VI.—IX., and to Calmet's Dictionary in his Article on the Deluge, Vol. I. The fact is, that such objections have been made through mere ignorance of the circumstances of the case; for example, one says that "not all the waters of the world, nor all the rain of heaven could cause such a catastrophe." Another remarks "All the air which encompasses the earth, if condensed into vapour, would not make thirty-one feet of water." These objections would never have been raised by any one who, in a proper spirit, had read the first Chapter of Genesis. There we find that, on the first day of the Adamic Creation, the Earth was WHOLLY SUBMERGED IN WATER, and on the second, God said, verses 6 and 7—

"Let there be a firmament in the midst of the waters, and

---

* See Bishop Wilkin's "Essay towards a Philosophical Character and Language."

let it divide the waters from the waters. And God made the firmament, and divided the waters which were under the firmament from the waters which were above the firmament, and it was so."

It was not until the third day that the DRY LAND appeared, and, when it did appear, it had still under it that vast abyss of waters out of which it was brought, and which, by inspiration, both Moses and Jacob called —" the Deep (*tehoom*) that coucheth beneath "— *Gen. xlix. 25, Deut. xxxiii. 13.* Above the Earth is the *reqio*, or firmament, which Job describes as being " strong as a molten mirror "—*Job xxxvii. 18,* and on it rests that portion of the waters which was divided from the waters of the Great Deep on the second day of that creation. It will, therefore, be seen that there was no difficulty whatever with God in overwhelming a guilty world with water, for—

" All the fountains of the Great Deep were broken up, and the floodgates of the heavens were opened, and the rain was upon the Earth forty days and forty nights "—*Gen. vii. 11, 12.*

SECTION 4.

THE EARTH NOT A PLANET, PROVED FROM THE WATERS FINDING THEIR OWN LEVEL ABOVE THE HIGHEST MOUNTAINS.

We are told—*Gen. vii. 20,* " fifteen cubits upwards the waters prevailed, and the mountains were covered," from

which I understand that the waters rose fifteen cubits
above the highest mountains, for in the preceding verse
we read—" All the high hills that were under the whole
heaven were covered."*   From this statement, as it is a
primal law of nature for water always to find its own
level, we have Divine assurance that the Earth was
completely under water.   The Jewish civil cubit was
measured from the point of a man's elbow to the tip of
his middle finger, and was reckoned as eighteen inches.
The Sacred Cubit (*Ezek. xliii. 13*) was a cubit and a
handbreadth, or about four inches longer.   Which of
these cubits was to be taken, in the measurement of the
Ark, we are not informed, but, if we reckon the lesser,
we find that the waters rose twenty - two and a half
feet above Mount Everest in Asia, the loftiest mountain in
the world.   Now, as the waters covered it, and, as they
always find their own level, it follows, as a matter of
necessity, that they also overspread the Mountains of the
Moon in Africa, Mont Blanc in Europe, the Andes in
South and the Rocky Mountains in North America, and,
of course, all lower elevations ; we have thus positive proof
that the Earth is not a Planet but a horizontal *Terra
Firma*.

The fact of water always finding its own level is so
apparent, from the water in the basin in which we wash
in the morning, to the water in the tumbler which we may
drink at night—from the duck's-pond in the village green
to the steamer's bowling-green of the broad Atlantic, that
it is a marvel that our modern Astronomers are still so
extremely foolish as to uphold convexity in water.   It is
one of these freaks of fashion which they still follow,

---

* See Ray's " Physico-Theological Discourses," 2nd Ed., 8vo., 1693.

in hopes of getting unthinking people to believe that the
world is globular; but daily are they "hoist by their own
petard," for the levelness of water meets them on every
hand. Even Sir Henry Holland, in his "Recollections
of a Past Life," second edition, p. 305, inadvertently lets
the cat out of the bag, when he refers to both the Sun
and the Moon being above the horizon at the occurrence
of an eclipse of the Moon. He says—

"This experience requires, however, a combination of circumstances rarely occurring—a perfectly clear Eastern and
Western horizon, and an *entirely level intervening surface, as
that of the Sea,* or an African desert."

Mr. C. Darwin, in his "Voyage of a Naturalist,"
p. 328, made a similar slip when he wrote—

"I am reminded of the Pampas of Buenos Ayres by seeing
the disc of the rising Sun intersected by a horizon, *level as the
ocean.*"

I confess I do not understand how Humboldt could
really have believed in the globularity of the world, when
he penned the following passage, knowing, as a Cos-
mogonist, that water occupies, at the very lowest compu-
tation, *at least three times the extent* of the surface of the
land—

"Among the causes which tend to lower the mean annual
temperature, I include the following:—Elevation above *the
level of the sea,* when not forming part of an extended plain."
"Cosmos," Vol. I., p. 326, Bohn's Edition.

Parallax believed that the proved levelness of
water would ultimately lead to the death of Modern
Astronomy. He remarks, as follows, in his "Zetetic
Astronomy," p. 362—

"The great and theory-destroying fact was quickly discovered that the surface of standing water was perfectly horizontal! Here was another death-blow to the universal ideas and speculations of pseudo-philosophers. Just as the 'universal solvent' could not be preserved or manufactured, and, therefore, the whole system of Alchemy died away, so the necessary proof of convexity on the waters of the Earth *could not be proved*, and, therefore, the doctrine of rotundity, and of the plurality of worlds, must also die. The death is now a mere question of time."

The Ark floated in perfect safety upon the waters, however tumultuous they may have been, for it was made in accordance with the instructions of God, and He Himself shut Noah in. The Ark was considered for ages to be a clumsy, strangely-shaped hulk, somewhat like the models sold in toy-shops for children, but, for nearly the last three hundred years, that idea has been entirely changed. In 1609 Peter Jansen, a Dutch ship-builder, determined to construct a ship on the lines given for the Ark, and, though much ridiculed at the time, he succeeded, and found that his ship would safely carry from thirty to forty per cent. more cargo in proportion to others, and his example was soon followed. In Appleton's Cyclopædia, Vol. XIV., Art. "Ship," we read—

"It is remarkable that its (the Ark's) proportions of length, breadth, and depth are almost precisely the same, considered by our most eminent architects the best for combining the elements of strength, capacity, and stability."

A later writer remarks—

"Ship-building was revolutionized, and the millions that go on the sea owe the change to the Bible. Since that the

Cunarders, the Collins, the White Star, and Inman line Companies have built their ocean steamships after the scientific pattern of Him, whose 'way is perfect,' and who designed Noah's Ark."*

When the Deluge began, what horror of soul must have been felt by those who had for so long heard the preaching of Noah, but who had refused to listen to his call for repentance, as they saw that his warning was now too late to be acted upon. Noah and those with him were safe, while they were doomed to death. Martin's famous Picture of the Deluge gives a vivid idea of their agonizing despair. Still, praise be to God, the door of mercy was not shut against these Ante-Diluvians for ever, for we read that, after the crucifixion of our blessed Lord—

"being put to death in the flesh, but quickened in spirit, in which also He went, and preached unto the spirits in prison, which aforetime were disobedient, when once the long-suffering of God waited in the days of Noah, when the ark was a preparing, wherein a few, that is, eight souls, were saved through water "
—*1 Pet. iii. 19, 20.*

"For to this end was the Gospel preached, even to the dead, that they might be judged, indeed, according to men in the flesh, but may live according to God in spirit"—*1 Pet. iv. 6*

---

* "Christianity and Science," by D. S. Taylor, p. 13; Marshall Brothers, Paternoster Row, London.
Since the above extract was written I have heard that some Atlantic Liners are now being built with a length nearly nine times their breadth, but such cannot be expected to have the *stability* of the Ark.

15

SECTION 5.

SUBSIDENCE OF THE WATERS, AND SAFE DEBARKATION OF NOAH AND ALL WITH HIM FROM THE ARK.

"And God remembered Noah, and every living thing, and all the cattle that was with him in the ark; and God made a wind to pass over the earth, and the waters assuaged. The fountains also of the deep and the windows of heaven were stopped, and the rain from heaven was restrained. And the waters returned from off the earth continually; and after the end of the hundred and fifty days, the waters were abated. And the ark rested in the seventh month, on the seventeenth day of the month, upon the mountains of Ararat. And the waters decreased continually until the tenth month; in the tenth month, on the first day of the month were the tops of the mountains seen. And it came to pass at the end of forty days, that Noah opened the window of the ark which he had made. And he sent forth a raven which went forth to and fro, until the waters were dried up from off the earth. Also he sent forth a dove from him, to see if the waters were abated from off the face of the ground; but the dove found no rest for the sole of her foot, and she returned unto him into the ark, for the waters were on the face of the whole earth; then he put forth his hand and took her, and pulled her in unto him into the ark. And he stayed yet other seven days; and again he sent forth the dove out of the ark; and the dove came in to him in the evening, and lo, in her mouth was an olive leaf pluckt off; so Noah knew that the waters were abated from off the earth. And he stayed yet other seven days, and sent forth the dove, which returned not again to him any more.

"And it came to pass in the six hundredth and first year, in the first *month*, the first *day* of the month, the waters were dried up from off the earth: and Noah removed the covering of the ark, and looked, and behold the face of the ground was dry. And in the second month, on the seven and twentieth day of the month was the earth dried.

"And God spake unto Noah, saying, Go forth of the ark, thou, and thy wife, and thy sons, and thy sons' wives with thee. Bring forth with thee every living thing that is with thee, of all flesh, *both* of fowl and of cattle, and of every creeping thing that creepeth upon the earth, that they may breed abundantly in the earth, and be fruitful and multiply upon the earth. And Noah went forth, and his sons, and his wife, and his sons' wives with him. Every beast, every creeping thing, and every fowl, *and* whatsoever creepeth upon the earth, after their kind, went forth out of the ark.

"And Noah builded an altar unto JEHOVAH, and took of every clean beast, and of every clean fowl, and offered burnt offerings on the altar. And JEHOVAH smelled a sweet savour, and JEHOVAH said in His heart, I will not again curse the ground any more for man's sake, for the imagination of man's heart is evil from his youth; neither will I. again smite any more everything as I have done. While the earth remaineth, seed-time and harvest, and cold and heat, and summer and winter, and day and night shall not cease "—*Gen. viii. 1—22.*

Noah was in the Ark for exactly one Solar year of 365 days. Should it be asked—How can this be correct, seeing that Noah entered into the Ark on the *17th* day

of the month Bul, and did not leave it till the *27th* day
of the same .month in the following year? I reply as
follows—The Ante-Diluvians were thoroughly acquainted
with the Solar period of revolution in 365¼ days, but
they reckoned by *Lunar* time, their year consisting of
354 days only, the eleven days of difference, called
"intercallery," being adjusted by a method which it
would take too long to enter into here, so that computations by Solar and Lunar time were made exactly to
correspond. Noah went into the Ark on Saturday, the
Sabbath, the Seventh day of the week, that being the *17th*
day of Bul, 1656 A.M., which was the beginning of the
new Solar year, when the people were in the midst of their
festivities—"eating and drinking," as described in
Matt. xxiv. 38. Counting from that day to Saturday,
the Sabbath or Seventh day of the week, the *27th* day of
Bul, in the following year, is precisely 365 days, as the
Lunar months intervening consisted only of 30 and 29
days alternately, so that the Solar year terminated on
the *27th* day of Bul, 1657; on which day Noah and all
with him came out of the Ark. For a full exposition of
this interesting subject, showing the extreme exactitude
of Biblical Chronology, I beg to refer my Readers to
Mr. Dimbleby's book, "All Past Time," mentioned
below.* The objector may cavil at, but he cannot elimi-
nate the essence of Truth; as the Bard of Erin sings—

> "You may break, you may ruin the vase as you will,
>   But the scent of the roses will hang round it still."

"All Past Time, ' by J. H. Dimbleby; E. Nestor, 28 Paternoster Row, London

SECTION 6.

THE NOACHIAN COVENANT.

On Noah leaving the Ark, God made the following Covenant with him, and with all who had been with him in that specially prepared rendezvous of safety—

"And God blessed Noah and his sons, and said unto them, Be fruitful and multiply and replenish the earth. And the fear of you and the dread of you shall be upon every beast of the earth, and upon every fowl of the air, upon all that moveth upon the earth, and upon all the fishes of the sea; into your hand they are delivered. Every moving thing that liveth shall be meat for you, even as the green herb have I given you all things. But flesh with the life thereof, *which is* the blood thereof shall ye not eat. And surely your blood of your lives will I require; at the hand of every beast will I require it, and at the hand of every man; at the blood of every man's brother will I require the life of man. Whoso sheddeth man's blood, by man shall his blood be shed, for in the image of God made He man. And you, be fruitful and multiply; bring forth abundantly in the earth, and multiply therein.

And God spake unto Noah and to his sons with him, saying, And I, behold, I establish My covenant with you and with your seed after you; and with every living creature that *is* with you, of the fowl, of the cattle, and of every beast of the earth with you; from all that go out of the ark to every beast of the earth. And I will establish My covenant with you; neither shall all flesh be cut off any more by the waters of a flood; neither shall there any more be a flood to destroy the earth. And God said,

This is the token of the covenant which I make between Me and you, and every living creature that is with you, for perpetual generations. I do set My bow in the cloud, and it shall be for a token of a covenant between Me and the earth. And it shall come to pass, when I bring a cloud over the earth, that the bow shall be seen in the cloud : and I shall remember My covenant, which is between Me and you, and every living creature of all flesh; and the waters shall no more become a flood to destroy all flesh. And the bow shall be in the cloud; and I will look upon it, that I may remember the everlasting covenant between God and every living creature of all flesh that *is* upon the earth. And God said unto Noah, This is the token of the covenant, which I have established between Me and all flesh that is upon the earth "—*Gen. ix. 1—17.*

Such is the Biblical account of the Deluge, and every word of it bears the stamp of truth. It is referred to as an accomplished fact several times in the New Testament, particularly by our Lord Himself. In His address on the Mount of Olives, shortly before He suffered, He spoke as follows to certain of His Disciples, who had asked Him respecting His Coming, and the end of the age—

" As the days of Noah, so shall also the Coming of the Son of Man be. For, as in the days that were before the flood, they were eating and drinking, marrying and giving in marriage, until the day that Noah entered into the ark, and knew not till the flood came, and took them all away; so shall also the Coming of the Son of Man be "—*Matt. xxiv. 37—39.*

Whoever, therefore, denies the fact of the Universal Deluge denies the truth of the words of our Lord Jesus Christ, and He hath said—" Whosoever shall deny Me before men, him will I also deny before My Father which is in heaven "—*Matt. x. 33.*

SECTION 7.

THE LAST JUDGMENT ON THE EARTH TO BE BY FIRE.

We learn from the Noachian Covenant that a Universal Deluge will never occur again, but God has told us in His Word that a still more terrible Judgment awaits the Earth—even its dissolution by Fire, before " the times of Restitution of all things, which God hath spoken by the mouth of all His holy prophets since the world began "—*Acts iii. 21.* It is written as follows; I quote from Rotherham's Emphasised Translation, as being the most literal—

"Howbeit the Day of the Lord will be here as a thief, in which the heavens with a rushing noise will pass away, while elements, becoming intensely hot, will be dissolved, and the earth and the works that are therein will be discovered. Seeing then that all these things are thus to be dissolved, what manner of persons ought (ye) all the while to be in holy ways of behaviour and acts of godliness, expecting and hastening the coming of the Day of God by reason of which, heavens being on fire will be dissolved, and elements becoming intensely hot, will be melted; but new Heavens and a new Earth, according to His promise, are we expecting wherein righteousness is to dwell "—*2 Pet. iii. 10—13.*

Scoffers may laugh at this prophecy of the Apostle Peter, just as they did at that of Noah, but it will be as assuredly fulfilled as that respecting the Deluge has already been. The very manner of dissolution has been foretold—the decomposition of what are called elements. This is one of those nuggets of knowledge hidden in the Bible, a problem which in its own way scientific chemistry has long been attempting to solve. The gases of water will then be resolved, and the Thames being set on fire will no longer be a mere figure of speech, but a terrific fact. Then will there be a true realization of the saying—Sic *transit gloria mundi*. The transit of Venus will occupy the attention of Astronomers no more. They will then have discovered that the Stars and planets are very different bodies from what they imagined them to be. The Apostle John, who became in spirit, not, as most Commentators tell us, on our Sunday, but, *en tē Kuriakē hēmera*, in the Lordly day, or, IN THE DAY OF THE LORD —*Rev. i. 10*, thus writes—

"And I beheld, when he had opened the Sixth Seal, and lo, there was a great earthquake, and the sun became black as sackcloth of hair, and the moon became as blood, and the stars of heaven fell unto the earth, even as a fig-tree casteth her untimely figs, when she is shaken of a mighty wind. And the heavens departed as a scroll, when it is rolled together, and every mountain and island were moved out of their places. And the kings of the earth, and the great men, and the rich men, and the chief captains, and the mighty men, and every bond-man and every freeman hid themselves in the dens and in the rocks of the mountains, and said to the mountains and rocks, Fall on us, and hide us from the face of Him that sitteth on the throne, and from the wrath of the Lamb, for the great day

of His wrath is come, and who shall be able to stand?"—
Rev. vi. 12—17.

It may be well to notice here two statements in the above passage, which are at utter variance with the teaching of Modern Astronomy. First, the Sun is said to become black as sackcloth of hair, and the Moon as blood, from which we may learn that these luminaries are entirely independent of each other, and that the Moon does not derive her light from the Sun. Secondly, it is declared that the Stars of heaven fell unto (*eis,* upon) the Earth, as a fig-tree casts her green figs, when shaken by a great wind, from which we may gather, that the Stars are at no great distance from the Earth, and are very much smaller than it, instead of their being, as Modern Astronomers say, untold millions of miles away, and immeasurably larger than our world.

The Ark is a type of our Lord Jesus Christ, the Way, the Truth, and the Life, our only means of salvation. May we all through Him be found in peace, without spot and blameless, so that, with holy expectation, we may look for "New Heavens and a New Earth, wherein dwelleth Righteousness"—*2 Pet. iii. 13.*

CHAPTER XII.

THE DELUGE: TRADITIONAL RECORDS.

SECTION   PAGE

1. MARKS OF THE DELUGE VISIBLE IN MANY LANDS - - -   234

2. THE ACCADIAN OR OLD CHALDEAN ACCOUNT OF THE DELUGE - - 237

3. EXTRACTS FROM OLD CHALDEAN EPICS, DECLARING THE REVOLUTION OF THE SUN, AND THE CREATION OF MEN AND ANIMALS - 247

4. BABYLONIA IDENTIFIED WITH THE GARDEN OF EDEN - 251

SECTION 1.

MARKS OF THE DELUGE VISIBLE IN MANY LANDS.

THOSE of our Modern Astronomers, who discredit the Biblical account of the Deluge, have not only done very wrong in denying what God has so explicitly stated to be true, but they have shown great want of judgment in rejecting a fact, the traditions concerning which have been recorded, with more or less accuracy, in so many different parts of the world. Even at a late Annual Meeting of the British Association, the President of that

Scientific Society spoke of the Deluge as if only a human legend, and not as an accepted Scriptural truth.   Besides, the great boulders, and other vestiges of that catastrophe, which are still seen in numerous places, prove the propriety of the old adage—"there are none so blind as those *who will not see.*"   In my own rambles in England and Scotland, especially in the latter, I have frequently observed such remains—immense isolated rocks, partly overgrown with moss or heather, lying in positions where they never could have been placed by human hands— lofty hills which appear to have been denuded of soil by vast masses of water rushing over their tops and down their sides—glens and valleys which have been scooped out or levelled by torrents of water, far, far exceeding in volume and power that of the rivers or smaller streams that have flowed through them since the memory of man, which excavatings and levellings the latter, as now existing, could never possibly have effected.   Any one who has visited the rent courses of the Wye, or the Find-horn—the levelled expanses of Strathmore or Strathfleet —the barren steeps of Ben Arkle, or the stony mountains of Assynt—will acknowledge the truth of my remarks. And these illustrations, from our own Island, are small in comparison of those which may be witnessed in America, Switzerland, New Zealand, and many other countries.

The learned Humboldt, though a Globist, strongly believed the fact of a Universal Deluge : he says—

"The ancient traditions of the human race which we find dispersed over the surface of the globe, like the fragments of a vast shipwreck, prevail among all nations, and bear a resemblance that fills us with astonishment.   There are many languages belonging to branches, which appear to have no

connection with each other, and these all transmit to us the
same fact. The substance of the traditions respecting the
destroyed races and the renovation of nature, is about everywhere the same, although each nation gives a local colouring."

The universality of the Deluge would never have been
questioned, but for the fads of certain Geologists, and the
exigencies of Modern Astronomers, who preferred
rejecting the Biblical account of the Flood to abandoning
their own theory of a Planetary Earth. Christian learned
men like Calmet and Dr. Adam Clarke, who had
thoroughly investigated the matter, considered the
Scriptural statements concerning it to be literally true,
even though they still clung to the Copernican system.
The marvel is how any one who has at all studied the
subject, with the records of past ages now disclosed,
and the silent but visible proofs of the catastrophe around
him, could ever believe otherwise, but there is no
gauging the eccentricity of the human mind. It would
occupy too much space to enter into the very numerous
national traditions of the Deluge, and I shall give only
one—that of the Old Chaldeans—but that is, indeed,
not only the most interesting, but the most ancient of any
with which I am acquainted. For other traditions I
beg to refer my Readers to Dr. Clarke's Commentary on
Genesis, Chapters vi.—ix., and to Calmet under the
articles named below.* Apolodorus wrote of it in his
History,† Ovid sung of it in his "Metamorphoses,"‡
Josephus referred to it in his "Antiquities,"§ and past

---

* Calmet's Dictionary of the Holy Bible:—"Ammon or no Ammon," "Ark,"
"Deluge"—Vol. I.; "Noah"—Vol. II.; "Judean History of Noah and the
Deluge," see "Fragments" xx.—Vol. III.; "Plates," "Construction of the Ark,"
"Dagon," &c.—Vol. V.
† Apolodor. Bib. lib. I. Cap. I.
‡ "Metam." lib. IV., 270.
§ "Antiq." Apion lib. I. S. 3, 19.

ages are full of its marvels, as Bryant, in his "Ancient Mythology," so clearly shows.

———

SECTION 2.

THE ACCADIAN OR OLD CHALDEAN ACCOUNT OF THE DELUGE.

The oldest and most remarkable Secular account of the Deluge appears to be that written in the Accadian, or Old Chaldean, cuneiform tablets about 4,000 years ago. The translation of these tablets into English is given in a small book, called the "History of Babylonia,"* a copy of which was kindly sent to me by Dr. Kenyon of the British Museum, to whom I had written, requesting information on this subject. I shall give some extracts from these ancient tablets, exhumed only in recent years, as if purposely to confute the infidelity of modern times, for they not only record the fact of the Deluge, in most unmistakable language, but also actually refer to several minute incidental particulars which occurred as stated in the Biblical account.

The Chaldeans were the earliest, and the most famous Astronomers of antiquity, and, in some fragments of their tablets on the Creation, we find, as side-lights by the way, that they did not demean themselves with the idea that they were derived from a monkey, nor did they

---

* "History of Babylonia," by the late George Smith, Esq., of the British Museum; edited by the Rev. A. H. Sayce, M.A., Society for Promoting Christian Knowledge, Northumberland Avenue, London.

imagine that the Earth was a rolling Planet, but declared that the Sun made its daily circuit round it, and its annual path through the Zodiac of the heavens. These tablets form a portion of a large Epic, discoursing chiefly on the Adventures of Gilmanes, a kind of early Hercules. The Author of " Babylonia," p. 41, says—

" The Chaldean legend of the Flood was in existence at least 2,000 years before the Christian era, and the events of the series of legends to which it belongs are carved on some of the most ancient Babylonian seals."

Noah, or Xisuthrus, as he is called in the Epic, was said to be the tenth in descent in the mythological Babylonian period before the Flood, thereby agreeing with the fact that he represented the tenth generation from Adam; but the length of the dynasty is entirely legendary, far exceeding the time occupied according to the Mosaic history. It is stated that, by reason of his virtues, he was exalted to dwell among the gods, which is probably a warped tradition of the translation of his ancestor Enoch, " who was not, for God took him "— *Gen. v. 24.*

Gilmanes became unwell and determined to seek recovery from Noah, who was said to be among the gods, somewhere about the Persian Gulf, and whom after various adventures he found. At the request of Gilmanes, Noah related to him the account of the Deluge, after which he instructed Nis Ea how to cure him of his disease. Gilmanes then returned to Erech (now Warka), the chief city of his dominion, which, with Babel, Accad, and Calneh, is mentioned in *Genesis x. 10,* as being the beginning of Nimrod's kingdom, in the land of Shinar.

It would seem, from the following quotation from "Babylonia," pp. 48, 49, that the story of Gilmanes had a latent allusion to certain facts of Astronomy, in which Science the Chaldeans so much excelled—

"It was to, this pre-historic epoch that the Adventures of Gilmanes, one of the most celebrated of the Chaldean heroes, was assigned. Gilmanes was originally a Solar hero, and the Great Epic in which his Adventures are described, is still conscious of the fact. The Epic is divided into twelve books, the subject matter of each book corresponding with the name of a Sign in the Zodiac. Thus the story of the Deluge is introduced as an episode in the eleventh book which answers to Aquarius, the eleventh Sign of the Zodiac, while the bull slain by Gilmanes in the second book is Taurus the second Sign of the Zodiac. The Adventures of the hero thus represent the passing of the Sun through the twelve months of the year, and his illness and retreat to the ocean, which surrounded the world, symbolize the paling strength of the Sun of winter, and his declension towards the western ocean. Through the medium of the Phœnicians or Syrians, the story of Gilmanes seems to have been carried to Europe, at all events the Greek Herakles, and, to a lesser extent, Perseus, is a reflection of the Chaldean Gilmanes, being the prototype of Herakles."

EXTRACTS FROM THE ELEVENTH TABLET OF THE ISHDUBAR LEGENDS, GIVING THE ACCADIAN ACCOUNT OF THE DELUGE.*

Column I.

* * * * * * *

LINE

8 Xisuthrus speaks to him, even to Gilmanes,

9 Let me reveal to thee, Gilmanes, the story of my preservation,

---

* "The History of Babylonia," pp. 33-40.

LINE

10 And the oracle of the gods let me tell it to thee.

11 The city of Surippak, the city which as thou knowest, is built on the Euphrates.

12 This city was already ancient when the gods within it

13 Set their hearts to bring on a deluge, even the great gods,

14 As many as there are—their father Anu,

15 Their King the warrior Bel,

16 Their throne-bearer Ninup,

17 Their prince the lord of Hades.

18 Ea, the lord of wisdom, conferred with them and repeated their decree to the Reed-bed: Reed-bed, O Reed-bed, frame, O frame,

19 Hear, O reed-bed, and understand, O frame!

20 O man of Surippak, son of Ubara Tutu:

21 Frame the house, build the ship, leave what thou canst, seek life.

22 Resign thy goods, and cause thy soul to live,

23 And bid the seed of life of every kind mount unto the midst of the ship,

24 The ship which thou shalt build.

*   *   *   *   *   *   *

38 . . . . I will judge above and below;

39 (But as for thee), shut (not) the door

40 (Until) the time come of which I will send thee word.

41 (Then) enter and turn the door of the ship (and)

42 Bring into the midst of it, thy corn, thy property, and thy goods,

43 Thy (family), thy household, thy concubines, and the sons of the people,

44 The (cattle) of the field, the wild beast of the field, as many as I would preserve.

LINE

45 I will send unto thee, and the door of thy ship shall preserve them.

46 Xisuthrus opened his mouth and speaks,

47 He says to Ea his lord,

48 (O my lord) no one yet has built a ship (in this fashion),

49 On land to contain the beasts (of the field),

50 (The plan?) let me see, and the ship (I will build),

51 On the land the ship (I will build),

52 . . . . As thou hast commanded (me).

Column II.

*   *   *   *   *   *   *

5 I made its side and I enclosed it.

6 I built six storeys, I divided (its passages) seven times.

7 I divided its interior nine times.

8 I cut (worked) timber within it.

9 I saw the rudder, and what was wanting I added.

10 Six sari of bitumen I poured over the outside,

11 Three sari of bitumen I poured over the inside,

*   *   *   *   *   *   *

23 I caused the tackle to be carried above and below.

24 (Then there went into it) two-thirds (of my household),

25 All that I had I put into it, all that of silver I had I put into it,

26 All that of gold I had I put into it,

27 All that I had of the seed of life I put into it. The whole

28 I brought up into the ship, all my slaves and concubines,

29 The cattle of the field, the beasts of the field, the sons of the people, all of them did I bring up.

30 The season Samas fixed, and

LINE

31 He spake, saying, "In the night will I cause the heaven
     to rain destruction."

32 Enter into the midst of the ship and shut the door.

33 The season came round (of which)

34 He spake, saying, "In the night will I cause the heaven
     to rain destruction."

35 I watched with dread the dawning of the day.

Column III.

1 (The surface) of the land like (fire) they wasted,

2 (They destroyed) all life from the face of the land.

3 To battle against men they brought (the waters)

4 Brother saw not his brother; men knew not one another.
     In heaven

5 The gods feared the flood, and

6 Hastened to ascend to the heaven of Anu (i.e. the highest
     heaven).

    *   *   *   *   *   *   *

19 Six days and nights

20 The wind, the flood, and the storm go on overwhelming.

21 The seventh day, when it approached, the flood subsided,
     the storm,

22 Which had fought against men like an armed host,

23 Was quieted. The sea began to dry, and the wind and the
     flood ended.

24 I beheld the sea and uttered a cry,

25 For the whole of mankind was turned to clay;

26 Like trunks the corpses floated.

27 I opened the window, and the light smote upon my face,

28 I stooped and sat down, I wept,

29 Over my face flowed my tears.

30 I beheld a shore beyond the sea;

31 A district rose twelve times distant.

32 On the mountains of Nizir the ship grounded,

33 The mountains of Nizir stopped the ship, and it was not able to pass over it.

34 The first day, the second day, the mountains of Nizir stopped the ship.

35 The third day, the fourth day, the mountains of Nizir stopped the ship.

36 The fifth day, the sixth day the mountains of Nizir stopped the ship.

37 The seventh day when it approached

38 I sent forth a dove and it left. The dove went and returned, and

39 Found no resting place, and it came back.

40 Then I sent forth a swallow and it left. The swallow went and returned, and

41 Found no resting place, and it came back.

42 I sent forth a raven and it left.

43 The raven went and saw the going down of the waters, and

44 It approached, it waded, it croaked; it did not return.

45 I sent (the animals) forth to the four winds, I sacrificed a sacrifice,

46 I built an altar on the peak of the mountain,

47 I sent vessels (each containing the third of an ephah), by sevens.

48 Underneath them I spread reeds, cedar wood, and herbs.

49 The gods smelt the savour, the gods smelt the good savour.

50 The gods gathered like flies over the sacrifices.

51 Thereupon the great goddess at her approach

52 Lifted up the mighty bow, which Anu had created according
   to (his) wish.

53 The gods by my necklace never will I forget.

Column IV.

*   *   *   *   *   *   *

12 Ea opened his mouth, and he says to the warrior Bel;

13 "Thou, O warrior, art the seer of the gods,

14 Why, why didst thou not consider, but caused'st a flood?

15 Let the doer of sin bear his sin, let the doer of wickedness
   bear his wickedness.

16 May the just prince not be cut off, the merciful that he be
   not (destroyed).

17 Instead of causing a flood, let lions come and minish men,

18 Instead of causing a flood, let hyenas come and minish men,

19 Instead of causing a flood let a famine happen, and let it
   (devour) the land.

20 Instead of causing a flood let plagues come and minish men.

21 I did not reveal the determination of the great gods.

22 To Xisuthrus alone a dream I sent and he heard the determination of the gods."

23 When Bel had again taken council he went up to the midst of
   the ship.

24 He took my hand and bade me ascend,

25 Even me he bade ascend, he united my wife to my side.

26 He turned himself to us, and stood between us, he blessed
   us (thus)

27 "Hitherto Xisuthrus has been a mortal man,

28 But now Xisuthrus and his wife shall be like the gods, even us.

29 Yea, Xisuthrus shall dwell afar off, at the mouth of the
   rivers.

30 They took us afar off at the mouth of the rivers they made
   us dwell."

The above extracts, from this ancient Epic, show
decidedly that the Chaldeans believed in a Universal
Deluge; the very differing in certain points from the
Biblical account, only proving that there was no collu-
sion; such, indeed, was impossible, seeing that the Epic
was written several hundred years *before* the birth of
Moses. The Author was not a worshipper of the one
God JEHOVAH, but was a polytheist, reverencing Ea, Anu,
Bel, Ninup, Merodach, Nergal, and others, who, in
Column III., line 50, he says, gathered as flies around
Noah's sacrifice. Again, the Epic speaks of there being
only six days occupied in overwhelming the world with
water, whereas the Bible states that the waters prevailed
for an hundred and fifty days, and that Noah was a whole
year in the Ark. The Epic says that Noah took with
him into the Ark, not only his family, cattle, and beasts
of the field, but his slaves and concubines and sons of the
people, while the Bible distinctly avers that only Noah,
his wife, his three sons, and their wives, in all eight
persons, were saved, besides a certain proportion of
animals, clean and unclean, fowls of the air and creeping
things of the Earth. Again, Xisuthrus or Noah tells
Gilmanes that he belonged to Surippak, a city on the
Euphrates, not far from the Persian Gulf, whereas the
Bible makes no allusion to it; but this is a matter of no
consequence, and it was by no means improbable that
Noah came from there, as Mesopotamia was doubtless
the original habitation of the Ante-Diluvians.

Several important and interesting particulars, narrated

in the Epic, agree with those mentioned in the Biblical account, some of which may be noticed here—

1. The wickedness of man was the cause of the Deluge; compare Epic, Column IV., 12—16 with *Gen. vi. 5—8.*

2. The command of God to Noah to build the Ark; Col. I. 21—45 with *Gen. vi. 14—16.*

3. The preservation of animals, &c.; Col. I. 44, 45 with *Gen. vi. 19—21* and *vii. 2, 3.*

4. Pouring bitumen outside and inside the Ark; Col. II. 10, 11 with *Gen. vi. 14.*

5. The utter destruction of all life on the Earth; Col. III. 1—26 with *Gen. vii. 21—23.*

6. Noah sends forth a raven; Col. III. 42—44 with *Gen. viii. 7.*

7. Noah sends out a dove; Col. III. 38, 39 with *Gen. viii. 8, 9.*

8. In Col. III. 32—36, the Ark is said to have grounded on the mountains of Nizir, which, it is believed, are not far from the mountains of Ararat on which it rested, according to *Gen. viii. 4.*

9. On the ground becoming dry Noah sent forth the animals, &c., out of the Ark; compare Col. III. 45 with *Gen. viii. 18, 19.*

10. On leaving the Ark Noah offered sacrifice; Col. III. 46—50 with *Gen. viii. 20.*

11. The bow in the cloud is set; Col. III. 52 with *Gen. ix. 13.*

12. The world is to be destroyed no more by a flood; Col. IV. 17—20 with *Gen. ix. 15.*

After such confirmatory proofs as have now been given, I pity any who, either from prejudice or from want of mental capacity, may still decline to believe the fact of a Universal Deluge. Very grateful should we be to those able and self-denying men, who have given their time and talents in recovering and deciphering such important relics of antiquity. I cannot here enter into the story of the Monuments, but beg to refer my Readers to the works I have already mentioned, p. 50, in which, with respect to them, will be found most interesting and useful information. Gradually the statements of Old Testament history are being corroborated by the discovery of tablets and other memorials of past ages, which are being brought forward in testimony of Scriptural truth. I would not, indeed, be much surprised, were the veritable Ark of Noah some day discovered among the mountains of Ararat, and the Ark of the Covenant exhumed from the ruins of ancient Jerusalem.

SECTION 8.

EXTRACTS FROM OLD CHALDEAN EPICS, DECLARING THE REVOLUTION OF THE SUN, AND THE CREATION OF MEN AND ANIMALS.

As bearing on certain Astronomic facts contended for in this book, I beg to subjoin the accompanying extracts from some other old Accadian Epics, showing the belief of the Chaldeans in the Revolution of the Sun and a regular Creation. The following was discovered by the late Mr. George Smith of the British Museum, who was of opinion that much would yet be found, confirmatory of the truth of the early histories mentioned in Genesis. The Epic begins,* pp. 43, 44—

" When on high the heavens proclaimed not,
(And) earth beneath recorded not a name,
Then the abyss of waters was in the beginning their generator.
The chaos of the deep (Tianat) was she who bore them all.
Their waters were embosomed together, and
The plant was ungathered, the herb (of the field) ungrown.
When the gods had not appeared, any one (of them)
By no name were they recorded, no destiny (had they fixed),
Then were the (great) gods created—
Lakhmu and Lakhamu issued forth (the first),
Until they grew up (and waxed old).
When the gods Sar and Kisar (the upper and lower firmaments)
         were created ;
Long were the days (until)
The gods Anu (Bel, and Ea were created),
Sar (and Kisar created them)."

From the Fifth tablet ; pp. 44, 45.

" (Merodach) prepared the mansions of the great gods,
He fixed the stars that correspond with them, even the Twin-
         stars.
He ordained the year, appointed the signs of the Zodiac over it.
For each of the twelve months he fixed three stars,
From the day when the year issues forth to its close.
He founded the mansions of the Sun-god who passes along
         the ecliptic, that they might know their bounds,
That they might not err, that they might not go astray in any
         way ;

---

* "History of Babylonia," pp. 43, 45.

He established the mansions of Bel and Ea along with himself.

Moreover he opened the gates on either side.

He strengthened the bolts on the left hand and on the right,

And in the midst of it he made a staircase.

He illuminated the Moon-god that he might be watchman of the
    night,

And ordained for him the ending of the night, that the day may
    be known.

(Saying), month by month, without break, keep watch in (thy) disc.

At the beginning of the month rise brightly at evening

With glittering horns, that the heavens may know.

On the seventh day halve (thy) disc."

I also quote the following lines from another old
Accadian Epic found by Mr. Pinches, p. 47—

   *   *   *   *   *   *   *

"Merodach bound together the slime (?) before the waters,

Dust he made, and poured it out with the flood.

The gods were made to dwell in a seat of joy of heart,

He created mankind

The god Aruru, the seed of mankind, they made with him.

He made the beast of the field, and the living creatures of the
    desert

He made the Tigris and Euphrates and set (them) in (their) place,

Well proclaimed he their name.

The *ussa* plant, the *ditta* plant of the marshland, the reed and
    the forest he made.

He made the verdure of the plain,

The land, the marshes, and the greensward, also,

Oxen, the young of the horse, the stallion, the mare, the sheep
    the locust;

Meadows and forests also;

The he-goat and the gazelle brought forth (?) to him."

Let us look at a few things in which the Chaldeans believed, which we may gather from the foregoing extracts from these Epics on Creation.

1. That, before the appearance of the Heavens and the Earth, there existed a great Abyss or Deep of waters. The classical reader will doubtless remember that Homer and the great Greek philosopher, Thales, also considered water to be the principle of everything, all confirmatory of the " Great Deep " of Scripture, in which the foundations of the Earth were laid.

2. That Merodach made the Stars, ordained the year, appointed the Signs of the Zodiac, and for each of the twelve months fixed three Stars (or constellations), and the path of the Sun in the ecliptic.

3. That he established the Moon-god as the watchman of the night, to give light quite independently of the Sun.

4. That mankind were created as mankind, and not evolved out of a lower order of being.

5. That beasts and all other animals were created in their own particular species, and no hint whatever is given of any change or modification in their form or nature. What a contrast is this to the statement made by Sir Michael Foster, M.P., President of the British Association, at the meeting held at Dover in September, 1899—

" That the shifting scenes of embryonic life are hints and tokens of lives lived by ancestors in time long past ! "*

Were this statement true there would be a serious " missing link " in Debrett's Peerage, for the chimpanzee,

---

* *The Birmingham Daily Gazette,* 14th September, 1899.

in its connection with the "upper ten," is altogether omitted there.

6. That men, animals, rivers, mountains, forests, &c., were all specially created, and did not spring spontaneously out of debris from a nebulous Sun, as so many of our Astronomers so foolishly imagine.

The Chaldeans were doubtless idolaters, and worshipped many gods, but as far as regards matters of nature, they appear to have been much more gifted with common sense than most of the Scientists of our own times. When they saw the Sun in his daily journey moving round the world, they did not say that it was the world that moved round it; and, when they saw the Moon put forth her pallid light, they did not suppose it to be reflected from the fiery rays of the Sun; nor did they ever dream, like the night-mared Evolutionist, that the monad could ever become a whale, or the monkey a man!

SECTION 4.

BABYLONIA IDENTIFIED WITH THE GARDEN OF EDEN.

There is one other passage in "Babylonia" to which I would like to allude—the situation of the Garden of Eden—as described by the late Mr. George Smith, for, although it does not bear directly on the Deluge, it does so indirectly, by testifying to the veracity of those

Scriptures which have so emphatically recorded the fact of the Deluge.

"The plain or 'Field' of Babylon was called Edinna in the old Accadian language, a word which was borrowed by the old Semitic conquerors of the country, under the form of Edinu or Edin. This is clearly the Eden of the Old Testament, so that it is not surprising that the two main rivers of the Garden of Eden are said to have been the Euphrates and the Hiddekhel. Hiddekhel is the Accadian name of the Tïgris *id idikla*, or stream of Idikla. The garden planted in Eden may have been near the town of Eridu, now marked by the ruins of Abu-Shahrein, in the south of Babylonia, which in the second millenium before the Christian era stood on the sea shore. At all events Eridu is reckoned as a sacred city in Babylonian literature; it is frequently termed 'the good,' or 'holy,' and near it was a forest or 'garden,' where grew 'the holy palm-tree,' identified with the 'Tree of Life.'"*

Another most interesting relic of Babylonian antiquity, bearing on Eden, has been exhumed from this now desert land. It is an engraving on a Babylonian Seal, representing the Temptation in the Garden of Eden.† Adam is depicted as seated on the right, and Eve on the left, with the Tree of Life between them, and an erect Serpent standing behind Eve. Here is a direct testimony that the Bible account of the Fall is no myth, as even some of our modern divines suppose, but a veritable reality.

"Some of the Pharisees from among the multitude said unto Him (Jesus), Master, rebuke Thy disciples. And He

---

* "History of Babylonia," pp. 53, 54.
† A copy of this Seal will be found facing p. 152 of "Babylonian Life and History," by E. A. Weller Bridge, Esq., M.A., of the British Museum; Religious Tract Society, 56 Paternoster Row, London.

answered and said, I tell you that if these should hold their peace, the stones would immediately cry out "—*Luke xix. 39, 40.*

And so the very stones of Babylon cry out against the infidelity of this pretentious age.

Infidels have long sought to throw discredit on the Holy Scriptures, and with them the Deluge has been a subject of special obloquy. Many of our Modern Astronomers, Scientists, and Hyper-critics have of late joined in the attack against it, and I have, therefore, been the more anxious to prove its truth, not only from Sacred, but from Secular authority, and trust I have been successful. I am grieved to say that, such is the perversity of the human mind, even some Ministers of the Gospel have not scrupled to assert their disbelief in the Deluge. For example, in *The Christian World Pulpit* of 14th June, 1893, a well-known Minister of Liverpool is reported to have said—

" No student of science is able to believe that any such flood as that recorded in the early Chapters of Genesis ever took place in the history of the human race. . . . . The flood story is nothing but a *myth.*"

Seeing, then, the wide-spread mutiny which has arisen against the Deluge, that just judgment of God upon a sinful world, every true Christian should be firm as a rock in upholding the truth of the Sacred Record. Let no one be faint-hearted; the promise has been given— " When the enemy shall come in as a flood, the Spirit of JEHOVAH shall lift up a standard against him "— *Isa. lix. 19.* Let me remind the gainsayer of the rebuke of JEHOVAH—

"Who is this that darkeneth counsel
  By words without knowledge? . .   .
Who shut up the sea with doors,
  When it brake forth and issued out of the womb?
When I made the clouds the garment thereof,
  And thick darkness a swaddling band for it,
  And prescribed for it my decree,
  And said, 'Hitherto shalt thou come and no further,
  And here shall thy proud waves be stayed'"

                              Job xxxviii. 2, 8—11.

Some of the over-zealous opponents of the Book of
Genesis have stated that the art of writing was unknown
in the days of Moses, and that 700 or 800 years after his
time, some impostor forged his name to the Pentateuch,
thus seeking, by a side-issue, to overthrow its authority.
I have not the slightest doubt, from the collateral
evidence afforded by Scripture, that writing was practised
from the time of Adam. But, be that as it may, the
Chaldean tablets, *written some hundreds of years before
the birth of Moses,* now stare such critics in the face, and
as living witnesses attest the truth of Scripture. But
we are told that in the last days "evil men and imposters
shall wax worse and worse, deceiving and being deceived"
—*2 Tim. iii. 13,* so that we need not be surprised if
infidel objections will be continued to the end of time.
Dear Cowper wrote more than a century ago—

      "The infidel has shot his bolts away,
        Till his exhausted quiver, yielding none,
      He gleans his blunted shafts that have recoil'd,
      And aims them at the shield of Truth again."*

---

* "The Task," Book VI.

Blessed are they who, trusting alone to the finished work of our Lord Jesus Christ, can look beyond the darkness for

" A morning without clouds, when the tender grass springeth up out of the earth through clear shining after rain "— *2 Sam. xxiii. 4.*

" Unto you that fear My name, saith JEHOVAH, shall the Sun of Righteousness arise with healing in His wings "—*Mal. iv. 2.*

Since the above was written, I have read in the *Standard* of 27th September, 1899, a most interesting article, headed " The Oldest Poem in the World," with a reference to which I shall now close this Chapter. A few years ago Professor Petrie, while exploring the Pyramid at Illahum, discovered a number of papyri, which were found to give many particulars of ancient Egyptian life. Among them was a Royal Ode, addressed to Usentisen III., regarding which the writer of the article says—

" Its value lies in its being certainly the oldest Poem in the world, nearly fifteen (?) centuries before the time of Moses; and also in the wonderful way in which it describes, in most figurative language, the great work that the King had done in the expansion of the Egyptian empire."

The work is published by Mr. Quaritch, and the autotype representations are said to be beautifully executed. I refer to these papyri, as a corroborative proof of the very early period in which the art of writing was known, and also to show that the Ancients were by no means the ignorant barbarians which some Modern Scientists, " dressed in a little brief authority," so erroneously consider them to have been.

CHAPTER XIII.

THE GREAT DEEP, A PROOF THAT THE EARTH IS NOT A PLANET.

SECTION   PAGE

1. THE EARTH IN SOLUTION BEFORE THE ADAMIC CREATION, SHOWING HORIZONTALITY BY ITS STRATA - - - - - 256

2. THE TIDES AND THE GREAT DEEP - - 258

3. THE GREAT GULF STREAM AND CURRENTS OF THE GREAT DEEP - - - - 265

4. THE RIVERS COME FROM AND RETURN TO THE GREAT DEEP - - - - - - 267

SECTION 1.

THE EARTH IN SOLUTION BEFORE THE ADAMIC CREATION.

THE late Dr. Woodward was of opinion that, at the time of the Noachian Deluge, the substance of the Earth was completely dissolved. But this could not possibly have been the case then, because we read—" All the mountains which were under the whole heaven were covered "—*Gen. vii. 19 ;* which shows that there were still mountains in existence ; and again, we find that, when the waters were subsiding, the Ark rested on the mountains of

Ararat—*Gen. viii. 4,* the loftiest of which range is, according to the British Almanac for 1900, 19,916 feet in height.* I believe, however, that BEFORE the Adamic Creation, the Earth was in a state of solution, which will account for the stratification of the different kinds of rocks, &c., laid for the most part according to their specific gravity or weight. This idea is strengthened by the words in *Genesis i. 2,* where the Earth is said to be *tehu vebehu,* "without form and void," when darkness was on the face of the Deep. *Tehu* signifies unformed, confused, and *behu,* empty, void, loose, just like what the Earth might be expected to be before it was constituted, by the action of the water, into the level stratification of the rocks. These words, *tehu, vebehu,* occur together in two other passages of Scripture, illustrative of their meaning, namely—" He shall stretch out upon it the lines of *confusion,* and the stones of emptiness "—*Isa. xxxiv. 11*—" I beheld the Earth, and lo, it was *without form and void,* and they had no light there "—*Jer. iv. 22.*

There is a remarkable verse, *2 Pet. iii. 5,* which particularly confirms this view—" For they wilfully forget that there were heavens from of old, and an Earth compacted out of water, and amid water, by the Word of God." (R.V.) Rotherham's translation, *in loco,* is still more emphatic—" For this they wilfully forget, that there were heavens from of old, and an Earth, on account of water, and by means of water, compacted by the Word of God." The Authorised Version, has missed the full interpretation of this important passage, by not giving the complete meaning of the word *sunestōsa,* made to stand together. In *Job* we find it asked—"Where wast thou when I laid the foundations of the Earth? Declare if thou hast understanding. Who hath laid the measures thereof, if thou knowest? Or who hath stretched the line upon it?"—*Job xxxviii. 4, 5.* Here the word *yasadi*, foundations, in verse 4, may refer to the granite bases of the mountains, and the word *mamdiah*, in verse 5, to the strata laid upon them, for it is derived from the root *madad* to extend or stretch. I would also observe that the strata are all *horizontal*, with the exception, of course, of those places where what are called "faults" or displacements occur, which have been caused, either by the breaking up of all the fountains of the Great Deep (*tehoom rabah*), at the time of the Deluge, or by volcanic disturbances in the Earth *after* the strata had been laid. The horizontality of the layers proves that the Earth never whirled round the Sun, nor any other heavenly body, for, had it done so, the strata would undoubtedly have been *curved*, instead of which they are all *straight*. And here I may add another proof that the Earth is not a revolving Planet, but is horizontally fixed on the waters of the Great Deep, from the fact that on every rock-bound coast, where the mark of the tide may be seen, the line traced by the action of the sea is found to be *straight*, without any curvature whatever.

SECTION 2.

THE TIDES AND THE GREAT DEEP.

The tides of the ocean have for long been considered as being caused by the "attraction" of the Moon, but latterly this has been seriously questioned even by some of our Modern Astronomers, owing to certain discrepancies which have been discovered between theory and fact. Indeed, the Moon, as has been previously remarked, has been a source of great trouble to our Astronomers, as she persists in acting in so many ways in direct opposition to what their theories require. Even Sir Isaac Newton himself confessed that the explanation of the Moon's action on the Tides was the least satisfactory part of his theory of Gravitation. This theory asserts that the larger object attracts the smaller, and the mass of the Moon being reckoned as only one-eighth of that of the Earth, it follows that, if, by the presumed force of Gravitation, the Earth revolves round the Sun, much more, for the same reason, should the Moon do so likewise, instead of which that wilful orb still continues to go round our world.

Tides vary greatly in height, owing chiefly to the different configurations of the adjoining lands. At Chepstow it rises to 60 feet, at Portishead to 50, while at Dublin Bay it is but 12, and at Wexford only 5 feet. The late Captain George Peacock of the Royal Navy writes as follows :—

"At Holyhaven, near the mouth of the Thames, the tide is actually falling, and running *down* rapidly, while, *at the same moment*, it is running *up* rapidly at London Bridge, and still rising. . . . There are four high waters and three low waters on the river St. Laurence (North America) *at the same time*, and in the river Amazon (South America), there are no less than six high waters and five low waters at the same time, and, in the dry season, as many as seven high waters and six low waters at the same time have been known."[*]

---

[*] " Is the world Flat or Round," by Captain George Peacock, R.N., F.R.G.S.; Bellows, Gloucester.

In the Mediterranean the tide is so small that, in one of his hymns, Mr. McCheyne poetically called that great expanse a " tideless sea," and, in the extreme South, the tides in some parts are scarcely perceptible.

The Earth is stated, on infallible authority, to be " founded upon the seas and established upon the floods " —*Psa. xxiv. 2*, and, in my opinion, the Tides are for the most part caused by the flux and the reflux of the waters of the Great Deep, with which the Earth is assuredly most closely connected—" He gathereth the waters of the sea together as an heap. He layeth up the depth in storehouses "—*Psa. xxxiii. 7*. Such a cause of the Tides was given by Parallax, who did such great service to true science by exposing the fallacies of Modern Astronomy, and Mr. Winship of Natal, in his excellent work, " Zetetic Cosmogony,"* p. 131, thus comes to the same conclusion—

" Tides are caused by the gentle and gradual rise and fall of the Earth on the bosom of the mighty deep. In inland lakes there are no tides, which also proves that the Moon cannot attract the Earth or water to cause tides. . . . . The Moon is the TIDE-KEEPER for the tides, nothing more. The ' phase ' of the Moon tells what kind of a tide may be expected, but she does not and cannot ' attract ' either the solid body of the Earth or the waters."

That the Earth itself has a slight tremulous motion may be seen in the movement of the spirit-level, even when fixed as steadily as possible, and that the sea has a fluctuation may be witnessed by the oscillation of an anchored ship in the calmest day of summer. By what

---

* T. L. Cullingford, 40 Field Street, Durban, Natal; John Wilson, 54 Bourne Street, Netherfield, Notts.

means the tides are so regularly affected is at present only conjectured; possibly it may be by atmospheric pressure on the waters of the Great Deep, and perhaps even the Moon itself, as suggested by the late Dr. Rowbotham, " may influence the atmosphere, *increasing or diminishing its barometric pressure,* and indirectly the rise and fall of the Earth in the waters." Of this we cannot now be sure, but of one thing we may be certain, that it is just as easy for God to adjust the courses of the Tides, as it is for Him to regulate the motions of the heavenly bodies.

Occasionally the sea coast is swept by what is called a Great Tidal Wave. Some years since such occurred in the Sunderabad, a low-lying woody district near Calcutta, which caused much loss of life to men and animals; and another, still more disastrous, happened not long ago in Japan, by which, if I remember rightly, 24,000 persons were drowned, and ships were carried about two miles inland. How these abnormal tides arise is a moot point, but I think it is most probable that they are caused by means of Earthquakes displacing the land, and, by this means, letting the volume of the sea roll far beyond its usual boundary.

The great Earthquake, which occurred on the morning of 1st November, 1755, generally called that of Lisbon, as that city suffered most from its terrible effects, was the cause of immense loss of life and property by sea as well as by land. According to the writer of the article " Earthquake," in the edition of the Encyclopædia Britannica now before me, it extended over an area of at least four millions of square miles, and particulars of it were noted in many places from Morocco to Norway, and from

Antigua to Bohemia. With regard to its effects at Lisbon he remarks—

"The bed of the river Tagus was in many places raised to the surface. Ships were driven from their anchorage, and jostled together with great violence, nor did their masters know whether they were afloat or aground. A huge new quay sunk to an unfathomable depth, with several hundreds of people who were upon it, nor was one of the dead bodies ever found. The bar was at first seen dry from shore to shore, but suddenly the sea came rolling in like a mountain, and about Belein Castle the water rose 50 feet almost in an instant."

It is interesting to notice what great disturbances this Earthquake caused at that time in *distant* lakes, ponds, springs, and rivers, where the shock itself was scarcely felt or not felt at all. I quote a few instances from the same writer—

"At Loch Lomond, in Scotland, about half an hour after nine in the morning, all of a sudden, without the least gale of wind, the water rose against its banks with great rapidity, but immediately subsided till it was as low in appearance as anybody then present had ever seen in the greatest summer-drought. Instantly it returned toward the shore, and in five minutes' time rolled again as high as before. The agitation continued at the same rate till fifteen minutes past ten the same morning, taking five minutes to rise and as many to subside. From fifteen minutes after ten till eleven the height of every rise became somewhat short of the immediately preceding, taking five minutes to flow, and as many to ebb, till the water was entirely settled. The greatest perpendicular of the swell was two feet four inches."

"At Loch Ness, about half an hour after nine a very great

agitation was observed in the water. About ten the river Oich, which runs on the north side of Fort Augustus into the head of the loch, was observed to sink very much, and run upwards from the loch with a pretty high wave, about two or three feet above the ordinary surface. The motion of the wave was against the wind, and it proceeded rapidly for about 200 yards up the river. It then broke on a shallow, and flowed three or four feet on the banks, after which it returned immediately to the loch. It continued ebbing and flowing in this manner for about an hour without any such remarkable wave as at first, but, about eleven o'clock a wave, higher than the rest, came up and broke with so much force on the low ground on the north side of the river, it ran upon the grass about thirty feet from the river's bank."

"At Cobham in Surrey, between ten and eleven o'clock, a person was watering a horse at a pond, fed by springs. While the animal was drinking, the water suddenly ran away from him, and moved toward the south with such swiftness that the bottom of the pool was left bare. It returned again with such impetuosity that the man leaped backwards to secure himself from its sudden approach."

"A very remarkable change was observed in the waters of Toplitz (Carlsbad), a village in Bohemia, famous for its baths. The waters were discovered in the year 762, from which time the principal spring of them had constantly thrown hot water in the same quantity, and of the same quality. In the morning of the Earthquake, between eleven and twelve of the forenoon, the principal spring cast forth such a quantity of water, that in the space of half an hour, all the baths ran over. About half an hour before this great increase of the water, the spring flowed turbid and muddy, then, having stopped entirely for a minute, it broke forth again with prodigious violence, driving before it a considerable quantity of reddish ochre. After that it became clear, and flowed pure as before. It still continues to do so, but the water is in greater quantity, and better than before the Earthquake."

From facts such as the above we may learn something of the great ramifications which must exist in chambers and channels under the Earth, evidently connected with the waters of the Great Deep.

Job was asked many questions by JEHOVAH, which he was unable to answer, a few of which are as follows—

" Where wast thou when I laid the foundations of the earth?
Declare if thou hast understanding.
Who determined the measures thereof, if thou knowest?
Or who stretched the line upon it?
Whereupon were the foundations thereof made to sink?
Or who laid the corner-stone thereof? . . . .
Hast thou commanded the morning since thy days *began*,
And caused the dayspring to know its place,
That it might take hold of the ends of the earth? . . . .
Hast thou entered into the springs of the sea?
Or hast thou walked in the recesses of The Deep?"

Job xxxviii. 4—6, 12, 13, 16.

Well would it be for our Astronomers, if, in considering such questions, they were brought into the same state of profound humility as that noble Patriarch, when he said to JEHOVAH—

" I have heard of Thee by the hearing of the ear,
But now mine eye seeth Thee,
Wherefore I abhor *myself*, and repent in dust and ashes."

Job xlii. 5, 6.

SECTION 8.

THE GREAT GULF STREAM AND CURRENTS OF THE GREAT DEEP.

Besides Tides, whose flux and reflux is not felt for more than forty miles from land, there are mighty Gulf streams or Ocean Currents, some of which are from 200 to 400 miles in breadth, and from 3,000 to 4,000 miles in length. They are deep, calm, and steady, and flow with an average speed of one and a half to two miles per hour. The courses of these immense currents, which flow in various opposite directions through the ocean, afford another convincing proof that there cannot possibly be any globularity there, because courses such as described could not exist on a convexity. These are vast Ocean Rivers which cannot flow *upwards* in their routes, any more than the Rivers of the Earth can do in theirs, the *upward* flow of running water being entirely contrary to the laws of nature. In *Psalm xxiv. 2*, we read that God founded the Earth " upon the seas, and established it upon the floods." The Hebrew word here used for " floods " is *naharoth*, which literally means " rivers," and the rivers referred to there must doubtless be those mighty ocean currents, which so majestically flow from the fountains of the Great Deep.

One of the most noted of these vast Currents in the Atlantic Ocean is the Great Gulf Stream, which flows from the Gulf of Mexico, where the temperature of the water is about 86 degrees; it then sweeps through the Straits

of Florida northwards as far as latitude 31 degrees N.,
when it takes a north-eastern direction to about latitude
36 degrees N.; it then crosses the Atlantic, past the
western side of the Azore Islands, up to the Western Coast
of Europe. When it issues from the Straits of Florida it
is of a dark blue indigo colour, and can be distinguished
from the green waters of the Atlantic for hundreds of
miles. Its mean breadth is about 350 miles.

In the same ocean there are other immense currents
—the Equatorial—the North African and Guinea—the
Southern Connection—the Southern Atlantic—the Cape
Horn—Rennels and Arctic Currents. The Arctic
comes from the Polar regions, bearing immence icebergs,
some of which are 200 feet high, which means a depth of
1,400 feet below the surface of the water. Many of these
are left on the west coast of Greenland, and others are
drifted south to warmer regions where they are gradually
dissolved.*

The Arctic Current, believed to arise at the North
Pole, runs along the east coast of Greenland, and, after
doubling Cape Farewell, flows up the west coast of Greenland to about Latitude 66 degrees N., when it turns
south along the west of Labrador. On reaching the
northern end of Newfoundland it divides, the smaller
portion passing through the Straits of Belle Isle, and the
main body going between the great and outer bank of
Newfoundland, and ultimately joins the Great Gulf
Stream between Latitudes 44 degrees and 47 degrees N.

Whence do these vast currents proceed? " the cause of
which," as the writer of the article " Atlantic Ocean " in

---

* See article " Atlantic Ocean " in " The Imperial Gazetteer "; Blackie & Son,
Glasgow, Edinburgh, and London.

the " Imperial Gazetteer," p. 244, confesses, " are but imperfectly, known." I am not at all surprised at Geographers and Astronomers being unable to account for these great bodies of water flowing through the oceans, so long as they imagine the Earth to be a whirling Planet, and ignore the Scriptural declaration that it " is founded upon the seas and established upon the floods "—*Psa. xxiv. 2.* My own opinion is that these Currents flow from some of the fountains of the Great Deep, and, like all the works of God, are meant for special service, for He makes nothing without use. Part of that service may be for promoting the circulation of the waters of the ocean, for it is known that the greatest storms do not disturb the sea deeper than about 90 feet, below which there is a perfect calm. In deep soundings delicate shells are often taken up, which have not the slightest signs of abrasion. These Currents are also of use in navigation, and are also thought to have a considerable climatic influence on the neighbourhoods through which they pass. Our own Islands of Great Britain and Ireland are believed to owe much of their verdant beauty, and their comparatively mild temperature, to their being washed by the waters of the Great Gulf Stream.

SECTION 4.

THE RIVERS COME FROM AND RETURN TO THE GREAT DEEP.

It was said by Solomon who " was wiser than all men " —*1 Kings iv. 31*—

" All the rivers run into the sea, yet the sea is not full;

unto the same place from whence the rivers come, thither they
return again "—*Ecc. i. 7.*

There is more true science taught in this one verse than
all our Modern Astronomers have ever known, else they
never would have imagined a Planetary Earth. It unfolds
to us the fact that the Earth is founded upon the Great
Deep, part of the waters of which percolate or flow
through its body in various channels, forming the springs
in lakes, hills, and valleys, from which the rivers take
their rise. Rivers have all a *downward*, and never an
upward course in any part of their journey to the sea,
thus proving that the Earth is not globular, and therefore
not a Planet. Perhaps this continual interchange in their
flow from and to the Great Deep, may be one of the
elements towards solving the problem of the Tides.
There are known to be many lakes and rivers which have
great springs in them, and even sprudels or fountains of
water, which burst from them with great force, notably
the hot sprudel in the river Toplitz at Carlsbad. There
are also hot springs in New Zealand, Iceland, and many
other parts of the world.

As the Psalmist sings—

> "He sendeth forth springs into the valleys;
> They run among the mountains."
>
> *Psa. civ. 10.*

The working of mines and quarries has sometimes to be
altogether abandoned, owing to the influx of water being
much more than the engine-pumps are able to carry away.
By sinking Artesian wells water may be found in most
parts of the Earth, and, as a general rule, the deeper
they are sunk the greater will be their flow. Such waters

cannot be deposited by rain, for we know, from carefully conducted experiments, that even in the most porous soil, water does not penetrate more than a few feet, so that these supplies must come either from the Great Deep direct, or from reservoirs of water connected with it in caverns of the Earth.

There are also wind caverns or vents in various parts of the world, from which the air occasionally issues with great violence. For example, Mr. Bryden, in his travels in Sicily, says, in the mountain of Neptune, there is

"A gulf or crater on the summit, from which at particular times there issues an exceedingly cold wind with such violence that it is difficult to approach it."

In the Lake of Geneva there is what is considered to be a subaqueous current, which occasionally makes the waters to rise like a Tidal wave; and there is a lake of unknown depth, near Boleston, in Bohemia, which is sometimes so disturbed that "masses of ice are said to be thrown up to some height from its surface."

Although I do not agree with Mr. Macdonald in his exposition of Parkhurst's Theory of the Earth, he is well worthy of respect as a Christian and a scholar, and I have much pleasure in quoting the following extract from his previously mentioned work, "The Principia and the Bible," pp. 139—141, as it fully corroborates the truth taught in *Ecc. i. 7*—"All the rivers run into the sea, yet the sea is not full; unto the place from whence the rivers come, thither they return again."

"Varinius and other competent authorities estimate that each of the larger rivers pours into the sea, in a single year, a quantity of water sufficient to cover the whole surface of the

earth. But the number of the considerable rivers in the old
continent amount to 430, and those of the new may be estimated
at 140. The comparative smallness of some of the former is
amply compensated by the vastness of the latter; to this if we
add all the minor streams, which flow in every quarter of the
globe (!), we may safely conclude that a quantity of water is
annually poured into the ocean, which, if collected, would
cover the earth 570 times. The first grand question then is—
Unless the heads of these rivers communicate with a great
central abyss of water, whence does this prodigious quantity of
water come? The second question is equally pertinent: Unless
the ocean communicates with the same great abyss, and thereby
maintains the circulation of the rivers, how does it happen that
no perceptible variation in the water level results from this
immense supply? Our philosophers attempt to explain these
facts by assuming that rivers are supplied by vapours precipitated upon the earth in rain, snow, dew, &c., and that a quantity
of water is exhaled from the ocean by the solar heat equal to
that contributed by the rivers. The utter insufficiency of this
explanation, however, will be obvious from the following con-
siderations.

"The highest estimate of the mean annual fall of rain,
dew, &c., throughout the world in our meteorological treatises
is 34 inches. Let it now be remembered that only one-third of
the surface of the earth is dry land, so that only one-third of
the quantity of rain that falls would be available for the supply
of the rivers. This would be a quantity little more than
sufficient to cover the entire surface of the earth to the depth
of eleven inches. What proportion, then, does this bear to the
volume of water thrown into the sea by a single great river,
which is estimated, as we have seen, to submerge the highest
mountains—not to mention the aggregate volume from all the

rivers of the globe (!) So far from being sufficient to feed all the rivers, it is questionable whether, after deducting what is resumed into the air from the earth by evaporation, the rain which falls upon the land is sufficient without foreign aid, to supply the wants of vegetable life. By a series of experiments, Dr. Dobson of Liverpool found the mean annual evaporation from a cylindrical vessel, twelve inches in diameter, to be 36.78 inches, while the mean rain measured in another vessel of the same aperture, during the same period, was 37.48 inches, leaving a residue of only 1.30 inches. Then the experiments of M. de la Hire show that a single fig-tree, furnished with 130 leaves, absorbed 2½ lbs. of water in five hours, or at the rate of 3,194 lbs in a year. With what reason, then, can it be maintained that, after meeting the demands of evaporation and sustaining vegetable life and growth, the rain is sufficient to supply all the rivers that fall into the sea? Ray has also well observed that the tops of the mountains above the sources of the Rhine, Rhone, Danube, and Po are during the winter half of the year constantly covered with snow to a great thickness, so that no vapours could touch them, and yet these rivers run as steadily in winter as in summer. Now this is inexplicable upon any other supposition than that of Solomon, viz., that rivers draw their supplies from the subterranean abyss into which they return them again."

I sincerely trust that, after considering the evidence which has been brought before him, the thoughtful Reader will clearly see that this world of ours is not a Planet, as supposed by our Modern Astronomers, but a real *Terra Firma*, founded upon the waters of the Great Deep, from which come and to which return, with unceasing flow, the rivers of the Earth, in accordance with the wise and beneficent purpose of our Divine Creator.

CHAPTER XIV.

FRAGMENTS GATHERED UP.

SECTION		PAGE
1. LOCALITY · · · · · ·		272
2. UP AND DOWN · · · · ·		274
3. SOME OTHER REASONS WHY THE EARTH IS NOT A PLANET · · · ·		278
4. CONCLUDING REMARKS ·		283

SECTION 1.

LOCALITY.

EVERY human being has

"A local habitation and a name,"

by which I mean that the veriest wanderer on the face of the Earth must occupy some particular place every moment of his life, for he is not ubiquitous, and cannot be in two places at the same time.

The Compass, except for the variations previously referred to, which are too unimportant to affect its general character, always points *straight* to the North centre, the opposite point, wherever it may be, being the South. If we look from the North to the South, the East will be on our left hand, and the West on our right, and, if we look from the South to the North, the East will be on our right hand and the West on our left.

When the dying gladiator fell in the Coliseum,

"Butchered to make a Roman holiday,
His thoughts were with his heart, and that was far away,"

but his body remained in the arena till it was sent to the lions. It disappeared, but the Coliseum is still in Rome, and Rome is still in Italy, and Italy is still in Europe, and Europe is still in the world, and the world is still where it has been since the Adamic Creation, with the Pole Star of the heavens shining over its Northern centre, as it is written—"He spreadeth out the North over the desolate place, and supporteth the Earth upon fastenings "—*Job xxvi. 7.*

Since I came to this house some years ago, both by compass and observation, it faced the *South*, even as it does to-day, as it has not moved one inch. But, six months ago, according to the theory of our Astronomers, it should then have looked towards the *North*, as the Earth would at that time have performed one half of its journey round the Sun. But, alas! for the poor theory, since ever I have been here it is only from the *back windows* that the North has been visible, and the South still faces me from *those of the front.* "Ah!" say our Astronomers, "you must not trust your own senses, but believe what our system demands"! They seem to think we are geese, and would thrust their crude conjectures down our throats with their theoretic air-pump, as the poulterer crams fowls for the market. What a parody on true science! What a climax to our boasted civiliza-

tion at the close of the nineteenth century! For myself
I utterly reject such teaching, and trust that all my
Readers may do so likewise. False Science has already
kept the wickets too long, and it is high time for Common
Sense to have its innings now. Surely we may say, with
respect to Modern Astronomy, as the Poet sang of
ancient Ilium, that the day draws nigh,

> "When even thou, Imperial Troy, must bend,
> Must see thy warriors fall—thy glories end."

Let us even hope, with regard to this barbaric system, that
we may be soon able to exclaim—*Troja fuit*—Troy has
been, but exists no more!

SECTION 2.

UP AND DOWN.

With the Modern Astronomer there is theoretically
neither "Up" nor "Down," though his experience belies
his assertion, every time he looks "up" to the heavens
or "down" to the ground. Such aberration of intellect
is really to be pitied. Yet it is painful to find that even
the minds of some Christian authors have been so warped
by this erroneous teaching, that they speak of the Earth
as "our globe" with the greatest *nonchalance*. I was
particularly struck with this some years ago when reading
Olam Haneshamoth, or "A View of the Intermediate
State," written about a century since by a great scholar,
the Rev. George Bennet of Carlisle. It is a most learned

and interesting work, and was highly commended by
Bishop Horsley.   Much useful information may be
gathered from the pages of this estimable author, but,
when he speaks of the situation of Sheol or Hades, the
place of departed spirits, he must have been sadly
hampered by the net of Modern Astronomy, as may be
seen from the following extract, p. 285—

"In the boundless regions of space *ascent* and *descent* are
lost; these being merely ideas impressed upon us from our
earliest infancy by reason of our union to matter. We are
naturally led to annex cheerfulness to *ascent*, by reason of the
bright splendour of the firmament above, and gloom to *descent*,
because of the interminable depth of earth, and its supposed
dark caverns, presenting themselves to the imagination from
below; yet the skies are everywhere, and spirits, whatever
may be their motion, or particular mode of existence, have
nothing to do with the influence of attraction or gravitation,
this more naturally agreeing with the properties of body."

Now this good man could never have written thus,
had he not been inoculated as a boy with the virus of
Modern Astronomy.   He would have been open to
receive the explicit teaching of Scripture, that THERE is
an "ascent" and "descent," an "Up" and a "Down,"
as it is written—

"A fire is kindled in Mine anger, and shall burn unto *the
lowest* Sheol"—*Deut. xxxii. 22.*

"As *high* as heaven what canst thou do? *Deeper* than Sheol,
what canst thou know?"—*Job xi. 8.*

It is much to be regretted that the Translators of our
Authorised Version made such a serious mistake as to

render the words "Sheol" and "Hades," "hell" and
"the grave," instead of giving their proper meaning—the
place of the dead—which is situate somewhere about the
centre of the Earth, as may at once be seen by comparing
the two following passages of Scripture, respecting the
place to which our Lord went at His death—

"Thou wilt not leave my soul in *Sheol*, neither wilt Thou
suffer Thine Holy One to see corruption"—*Psa. xvi. 10.*

"As Jonah was three days and three nights in the belly of
the great fish, so shall the Son of Man be three days and three
nights, *en tē kardia tēs gēs, in the heart of the earth*"—
Matt. xii. 40.

Sheol is thus shown to be in the heart or central part
of the Earth. The study of this subject is most important
and deeply interesting, and I respectfully beg to refer any
of my Readers, who may wish to consider it, to my own
work, "Hades and Beyond," where this matter has been
investigated to the best of my ability.*

To prove an "Up" and a "Down" really seems to me
a work of supererogation, as the fact of there being such
is so patent to the perception of all who have eyes to
see and judgment to discriminate; still, for the sake of
some, it may perhaps be well to give a few Scriptural
illustrations—

"So they, and all that pertained to them *went down* alive
into Sheol"—*Num. xvi. 33.*

"Elijah *went up* by a whirlwind into heaven"—*2 Kings ii. 11.*

"If I *ascend up* to heaven Thou art there; if I *make my bed
in Sheol*, behold, Thou art there"—*Psa. cxxxix. 8.*

---

* See note on p. 55.

"He knoweth not that the Rephaim are there, and that her guests are in *the depths* of Sheol "—*Pro. ix. 18.*

"The way of life is *above* to the wise, that he may depart from *Sheol beneath* "—*Pro. xv. 24.*

"I will *ascend above* the heights of the clouds; I will be like The Most High; yet thou shalt be brought down to *Sheol*, to the *uttermost parts of the pit* "—*Isa. xiv. 14, 15.*

"Thus saith JEHOVAH, If *the heaven above* can be measured, and *the foundations of the earth searched out beneath*, then will I also cast off all the seed of Israel for all that they have done "—*Jer. xxxi. 37.*

"I made the nations to shake at the sound of his fall, when I cast him *down to Sheol*, with them that *go down into the pit* "—*Ezek. xxxi. 16.*

"The strong among the mighty shall speak to him out of the midst of *Sheol*, with them that help him, they are *gone down*, they are uncircumcised, slain by the sword "—*Ezek. xxxii. 21.*

"Ye men of Galilee, why stand ye looking into heaven? This same Jesus which is *taken up from you* into heaven, shall so *come* in like manner as ye beheld Him *going into heaven* "—*Acts i. 11.*

"Now that He *ascended*, what is it save that He also first *descended into the lower parts of the earth*. He that *descended* He it is who also *ascended* even *above all the heavens*, that He might fill all things "—*Eph. iv. 9, 10.*

"And they heard a loud voice out of heaven saying—*Come up hither;* and *they went up to heaven* in the cloud, and their enemies beheld them "—*Rev. xi. 12.*

He must, indeed, have but a poor understanding, who does not see from the foregoing passages, that there is an "Up," and that there is a "Down"—that Heaven is *above*, and that Sheol is *beneath* the surface of the Earth. No reasoning mind can question the matter.   In the book of *Ecclesiastes* alone, Solomon uses the expression " under the Sun " no less than twenty-five times, bearing reference to the Earth, or things pertaining thereto.   He who was wisest among men could never have been guilty of such arrant folly, as to suppose that the Earth was only a Planet, whirling round the Sun.

———

SECTION 3.

SOME OTHER REASONS WHY THE EARTH IS NOT A PLANET.

In the course of my reading and meditations, I have found other Reasons, besides those previously given, that the Earth is not a Planet.   Those already mentioned ought, I think, to be quite sufficient to convince any ordinary mind that it is not, but, in case they may have failed to do so, I beg to quote a few other Reasons from a very able pamphlet,* written by the late Mr. William Carpenter of Baltimore, in the hope that they may be more successful, my desire being that every Reader of this book may be as assured, as I am myself, that this Earth is not a Planet.

" 11. As the Mariner's Compass points North and South at the same time, and as the North, to which it is attracted, is that part of the Earth where the North Star is in the zenith, it

---

* " One Hundred Proofs that the Earth is not a Globe."   John Williams, 54 Bourne Street, Netherfield, Notts.

follows that there is no South 'point' or 'pole,' but while the centre is North, a vast circumference must be South in the whole extent. This is a proof that the Earth is not a Globe.

"12. As we have seen that there is really no South point (or pole), but an infinity of points, forming together a vast circumference—the boundary of the known world with its battlements of icebergs, which bid defiance to man's onward course in a Southerly direction—so there can be no East or West 'points,' just as there can be no 'yesterday' or 'to-morrow'! In fact, as there is one point that is fixed (the North), it is impossible for any other point to be fixed likewise. East and West are, therefore, merely directions at right angles with a North and South line, and, as the South point of the Compass shifts round to all parts of the circular boundary (as it may be carried round the central North), so the directions East and West, crossing this line continued form a circle at any latitude. A Westerly circumnavigation is a going round with the North Star continually on the right hand, and an Easterly circumnavigation is performed only when the reverse condition of things is maintained, the North Star being on the left as the journey is made. These facts, taken together, form a beautiful proof that the Earth is not a Globe.

"13. As the Mariner's Compass points North and South at the same time, and as a meridian is a North and South line, it follows that meridians can be no other than straight lines. But, as the meridians on a globe are semi-circular, it is an incontrovertible proof that the Earth is not a Globe.

"14. Parallels of latitude only—of all imaginary lines on the surface of the Earth—are circles, which increase progressively from the Northern centre to the Southern circumference. The mariner's course in the direction of any one of these con-

centric circles is his longitude, the degrees of which INCREASE
to such an extent beyond the Equator (going Southwards), that
hundreds of vessels have been wrecked, because of the false
idea created by the untruthfulness of the charts, and the
globular theory together, causing the sailor to be continually
getting out of his reckoning. With a map of the Earth in its
true form, all this difficulty is done away with, and ships may
be conducted anywhere with perfect safety. This, then, is a
very important proof that the Earth is not a Globe."

" 16. If the Earth were a Globe the distance round the surface, say at 45 degrees South latitude, could not possibly be
any greater than at the same latitude North, but, since it is
found by navigators to be twice the distance—to say the least
of it—or double the distance it ought to be according to the
globular theory, it is a proof that the Earth is not a Globe."

" 21. Man's experience tells him that he is not constructed
like the flies that can live and move upon the ceiling of a room,
with as much safety as on a floor, and, since the modern theory
of a planetary Earth necessitates a crowd of theories to keep
company with it, and one of these is that men are really bound
to the Earth by a force which fastens them, 'like needles round
a spherical loadstone,' a thing perfectly outrageous, and opposed
to all known experience, it follows that, unless you trample
upon common sense, and ignore the teaching of experience, we
have an evident proof that the Earth is not a Globe."

" 24. When a man speaks of a 'most complete' thing
amongst several things which claim to be what that thing is,
it is evident that they must fall short of something which the
'most complete' thing possesses. And when it is known that
the 'most complete' is an entire failure, it is plain that the
others, all and sundry, are worthless. Proctor's 'most com-

plete proof that the Earth is a Globe,' lies in what he calls the 'fact' that distances from place to place agree with calculation. But, since the distance round the Earth at 45 degrees South of the Equator is twice the distance it would be on a globe, it follows that what 'the greatest astronomer of the age' calls a 'fact' is NOT a fact, that his 'most complete proof' is a most complete failure, and that he might as well have told us that he had NO PROOF to give at all. Now since, if the Earth be a Globe, there would necessarily be piles of proof of it all round us, it follows that when Astronomers, with all their ingenuity, are utterly unable to point one out—to say nothing of picking one up—that they give us a proof that the Earth is not a Globe."

"28. Astronomers are in the habit of considering two points on the Earth's surface, without, it seems, any limit as to the distance that lies between them, as being in a level, and the intervening section, even though it be an ocean, as a vast 'hill' of water! The Atlantic Ocean, in taking this view of the matter, would form a hill of water more than a hundred miles high! The idea is simply monstrous, and could only be entertained by scientists, whose whole business is made up of materials of the same description, and it certainly requires no argument to deduce, from such 'Science' as this, a satisfactory proof that the Earth is not a Globe."

"35. If we examine a true picture of the distant horizon, or the thing itself, we shall find it coincides exactly with a perfectly straight and level line. Now, since there could be nothing of the kind on a globe, and we find it to be the case all over the Earth, it is a proof that the Earth is not a Globe."

"41. When Astronomers assert that it is 'necessary' to make 'allowance for curvature' in canal construction, it is, of course, in order that in their idea a level cutting may be had for

the water. How flagrantly, then, do they contradict themselves when they say the curved surface of the Earth is true
level ! What more can they want for a canal than a true level?
Since they contradict themselves on such an elementary point
as this, it is an evidence that the whole thing is a delusion,
and we have a proof that the Earth is not a Globe.

"42. It is certain that the theory of the Earth's rotundity,
and of its mobility must stand or fall together. A proof, then,
of its immobility is virtually a proof of its non-rotundity. Now,
that this Earth does not move, either on an axis, or in an orbit,
round the Sun, or anything else, is easily proven. If the
Earth went through space, at the rate of eleven hundred miles
in a minute of time as Astronomers teach us, in a particular
direction, there would unquestionably be a difference in the
result of firing off a projectile in that direction, and in a
direction the opposite of that one. But, as in fact, there is not
the slightest difference, in any such case, it is clear that any
alleged motion of the Earth is disproved, and that, therefore,
we have a proof that the Earth is not a Globe."

"44. It is in evidence that if a projectile be fired from a
rapidly moving body in an opposite direction to that in which
the body is going, it will fall short of the distance at which it
would reach the ground if fired in the direction of motion.
Now, since the Earth is said to move at the rate of nineteen
miles in a second of time, from West to East, it would make all
the difference imaginable if the gun were fired in an opposite
direction. But, as in practice, there is not the slightest difference whichever way the thing may be done, we have a forcible
overthrow of all fancies relative to the motion of the Earth, and
a striking proof that the Earth is not a Globe."

Want of space forbids my giving farther extracts from

this vigorous pamphlet, to which I would refer any Reader who may unfortunately still cling to the theories of Modern Astronomy, though, I must confess, I cannot conceive how any sane person, unless mailed in prejudice, can possibly resist the plain and ample evidence, which has been previously adduced, to prove that the Earth is not a Planet.

————

SECTION 4.

CONCLUDING REMARKS.

I am thankful to have now come to the closing pages of my book, a work which I would never have undertaken, had I not known the urgent necessity for a strong protest against the assumptions of a false science, which has so greatly tended to foster and increase the infidelity of the day. Owing to the badness of my sight, during a great part of its progress, both reading and writing have been very trying, and I believe that I never could have done as I have, had it not been as an answer to much prayer, and I can, therefore, the more readily hope for its success. If I have made any mistakes, I shall consider it a real kindness to be corrected, but I have endeavoured to be very careful, as to the truth of every statement which I have made, and every passage which I have quoted. Of one thing I am perfectly certain, namely, that I have proved that the Earth is NOT a Planet, and all the Astronomers of Christendom will never be able to overthrow that fact. I confess that at times I have felt sad that the

stability of the Earth should ever have required proving
at all, as such shows into what a low condition sin has
brought the erring intellect of man.

Another matter, which caused me much pain, arose
from reading certain attempts, made by some Christian
writers, to reconcile Scripture with Modern Astronomy.
It seemed to me as if Christ were again being wounded
in the house of His friends—*Zech. xiii. 6,* and Moore's
lines in " The Fire-worshippers " rushed into my mind—

> " Oh ! colder than the wind that freezes
>
> Founts that but now in sunshine play'd,
>
> Is that congealing pang which seizes
>
> The trusting bosom when betray'd."

Instead of boldly upholding Scripture, which " cannot be
broken "—*John. x. 35,* they coolly speak of this world as
" our globe," as if it were one in reality, and plausibly
seek to *accommodate* the phrase to the teachings of a
false Astronomy—a terrible mistake, and utterly useless,
for one might as soon essay to reconcile iron with clay,
as Scripture with Modern Astronomy. As a kind of
soporific to their conscience, they say that Scripture does
not attempt to teach science. Certainly not, as science
is taught in the schools, but it never contradicts facts,
and, to the true Christian student, it teaches more *real
science* than all the schools and colleges in the world.
Some foolishly say, " What does it matter to us whether
the Sun goes round the world, or the world goes round
the Sun ? " It OUGHT to matter very much indeed ; BOTH
statements cannot be true, and it matters everything
whether it be God or man who does not speak the truth.
I take my stand with Paul and say—" Let God be found

true, but every man a liar "—*Rom. iii. 4.* It is a matter of FUNDAMENTAL PRINCIPLE, and in charity I hope that those, who ask such a question, do not think of what it involves, for often, as Hood wisely said,

> "Evil is wrought by want of thought,
> As well as by want of heart."

What is there in Modern Science of which we may be so proud? It is only the old under another name, for as Solomon says—"There is no new thing under the Sun "—*Ecc. i. 9.* Adam, before the Fall, intuitively gave names, from their inherent properties, to every beast of the field and fowl of the air—*Gen. ii. 19, 20.* Before the Flood, his descendant Jubal was—"the father of every one handling harp and organ," and Tubal-Cain (the Vulcan of heathen mythology), was—"an instructor of every artificer in brass and iron "—*Gen. iv. 20, 21.* What could equal the grandeur of Solomon's Temple, the pillared halls of Tadmor, or the stately columns of Baalbac? Who could rebuild the wonderful Rameseion of Medinet Aboo, or the magnificent temples of Luxor and Karnak, all memorials of the No or No Ammon of Scripture*—the hundred-gated Thebes of which Homer sang?† Who could now reconstruct the Great Pyramid of Gizeh, with its Astronomic teachings, and its geometric proportions, or re-design the esoteric adaptations of its marvellous interior?‡ Mr. Alexander McInnes, a member of the Glasgow University Council, in his able pamphlet, "The Opposition of Science to Religion,"§ shows that

---

* Ezek xxx. 14 ; Nahum iii. 8.
† "Iliad," Book ix.
‡ See Professor Piazzi Smyth's most interesting work, "Our Inheritance in the Great Pyramid."
§ William Love, 221 Argyle Street, Glasgow.

even Electrical Science is only a revival, or rather a further development of the Magnetic Magic exhibited of old, when the statue of Memnon uttered a cry of joy as the Sun arose, and wept as it appeared to set—when a magnetic image of Venus, held suspended in the air, an iron one of Mars—and when Lucian declared he saw— "a very old image of Apollo lifted aloft by the priests, and left hanging without any visible support." It is fashionable now to exalt Neo-Science at the expense of the old, but I am ·inclined to think that many useful lessons may be learned from the past, and, that in more arts than one, the Moderns are only now nibbling the left parings of the cheese which the Ancients ate. With respect, at least, to the Science of the Heavens, our Astronomers have utterly failed to discern the truth, and it would be well for them to return to the "old paths," and humbly walk therein, with as little delay as possible.

Sir Isaac Newton said—" The Sun is the centre of the Solar system and is immovable," and on this theoretic basis, the calculations of Modern Astronomy have been made. When Sir William Herschel discovered that the Sun DOES MOVE, as he supposed towards Hercules, and others followed in his wake, surely in common honesty, our Astronomers were bound to confess that their previous theory of a stationary Sun was wrong, instead of which they still continued to palm the results of their former calculations on the public, as if there had been no cause for any change of opinion. Being a plain man I call such conduct "deceptive," though, perhaps, the Loyolas of the day would only consider it to be "smart." Some may probably imagine that on this point I speak too strongly, but I think not more so than the occasion demands. It is as useless to palaver with error as to soft-soap a crocodile. It was not with honeyed words that our Lord rebuked the Scribes and Pharisees, but he boldly exposed their hypocrisy—*Matt. xxiii. 13—33*. We are told that " the wisdom which is from above is *first pure*, then peaceable "—*James iii. 17*—" *resist* the Devil, and he will flee from you "—*James iv. 7*. If this had been done when Modern Astronomy was first introduced, its godless and absurd theories would never have saturated so many with infidelity as they have done—if Sacerdotal Ritualism had been nipped in the bud when it first appeared, our land would not now have been shadowed by the upas-tree of Rome.* My dear Reader, for your own sake, as well as for that of our beloved country, be bold and firm against error and evil of every kind.

I have no hesitation in saying that I believe the real source of Modern Astronomy to have been SATAN. From his first temptation of Eve in the Garden of Eden until now, his great object has been to throw discredit on the Truth of God—" Yea, hath God said that ye shall not eat of every tree of the garden ? " Here the Tempter insinuates the meanness of God in withholding even one fruit from man, and, when Eve replied, that they might eat of every tree except that in the midst of the garden, which they were not even to touch on the pain of death, he at once gave God the lie direct by saying—" Ye shall not surely die, for God doth know that, in the day ye shall eat thereof, your eyes shall be opened, and ye shall be as gods, knowing good and evil "—*Gen. iii. 1—5*.

---

* For a telling exposure of the evils of Rome and Ritualism, I beg to refer my Readers to the following excellent work, " A Strong Delusion, a Book for the Times," which may be obtained from the Author, Mr. Arthur Lee, Dudley, Worcester.—Post free, 2/6.

Just so, when God has so expressly told us in His own Word that the Sun moves round the world, and our own senses corroborate the fact, Satan, by his delusive teaching, daringly asserts that this fact is not true, but that our eyes deceive us, and that the world moves round the Sun. Thus again he seeks to make us believe that God is a liar, and many, alas! trust the lie of Satan before the truth of God. This is one of the chief causes of the abounding infidelity in this sceptical age. Say not, dear Christian Reader, that it matters little to you whether the Sun goes round the world, or the world goes round the Sun, because the PRINCIPLE is involved—whether God or Satan is to be believed.

But, while I am, for the reasons already given, so opposed to Modern Astronomy, I have not the smallest feeling of ill-will against Astronomers themselves, or, indeed, against anyone in the whole world. I therefore wish well for all our Astronomers personally, hoping the best for them in days to come, and trust that they will forgive any seemingly harsh expressions I may have used, kindly remembering that it was not against themselves, but against their erroneous theories, that my remarks have been made.

"Each one of us shall give account of himself to God"—*Rom. xiv. 12*, and I sincerely hope that each one of my Readers, as well as myself, may be found at last to have been true and faithful to Him. In His hands I leave this book, praying that it may be for His glory, and our fellow-creatures' good. Amen.

Lightning Source UK Ltd.
Milton Keynes UK
UKOW04f2006301117
313661UK00001B/124/P